OUR Faithful Companions

OUR *Faithful Companions*

EXPLORING THE ESSENCE OF OUR KINSHIP WITH ANIMALS

Aubrey H. Fine, Ed.D.

Professor and Licensed Psychologist
California Poly State University

Foreword by Dr. Stanley Coren

Photographs by David Sax

Alpine
PUBLICATIONS

Our Faithful Companions: Exploring the Essence of Our Kinship with Animals
Copyright 2014 by Aubrey H. Fine

ISBN 978-1-57779-162-1

Editing: Dianne Nelson

Design: Laura Newport

Photographs by David Sax unless otherwise indicated.

1 2 3 4 5 6 7 8 9 0

Printed in the United States of America.

CONTENTS

This book is dedicated to my human and non-human children and grand-kittens. All of you have blessed my life and collectively have made me a better person.

The book is dedicated to Sean, Corey, Nelli, PJ, Sasha, Goldie, Copper, Puppy, Shrimp, Hart, Magic, Ketzy, Tikvah, Snowflake, Coshi, Starlight, Boomer, Tilly, Oscar, Polly, Kitty, Sneaky, Houdini, Spikey, Tweedle, Hunter, and Colby.

ACKNOWLEDGMENTS

Borrowing from the phrase "It takes a village to raise a child," this book would not have come to fruition without the help and support of many.

I would like to acknowledge and thank David Sax for photographing the various scenes highlighted in the book. David is a talented photographer, and I am indebted to him for sensitively capturing the essence of our relationships with our faithful companions.

I would like to thank my friend Tom Zasadzinski for giving me permission to use his photograph of my "forever dog" PJ for the opening of Chapter 8. Gratitude is also expressed to Krista Trapani for designing the art that surrounds the picture. Krista also deserves many thanks for designing the template of the "PAWS for Thoughts" activities and the graphics for the healing workbook, which is incorporated in the appendix of this book to commemorate the lives of our faithful companions.

I am indebted to the following people for their support in gathering some of the research for this book and conducting some of the interviews: Julia Gimeno, Maureen Huang, Ellie Reimers, Joanne Cole, Michael Donato, India Wallace, Christine Bowers, Shawna Weaver, Michela Parisi, Jane Deming, Katenna Jones, Crystal DeArman, and Charlotte McKenny.

During the past year, several people read earlier drafts of the various chapters and provided input and editorial comments. I am sincerely indebted to these individuals for their suggestions: Rudi Gomez, Stephen Davis, Dale Salwak, Julia Gimeno, Ronald Kotkin, Jose Peralta, Sabrina Schuck, Bill McCullough, Christine Bowers, Jane Deming, Katenna Jones, India Wallace, Shawna Weaver, Pam Seggerman, Dana O'Callaghan, and Phillip Tedeschi.

I also wish to thank Dr. Stanley Coren, who wrote the foreword for this book, I value Dr. Coren's insights on human-animal interactions and am honored that he was willing to make this contribution.

Throughout this book you will find many amazing stories of companion animals and their human counterparts. I could not have accumulated such a vast store of knowledge without the assistance of these wonderful individuals who allowed me to interview them and relate their experiences in this book. Some names have been purposely changed to protect the privacy of the contributors. To all of you — my deepest thanks for sharing with me and permitting me to include your stories here.

FOREWORD

BY DR. STANLEY COREN

This book explores the nature of the bond that people have with animals. This bond can be extremely strong and, in fact, has been used by psychologists in the clinical practice of what has come to be known as animal-assisted therapy (AAT), which involves using an animal as a fundamental part of a person's treatment. Although the most common animal used in AAT is the dog, we also find cats. Other animals include rabbits, birds, fish, and gerbils, along with some large animals such as horses and some exotic species like elephants, dolphins, and lizards.

Over the past thirty years, we have seen a huge increase in the number of scientific studies that have looked at the human-animal bond and concluded that the emotional bonds we have with our companion animals help us cope with stress and assist with other therapeutic interventions. These studies tell us about how physiological mechanisms, such as the flow of the hormone oxytocin when we are in contact with a familiar and friendly animal, may play a part in our emotional link with them. The data also show us how the attachments we form with animals follow the same rules as the attachments we form with children and other loved ones.

Yet long before any scientific data existed to explain the nature of the human-animal bond, people sought comfort through their contact and interactions with animals. In an archaeological site known as Ein Mallaha, located on the coast of what is now Israel, we find the remains of a small Neolithic village built near the shore. This Natufian community dates to around 10,000 years ago, which would be toward the end of the Stone Age. Here, archaeologists found the grave of an elderly man buried in a curled position, with his knees up near his chin — the traditional burial posture of the time. As they uncovered the upper part of the body, they found the man's head resting on his left hand. Working to clear the area around the hand, they discovered that it had been gently placed on the chest of a four- or five-month-old puppy. The dog had clearly been placed in the grave to provide consolation and companionship to his master on his trip to eternity.

Gaining emotional support from companion animals has been so common through the ages that it is a wonder scientists did not recognize its psychological importance and clinical potential until more recently. Numerous examples reveal the importance of our human-animal bond. Throughout history, political and military leaders have felt lonely and isolated. Those in power often worry about exposing their concerns to others, fearing that their secrets might be deliberately used against them or inadvertently become known to enemies who might take advantage of them. For this reason, numerous people in power have turned to dogs as their most intimate companions. Take the case of General Dwight D. Eisenhower, who would go on to become President of the United States after World War II. In 1943, he was supreme commander of the allied military operation and coordinated the operations in North Africa that would finally wrest control from the Germans. While there, he wrote to his wife Mamie, "The friendship of a dog is precious. It becomes even more so when one is so far removed from home as we are in Africa. I have a Scottie. In him I find consolation and diversion . . . he is the 'one person' to whom I can talk without the conversation coming back to the war."

John F. Kennedy's presidency included nine dogs, but his favorite was a Welsh Terrier named Charlie, a scamp who would silently slip up behind a gardener who was digging or working the soil, then make a quick rush at the man, nipping him in the seat of the pants or grabbing at his leg. When a worker complained, he was told to forget the incident, because JFK was more likely to have the man dismissed than to take action against the dog. Charlie's real importance was as a source of comfort to the President. This was proved during the Cuban Missile Crisis when JFK interrupted deliberations of his advisors to have Charlie brought to him. For what seemed like a very long time, Kennedy sat stroking the dog, and those who were present report that, as he caressed the dog, the President gradually seemed to relax. Then, with a calm look of control, he put Charlie down and said, "I suppose that it's time to make some decisions."

History records that dogs have served in a quasi-therapeutic function many times, bringing consolation to people during times of pain or crisis and often serving the same psychological functions that a family priest might fulfill. Mary, Queen of Scots, for instance, spent her long hours of prison confinement in the Tower of London in the company of only her small spaniels. She spoke to them and they comforted her through the night. In 1587, when she was beheaded, it was reported that she walked to the block in a slow and stately manner, appearing to be quite composed. It was later discovered that she walked that way because she had hidden one of the toy dogs under her voluminous robes, obviously to provide herself with comfort and companionship in her final moments. Many years later, the person who had ordered Mary's execution, Queen Elizabeth I, also had few friends to ease her loneliness. She would spend her last night "consoled only by her dogge," a very similar toy spaniel.

The formal study of the human-animal bond and its use in psychological settings in North America can probably be traced to Boris Levinson and his 1969 book, Pet-Oriented Child Psychotherapy. The book resulted from observations Levinson made while treating children who had severe emotional and communicative problems, such as autism. Levinson noted an improvement in his ability to get through to these children when his dog was present during the therapy sessions. At the time Levinson was writing his book, I was teaching at the Graduate Faculty of the New School for Social Research, located in a building at the corner of Fifth Avenue and Fourteenth Street in New York City. Yeshiva University, where Levinson held a position as a professor, was located only a few blocks south on Fifth Avenue, and occasionally he would join me and other colleagues for coffee and conversation.

Although Levinson was a specialist in child psychology, he never struck me as a person who would get along with children. His angular face, deep-set eyes, and severe goatee made him look more like the stereotype of an evil sorcerer. Nonetheless, quite incongruously, he had a merry note to his voice. I later learned that most of his young patients referred to him as "Uncle Boris." One afternoon, Boris joined a colleague and me for coffee, and while we sat there, talking about random topics, I congratulated him on his new book about animal-assisted therapy. I then casually asked, "So tell me — what made you think that the emotional bond between dogs and people would be strong enough to be of value in therapy in the first place?"

Levinson smiled and said, "I never really planned in advance to use a dog as a co-therapist. The patient was a nine-year-old boy who was extremely withdrawn. In the past, his therapeutic experiences had not been very successful, and a number of psychologists and psychiatrists had already given up on him. The child acted in the way a lot of patients suffering from autism do. He simply would not communicate. You can't do therapy unless there is some kind of communication. Anyway, the boy's mother was quite desperate and asked me to at least look at the child and see if something could be done.

"Every now and then, when the opportunity arose, I would bring my Golden Retriever Jingles to work to keep me company. So it just happened that on the day when that mother and son arrived at my office, I happened to have Jingles with me. Jingles was a typical Golden Retriever, the sort of kissing-oriented dog who believes that 'You've got a face and I've got a tongue and I'm sure we can work something out.'

"When the boy walked into the room, Jingles jumped up and greeted him in the enthusiastic way that Golden Retrievers greet anything that might be alive. The results were remarkable, at least from a psychological point of view. The boy wrapped his arms around the dog's neck and actually spoke — not much, but a few words. It was a remarkable start given the fact that previous therapists had found this child was virtually impossible to communicate with.

"At the time, I didn't know of any data or historical precedents where dogs were being used to establish an emotional link with people or might serve to open some kind of communication channel that could be used therapeutically. In fact, my first predisposition was to think that the child was just having a particularly good day, or maybe even that the boy's mother had overstated the severity of his problem. The fact that my dog Jingles played such a significant role in the interaction really didn't occur to me until I thought about the situation later.

"It was when I was sitting down and organizing my notes about that day's intervention with the boy that something popped into my head. It was a story, a folktale, that I had heard, or maybe I had read, somewhere, sometime. From what I could remember, it belonged to the Plains Indians, maybe the Sioux Indians. Anyway, the way that I remembered the story was that after the world had been created, after the mountains and lakes and rivers had been shaped, and the forests had been filled with trees and bushes, and the plains had been covered with grass, and all of the animals had been made, the Great Spirit, or whatever the creator was then called, felt that there was one more task that he had to complete. So he sent out the word for all of the different species of animals and also for the humans to gather on one great plain on a particular day. And on that day, the Great Spirit placed the animals on one side and mankind on the other side and then drew a large line in the earth. And that line began to turn into a crevasse, which widened and became deeper and wider by the moment, with man standing on one side of the fissure and the animals on the other. Then, at the last moment, before the gap became unbreachable, dog leapt over and stood by man.

"You know, it is odd that that particular story, created by an unlettered and uneducated primitive group many years ago seemed to me to capture our forced estrangement from nature in general, and from animals specifically. It is worse now than it was back in the days when that story was created, since the difficulties and complexities of living in a highly technological environment have alienated us from our evolutionary origins and broken those relationships with nature that are essential for our emotional, if not biological, survival. But according to that story, there is one major exception, and that is the bond between humans and dogs. As the canyon between the rest of nature and mankind grows wider and wider, we can still look down and see that dogs are standing by our side. Our feeling for dogs is woven into the fabric of our souls, and as I thought about it, I knew that this folktale caught the fact that between dogs and humans there is an emotional link, a connection that I could use as a psychologist. I felt that the presence of Jingles as my co-therapist could help to establish an atmosphere of trust that could serve as the basis of a solid relationship with the child.

"So in the end, I placed my trust, not only in my clinical observations, but in the truth that that little folktale was wrapped around. That is what got me started, and it seems to be working."

We have come a long way since the Stone Age, but still, like that Natufian man, we draw comfort and reassurance from the presence of a companion animal. Through the ages, dogs and other pets have managed to sneak into our psyches, under the radar of our emotional defenses. And thus we find them by our side when we need emotional support and solace. The big difference between now and the Stone Age is that, in our modern era, science is beginning to systematically explore the nature of the human-animal bond, and as our understanding of our attachment to animals becomes clearer, our ability to use that relationship in therapeutic settings becomes easier and more effective. This new data also help to clarify the position that dogs fulfill in our lives as friends and family members. The material in this book will give you a glimpse of how far we have come in our study of this fascinating phenomenon.

Stanley Coren, PhD, DSc, FRSC
Professor Emeritus
Department of Psychology
University of British Columbia

CHAPTER ONE

DISCOVERING THE HEART AND SOUL OF OUR FAITHFUL COMPANIONS:
Connecting Souls and Developing Kinship

It was December 2001 and my boys were about to give me a gift that would alter my life: a note in an envelope. It wasn't what was in the envelope that was so remarkable but rather the sentiment it held. The boys knew me as a dad who loved to be surrounded by animals. Both of them had grown up with our pack of "four-leggers" and "two-wingers" and instinctively understood how essential my bond was with these other family members.

The note in the envelope was simple. It highlighted their desire to buy me my next Golden Retriever puppy. You see, we had lost our older Golden several months before, and although we had two other dogs, the boys were very much aware that I had a significant void in my life. As we all know, the sad part of our relationship with these unique creatures is that they have shorter life spans than we do. The joy we share with them is not long enough, and eventually we are confronted with loss. No loss can ever be replaced, and rightly so.

The gift wasn't really going to be the purchase of another dog but, more importantly, the recognition that my sons knew what brought me happiness. Tinsel and tin perhaps make many lives easier, but the soulful eyes of a living, breathing companion are priceless. It was my sons' understanding of this concept that made their gift the most special one of all.

1

That envelope my boys gave me was a gift of life . . . a life that I was so blessed to share. A day doesn't pass by without a generated smile or a sparkle in my eyes when I remember days shared with "PJ." She truly made me a better person.

—

We all have such stories, some of which make us laugh while others make us weep. Some stories take us back to a childhood companion long gone physically but not forgotten, while others help us celebrate a joyful journey with a companion right now, in the moment. It really doesn't matter. What ties all of these moments together is the tapestry of living memories of lives shared and their profound significance to us.

Our knowledge and awareness of the benefits of human-animal interactions and our bond to companion animals continues to evolve. Throughout this book, I will discuss some of the underlying ingredients that impact our relationships with companion animals and explain why they may occur. By integrating current scientific research with personal anecdotes and stories from many who have experienced these bonds, we will reveal what many have always known and taken for granted: our relationships with our companion animals are good for us.

In the upcoming chapters, we will unravel some of the mysteries of why we connect with other species of beings and examine the significance of these relationships in our lives. We will first clarify the essence of the human-animal bond and highlight the key ingredients of a healthy relationship. Throughout the following chapters, we will also examine ways in which animals enrich our well-being, improve our health, promote kindness, foster relationships, and generally make our lives richer. In later chapters, we'll explore how companion animals benefit children and their families, as well as their important roles as service and therapy animals. We will also give attention to the comforting roles that our companions have in supporting people with chronic illnesses and how we cope with their eventual death. We will unravel the essence of our unique relationships and suggest how we can make our bond more meaningful for both ourselves and our animal friends.

If you had told me forty years ago that I would be writing a book about our relationships with animal companions, I would have said, "Are you kidding me?" I was the boy who not only grew up without any pets but actually feared dogs. Perhaps it was my early upbringing. My mother didn't have any connection to four-legged creatures. In her eyes, pets were just another unwanted expense. My life would have been a different story if I had believed her and had never made an animal friend.

How do these relationships come about? Sometimes it is by conscious choice and planning. Often, however, companion animals come into our lives without our planning. Even when we do not anticipate taking in an animal, these beings find their way into our hearts and become an integral part of our lives. Sometimes life truly sends us serendipitous surprises. They become part of our family by way of a chance encounter.

The next three stories, on the surface, are all very different. However, all three reflect the unpredictable way in which animals came into the lives of the families and the special connection that resulted.

I am always amused when I look back over the years and reflect on when we got our first dog. I'll never forget that day in July; I was like a little boy at Christmas. There we were, my wife Nya and I in front of a store, when we encountered a young woman with a Golden Retriever puppy in a basket.

Over the previous couple of years, Nya and I had discussed the possibility of adopting a dog (a Golden Retriever was our breed of choice), and here we were with a Golden within our grasp. I quickly reverted to my five-year-old behavior and begged my wife to get the dog. Imagine a four-ring circus with me as the star attraction.

My wife was in her glory, acting like a mom and quizzing me on the responsibilities of having a puppy: "Who is going to do the feeding, walking, and cleaning up after him? You know having a puppy is a big job." Of course I knew, and like any other good five-year-old, I immediately responded with juvenile affirmative "yes"es to every question and continued my relentless begging. Finally, she gave in, and we were about to take Goldie home with us when my wife added one more condition to our deal: "Always remember, we can only have one pet at a time!" Who would have thought that years later we would live in an ark that resembled the home of Doctor Doolittle?

I often talk to my friend Laird Goodman, a veterinarian from Oregon, about people's unique relationships with their companion animals. Because he is in the field, he has witnessed firsthand many remarkable situations involving humans and animals, but when I talked to him about this book, he chose not to share the stories of others, but rather his own. He recalled with a smile on his face his tiny apricot Toy Poodle, Princess, who was a cherished member of the family. However, her initiation into it wasn't smooth. Laird explained, "We had a 'Daddy Date' planned — dinner at McDonalds and a movie; Disney's *Aladdin* had just opened, and my daughter Jenny and I were going to make an evening of it … right after I got off work. But, I was a veterinarian, it was a Saturday, and anything could happen — and it did."

At 11 A.M., an eight-week-old — as yet, unnamed — female Toy Poodle was rushed into Laird's clinic. She was comatose and severely traumatized by a neighbor's Pit Bull after she had accidentally wandered into his yard. After a quick evaluation, Laird recommended euthanasia to the family because she had lost a lot of blood; the internal injuries were just too extensive. His clients, who had witnessed the attack, were extremely upset. They just couldn't bear to let go. "Do everything you can to try to save her. We don't care how much it costs."

Modern veterinary medicine is incredible; we can do so much more for animal patients today. Still, this case had such a poor prognosis that Laird again suggested euthanasia as the most humane approach, but the family was determined to try and therefore his team went into action. It was all hands on deck; all of his afternoon appointments were cancelled, and the puppy was prepped for emergency surgery while a unit of blood was ordered from the animal blood bank in Portland.

Laird made an exploratory incision into the abdomen, where he found punctures and tears to the liver, spleen, and uterus. Multiple punctures to the intestinal tract meant the Poodle's abdomen was contaminated and infected. He attended to the most serious injuries first, but as the surgery progressed, he became more aware of the rhythmic "beep-beep" of the ECG (heart) monitor, and a deep foreboding began to creep into his consciousness as he anticipated the final squawk or "beeeeeep" indicating a flat line — no heartbeat — but he worked on, hoping against hope and trusting in his skills. He couldn't let this small being die.

They worked into the evening, and somehow she was still alive when the last stitch was placed. "She's a tough little gal," Laird said when he called the owners. "She's alive, but she'll need to be transferred to a critical-care unit if she has any chance of making it."

Before he was able to complete the sharing of his good news, on the other end of the phone he heard, "Well, Dr. Goodman, we talked it over and we really don't have any money to pay for her surgery and care. Just put her to sleep." Imagine his shock and disappointment. He and his team had worked tirelessly over the past several hours, and this tough little Toy Poodle had fought so hard to this point. Now, her owners were bailing out. To top it off, in the rush to save her, Laird had cancelled the afternoon's appointments, which was sure to upset his boss.

Laird stayed at the clinic until 10 P.M. looking in after the small poodle, but she never regained consciousness. He was tempted at that point to euthanize her because he doubted she would recover. The logical side of his brain said she had no chance, but in his heart he just couldn't let go after everything the team had done and how hard she had fought to cling to life. Instead, he elected to give her some more pain medication and left the little gal attached to her IV line.

When Laird got home, his daughter was already in bed. "Why didn't we go on our Daddy Date?" she asked. He explained about the puppy and the surgery. After listening wide-eyed, she asked what the puppy's name was. Although her owners had not given the clinic a name, Laird felt she deserved this last acknowledgment before she passed, and in deference to the *Aladdin* movie they had missed, he named her "Princess."

"Let's say a prayer for Princess, Daddy," Jenny said. Laird's immediate thoughts were, "She's going to be disappointed. There is no chance this dog is going to make it." He immediately began to ponder the difficult discussion he would need to have when prayers went unanswered. Different alternatives ran through his head, including, "Princess is in a better place now." It's a discussion that never seems to comfort anyone. As he kissed his daughter goodnight, she asked God to watch over Princess and help her get better.

The next morning, Laird got up early to go check on his patient. Jenny wanted to come with him. All the way to the hospital, he rehearsed his speech just in case they found little Princess not alive. To his complete and utter amazement, when they entered the clinic, Princess was not only alive but had pulled out her IV and was at the front of her kennel, yapping for breakfast! "Jesus listened to our prayer, Daddy!" Jenny cried. Indeed it appeared as if He had; it truly was a miracle. Upon her full recovery, Princess became a beloved member of the Goodman family until her death at age seventeen. Chance, however strange, had brought them together.

Laird's story shows that sometimes necessity and circumstances bring people and animals together, and the resulting link can lead to life-changing events. This was also the case with Sami Stoner and Chloe.

On Christmas Eve, ESPN aired an episode about a runner, Sami, who was legally blind and competing in the Ohio High School Athletic Association's program, running cross-country with the support of her service dog, Chloe. Her story was so intriguing, I knew I had to find her and hear it in person.

This high school senior was a charming, confident young woman who spoke with great poise as she explained that in eighth grade she had been diagnosed with Stargardt's disease, a hereditary form of macular degeneration that causes irreversible blindness. Today, Sami's vision is about 20/800; she can still see slightly peripherally, but her ability to see things straight ahead of her is blurry and quite dark.

Sami was a runner, and logically, the inability to see what was directly ahead of you would make running significantly challenging if not impossible. At the age of fourteen, she vowed that her visual impairments might restrict some of her life ambitions, but her dream to continue running would not be squelched.

She contacted Pilot Dogs, a service-dog organization based in Columbus, Ohio. They agreed that she was eligible for a dog and invited her to participate in a four-week program. Eventually, she was matched with a young, one-and-a-half-year-old Golden Retriever. "It was love at first sight. Chloe was by my side all the time." Their bond developed quickly. Although Sami had known other dogs in her childhood, this was different; these two would become inseparable soul mates.

Sami recalled their first practices and early races together. The team was very excited to have a new member, and once the Ohio state athletic governing body agreed to allow Sami and Chloe to run extramurally (with an adjustment that the pack of runners started the race twenty seconds earlier), the pair was ready to compete. Ironically, their first race together resulted in Sami's best competitive time. "When Chloe guides me through a race, she does it with tremendous vigilance. She always stays focused." When Chloe is about to race, Sami can feel her becoming more energized. "She's a ball of energy and is 100 percent focused." Since that first race, Sami has completed twelve more cross-country high school races, as well as multiple 5ks and 10ks for various organizations.

"Having a constant companion by your side is just a tremendous experience. She's given me my confidence and independence back again. Chloe allows me to live a normal teen life. I cannot imagine what life would be without her."

Today, Sami and Chloe are inseparable. They go to friends' houses to hang out, where Chloe is just one of the girls. In fact, this year Sami was elected her school's homecoming queen. A picture in the newspaper showcased Chloe lying right next to Sami, also wearing a tiara with a bouquet of flowers next to her. The caption below the photograph read "...Chloe the mini queen."

Even Sami's father has seen the unique dynamic of the relationship; Sami and Chloe seem to know what the other one needs, perhaps because they're around each other so much. He says that, although they have other family companions, Chloe and Sami are connected at the hip. It is a very reciprocal — almost symbiotic — relationship; they rely on each other. "Chloe belongs more to Sami than the rest of the family, and Sami really tries to take on that responsibility. She tries to meet Chloe's needs not only because Chloe meets her needs, but because they share their lives together."

Over the years, pet ownership has grown in America. According to the 2011–2012 American Pet Products Association (APPA) National Pet Owner Survey, 62 percent of households own a pet, which equates to about 72.9 million homes. In fact, in 1988 when the first study was done by the APPA, only 56 percent of U.S. households owned a pet, so we see a modest growth of about 6 percent over twenty years. Among families with children under eighteen years of age, 76 percent were pet owners in 2002, and most families reported more than one pet. In essence, pets are more likely to be found in households with children than in any other type of household. According to Gail Melson (2001), most parents acquire animals for their children in the belief that pets can teach lessons of responsibility and nurturing while also providing companionship and love. Families with young children make up about 60 percent of pet owners in this country and feel that having a pet is a healthy way for a child to learn responsibility and to demonstrate kindness. Most parents reveal that children maintain high levels of daily involvement in caring for, and playing with, the family pets as they grow from preschoolers to teens, even though children's family time decreases as they age. Importantly, despite the inevitable increase in a child's independence as he/she grows older, a pet can serve to both strengthen and maintain family ties.

The demographics of pet ownership become more striking when we look at the entire change in the human family structure. As many have realized since the baby boom, home family size has been dramatically shrinking and consequently we see fewer children per family. Under such conditions, pets can often provide effective and ongoing bonds for children within their homes.

Another important change to note is how much money we put into the care of our pets. Total spending on pets topped $50 billion in 2011. This money was used for a variety of supplies, equipment, and care. This spending has even expanded to include special grooming, daycare, and exercise classes. Pets are moving from background animals that need food and shelter to fully functioning members of the family that require all the same commodities and care as humans in the family.

Although cats and dogs are the most popular animals adopted by humans, birds, rabbits, ferrets, guinea pigs, reptiles, hamsters, and gerbils make up some of the other animals commonly adopted by families. In a later chapter, we will discuss how you can select the most suitable animal companion for you and your family.

Over the years, it's been amazing to see the transition of pets becoming family members rather than just pets. So many of us consider our pets as children, and we literally become designated mommies and daddies. Actually, 83 percent of people surveyed in a paper written by Young in 2003 saw themselves as "parents" rather than "owners." How many of you would agree that you sometimes talk to your pets using what some call "mother-ese," or baby talk? I admit that I do it with great zest but wouldn't want to be caught in public, although many people don't mind at all using baby talk with their pets in public.

Nevertheless, in our private moments, many of us talk to our beloved companions in an endearing, loving manner. In *The Pawprints of History* (2002), Stanley Coren notes that several psychologists have called the specific way we talk to dogs as "doggerel," which is not to be confused with bad poetry. The conversations are usually limited to four words and are simplified with the use of many commands in the interactions. Coren also points out that we use many tag questions in the conversations. These statements traditionally incorporate an observation that is then turned into a question like, "You want to play ball, don't you?" or "Would you like to go for a walk?"

In fact, our pets become so much a part of our daily lives that we often endow them with human characteristics. We talk to them like people and we attribute to them such human qualities as reason, intention, cognition, emotion, and perception. Most devoted animal owners will swear to the "fact" that their pets know far more than they are letting on!

Pets can also facilitate our social relationships. For example, we often connect with neighbors who have pets that intrigue us. Ironically, how many of you know your neighbor's pet's name but don't necessarily remember the actual neighbor's name? Again, our connection with animals seems to have a greater impact on our connections with others. Animals are easier to talk to than people, or they act as a bridge into an introduction.

Our link with animals is everywhere, but let's not forget that not everyone wants a companion animal. In a 2012 study, the American Humane Association attempted to research reasons why more families did not have a cat or a dog. Every year, three to four million healthy, adorable pets are euthanized in many shelters throughout the country. Why weren't families stepping forward to save these unfortunate animals? The American Humane Association, with funding from PetSmart Charities, conducted a survey that was administered to 1,500 respondents in February 2012. The survey looked at 1,500 consumers between the ages of eighteen to thirty-four and separated them into three groups of 500. One group had never owned a dog or a cat as an adult (and were considered "non-pet owners"), a second group had previously owned a cat but not within the last twelve months, and the third group had previously owned a dog but not within the past twelve months.

The study attempted to shed light on the barriers of pet ownership in order to understand the variables that seem to most strongly impact American households' decision to not keep pets. Out of 117 million households in the United States, only 38.9 million owned cats and 46.3 million owned dogs. Why was there such a large disparity between those families who owned pets and those who did not?

The first phase of the study revealed many interesting issues and drew four major distinct conclusions:

- Dogs were more likely considered as future pets than were cats.
- Previous dog owners were more likely to consider adding another dog to their household,
- Previous cat owners were not as likely to consider doing the same with another cat.
- Fewer owners had acquired their prior pet from shelters or rescues rather than from friends, families, or neighbors.

This research also revealed several barriers that discouraged the ownership of pets by families in general. Highest on the list were the cost of taking care of new pets and the resources needed to do it, followed by the lifestyle changes that occur in a family, the cleaning up and taking care of the animal's daily needs, and, last but not least, the grief over the loss of a beloved pet (and not wanting to experience it again).

According to the survey's respondents, the lifestyle issues that seemed to cause the most challenges were a lack of time to care for the animals and traveling away from home. Additionally, many talked about the expenses of veterinary and general care of the pets. An interesting trend to note was pet ownership dropping sharply because people had lifestyles that were no longer conducive to supporting a dog or a cat in their daily lives. This sentiment seemed to be most true in the older population.

When we look at these data, and the data gathered by APPA, we start to see a picture of a general shift in pet-ownership trends that reflect a larger shift in the part these animals play in our daily lives. This new, more complex dynamic means that animals are no longer just "pets." In order to understand why these shifts are occurring, we must reexamine their role in our lives.

WHY DO WE LOVE ANIMALS?

The natural question to ask is, why do people like to be surrounded by pets in general? Many pet owners view relationships with animals in humanistic terms. Most see their pets as companions or friends. Some believe that one of the reasons we see a growth in companionship over the years relates to many people humanizing their animal's characteristics. We call that anthropomorphic thinking. Basically, we sometimes perceive pets as substitutes for other people, and we attribute uniquely human characteristics and qualities to non-human beings or inanimate objects. Animals are frequently subjects of this form of anthropomorphic thinking.

According to James Serpell, a professor at the University of Pennsylvania, anthropomorphism is the attribution of human mental states from non-human animals. He suggests that this trait is almost unavoidable, especially considering that many pet owners name their companion animals with human names, celebrate their birthdays and feed them human products, and on occasion dress them as they would a child or loved one. Anthropomorphic thinking is sometimes unavoidable when we look at objects or animals from a human perspective. We attempt to understand their point of view from our own. This is done quite often in our world, and Serpell points out that "our willingness to anthropomorphize was critical to the domestication of wild animals and forming bonds with them.... We were particularly drawn to those species that seemed responsive to our Dr. Doolittle overtures."

Serpell also suggests that anthropomorphic thinking is important in some ways for what he calls "pet keeping," because we see some of these warmhearted features that entice us to want to adopt pets. In fact, research suggests animals with more infantile features are more likely to be adopted than animals with more adult features. Just as there is something cute in a baby or child's face that melts our hearts, there is something in an animal's "cuteness" that attracts us.

Alexandra Horowitz, author of *Inside of A Dog* and a professor at Barnard College in New York, believes that the animals we seem to most love are the ones that make expressions at us. She explains how both dogs and cats return our non-verbal gazes toward them and that dogs are even capable of raising their lips to appear as if they are smiling. For some of us, the sense of companionship and non-judgmental acceptance is crucial. It is amazing that many times we can have a full conversation with our pal without any verbal exchanges, and yet we feel heard. The eyes are the windows to their souls, and when they look right into ours, we feel that connection. There are times when we may communicate in silence, and just our close proximity, or being able to touch, seems to be what we both need. For example, the other day, my kitchen floor was being sanded and my dog found refuge under my desk and put her head on my foot. Nothing was said; we were just there for each other.

Perhaps one of the greatest reasons why we love being around our companions relates to the pleasure, the affection, the non-judgmental acceptance, or the love we receive from being around these animals. At one time or another, all of us have experienced a zealous greeting from our own or someone else's pet. When I come home on any given day, it's like the Calgary Stampede. All the animals are running to the door, barking; the cockatoo is squawking; they are all excited to see me and they let me know it. It is a beautiful welcoming ritual that is repeated daily.

For some, animals provide us with an outlet for our playfulness, while in other cases our companions become our excuse for staying engaged and/or exercising. According to Rebecca Johnson, a leading scientist in the field of human–animal interactions, "If we're committed to a dog, it enables us to commit to physical activity ourselves." It seems that our pets can be great motivators to get us off the couch and onto the walking trails, even if it's for a short distance.

ANIMALS AND THE MEDIA

Interest in human-animal interaction has increased in the past few decades as a direct result of mainstream media, social media, and coverage by the popular press of the impact of animals on human lives. This coverage has piqued the general public's curiosity of our unique relationships with animals. Magazines, newspapers, and newscasts are filled with stories that explore and highlight animals who have saved humans, and vice versa. These types of stories abound across cultures. Over time, they have played key roles in the formation of our human traditions and have influenced changes in literature, politics, and science. It is evident that many people romanticize their relationships with animals and have become infatuated with these connections. Perhaps this glamour of our unique affection for/connection with animals is directly related to the mystique of interspecies bonding. People seem intrigued by our similarities and differences and want to better understand our relationships with domestic and exotic animals.

Many authors have crafted children's literature about members of other species and used them as vehicles to help children and their parents make a better sense of their lives. Stories such as *Charlotte's Web, The Incredible Journey, White Fang, Lassie Come Home, The Rats of NIMH*, and *The Runaway Bunny* all have meaningful plots that teach the reader using animals as the basis for understanding.

In the twentieth century, many writers turned to old animal stories to produce revolutionary works that dealt with modern themes. Wonderful stories such as *The Tale of Peter Rabbit, Old Yeller,* and *The Black Stallion* are now part of our literary fabric. Perhaps one of the most influential series of books in this genre was written by James Herriot (his real name was Alf Wright), a British veterinary surgeon who helped bring animals into our daily lives. His stories were later reproduced in a ninety-episode BBC television series, *All Creatures Great and Small.* Beyond printed press, films such as *Babe, War Horse, Marley and Me, My Dog Skip, Seabiscuit,* and *Dolphin Tale* are just a few that highlight our intense interest in and curiosity about other living beings.

A special subgenre is the book written from the point of view of the animal, and many books have been written in the voice of a canine, such as *White Fang* and *The Incredible Journey.* I remember when I wrote *Afternoons with Puppy,* I wanted Puppy (my first therapy dog) to be the narrator and wrote all the stories in her voice. I thought the materials would be extremely powerful because readers would have the insights explained through canine eyes. At the time, only a couple of publishers thought that would work. Years later, writing in an animal's voice became a well-accepted approach in books like *The Art of Racing in the Rain* by Garth Stein and the *Chet and Bernie* mystery series by Spencer Quinn.

It is evident that the common denominator for all these books is the special bond between humans and other living beings. John Steinbeck's *Travels with Charley: In Search of America* is a prime example. The book details a road trip Steinbeck took with his ten-year-old male French Poodle, Charley. They traveled 10,000 miles from Long Island, New York, through Maine, the Pacific Northwest, California, Texas, and the South. It is a wonderful description of life in 1960s America.

However, the most poignant message is Steinbeck's intense connection with his road partner; throughout the book, readers can see how important Charley's relationship is to him. He shares the good times as well as the bad, and the conversations with Charley seemed to help Steinbeck deal with stress and, at times, loneliness. At one point, when he was feeling blue, Steinbeck writes, ". . . he [Charley] came into the bathroom and that old fool played with the plastic bath mat like a puppy. . . . Then he rushed to the door and barked as though I were being invaded" (p. 47). Steinbeck also writes about how he used Charley to meet other people on his trip. "In establishing contact with strange people, Charley is my ambassador. I release him, and he drifts toward the objective, or rather to whatever the objective may be preparing for dinner. I retrieve him so that he will not be a nuisance to my neighbors — *et viola!* A child can do the same thing, but a dog is better" (p. 65). He clarifies succinctly later in the book that "a dog, particularly an exotic like Charley, is a bond between strangers. Many conversations on route begin, 'What degree of dog is that?'" (p. 9). This book is one small example of the way in which literature and mass media have assisted in bringing different species closer together.

WHAT IS THE HUMAN-ANIMAL BOND?

So what is what we call the human-animal bond? In many ways, the definition captures the spirit of the infant/parent bond, which is actually the reason why the term was originally developed. People like Leo Bustad, one of the founders of the Delta Society (now called Pet Partners), basically believed that when they looked at the relationship we have with other species of animals, in many ways what we see is a support system that parallels the infant-parent relationship. In another sense, the phrase "human-animal bond" is a metaphor for the roles animals play in our lives.

Bill McCulloch, DVM, another Delta Society founder, explains a defining moment in 1959 early in his small-animal veterinary practice in Des Moines, Iowa. He recalls that when he left his veterinary practice to pursue a masters degree in public health at the University of Minnesota, a client who owned a Beagle came into the hospital to give him a present. "What they said was to be the seed of my eventual interest and efforts in the human-animal bond: 'Dr. McCulloch, you know that my husband and I could not have children and our Beagle was like a child and member of our family to us. Somehow, we sensed that you understood this attachment. We love you for that!'" In essence, Bill understood the impact of the bond.

While he may have emulated these feelings as a veterinarian, Bill's understanding of the importance of the bond was established as a young child. He grew up on his grandparents' farm in Minnesota in the late 1930s and 1940s, and his early life experiences helped form his impressions of what a veterinarian should be. His grandfather owned draft horses and never rode a tractor, even after a time when the family had three John Deeres on the property. He remembered with great emotion the day his granddad sold his two horses to a neighbor in the fall of 1994. "I saw tears in the old Swede's eyes as the horses left his land. Although they may have been draft horses to others, they were part of his life."

It seems apropos that a graduate of Iowa State University (ISU) would develop this keen sensitivity of what it means to be a caring doctor. ISU is home to one of the most famous statues in veterinary medicine, called the Gentle Doctor. In fact, the statue reminds all of us about the compassion that is often present in a patient/doctor relationship. Bill often sat in front of this wonderful piece of art, perhaps not even realizing its message. It doesn't take long to recognize that the image of the "gentle doctor" has been illuminated deep within his soul. Bill was the "gentle doctor" to that Beagle's family; he understood the value of the dog to its family, not because of his veterinary training, but because of a life built deeply on understanding the principles of the bond.

Today, Bill's story is increasingly more common. There is a new interdisciplinary field called anthrozoology that highlights the study of the relationships between humans and animals. One key area in the field is studying the bond.

Today, there are a number of ways to define this unique relationship. According to the American Veterinary Medical Association (AVMA), "the human-animal bond is a mutually beneficial and dynamic relationship between people and other animals that is influenced by behaviors that are essential to the health and well-being of both. This includes, but is not limited to, emotional, psychological, and physical interactions with people, other animals, and the environment." This is amazing when we think of the history of humans and companion animals, because this is a very long relationship. Historically, the human/canine relationship goes back almost 12,000 years and the human/feline relationship 9,500 years. Gregory Berns, director of the Emory University Center for Neuropolicy and the lead investigator of the center's dog project, posits that the close relationship between humans and dogs may have an evolutionary basis. He explains, "The dog's brain represents something special about how humans and animals came together. It's possible that dogs have even affected human evolution. People who took dogs into their homes and villages may have had certain advantages. As much as we made dogs, I think dogs probably made some part of us, too."

The relationship between humans and dogs is especially strong regarding tasks that involve social cognition. In fact, Brian Hare (2013) suspects that, in this area, the similarities between dogs and humans are even closer than between humans and other more closely related species such as the great apes. Like Berns, Hare hypothesizes that, over centuries, dogs and humans have shared "convergent cognitive evolution" that has resulted in mutually inheritable traits, particularly the ability to reach across species in order to cooperate and communicate in an almost human-like manner. Humans, too, have benefited from this relationship as our relationship with canine companions has shaped our own preferred methods of communication and even cognition.

So what is it that has caused us to become closer to these other species of animals? I believe one of the most critical aspects in this evolution is a growing respect and understanding that our companion animals are sentient beings with emotions and thoughts. Once we accept this position, it changes the way many of us view these animals. Let's scrutinize the American Veterinary Medical Association's definition at this point and identify a few of the factors that contribute to and strengthen this relationship.

The first factor is the interpretation, or sometimes the misinterpretation, of certain behaviors that are human-like. Again, we return to the anthropomorphic position that suggests our relationships with animals have these human qualities. For some of us, our animal companions are humans, although we're going to need to talk about the fact that in some ways this may not be the healthiest way to look at this relationship.

The second factor is the animal's dependence on its human counterpart, which has probably become an even more significant contributor to the relationship. When people have pets, they begin to appreciate and recognize the importance of that pet in their daily lives and how dependent that animal is on them. For those who have really become connected, there is a sense of pride that they have accepted the responsibility. Perhaps one of the biggest changes that has occurred in the last 50 to 100 years is our understanding of our relationship with other species. Rather than viewing the relationship as a utilitarian role, our animals now play more of a companionship role. Understanding this change is crucial, because we recognize that we don't just take from animals. They are not subordinates; rather, they are companions. The key concept is that many of us recognize our pets as friends and members of our own family, and over the years, we have seen these pets leave the backyard and garage to enter our homes and bedrooms and really become an integral part of our family life.

The third factor pertains to our daily routines. The companion animal's residence in the home allows both humans and animals to share daily routines. It's not uncommon for all of us to walk with our companion animals and to do things with them that enhance and even enrich our daily lives.

Finally, for some people, companion animals provide a sense of security. They serve not only as protectors of the home but also as a sympathetic ear in the late evening.

I recently had a conversation with Richard Timmins, DVM, to get his opinion on the AVMA's definition of the bond. I met Rick when he was the director of the Center for Animals in Society at the University of California–Davis, and he is now on the faculty of Carroll College in Montana. I have been very impressed with his knowledge and tremendous insight into human-animal interactions:

> My veterinary education in the 1970s trained me to be a pretty successful dog and cat repairman, but it had not prepared me for that unique and dynamic relationship that defined each owner/pet dyad that entered my clinic. The depth of that relationship and its impact on the decisions and actions of the clients certainly varied, but there was at least one underlying commonality: the pet was meaningful to the human in some specific and important fashion. Now, of course, we know about the physiology of the relationship — the cardiovascular effects, the flow of neurochemicals, the relaxation response, etc. But at that time, when the term "human-animal bond" was just entering the lexicon, I focused on trying to grasp what that "meaning" was for the individual client and his or her pet. Only when I began to understand it could I be effective in my work. It was essential to determine which roles the pet played in the daily lives of the human family and to recognize how the roles changed over time. This allowed a more cogent communication regarding the development of a wellness plan that could satisfy the health needs of the pet and the needs of the client. This eventually evolved into the concept of Veterinary Family Practice (www.avfp.org). During the many iterations of my thirty-plus years in veterinary medicine — moving from practice to industry to academia, I have come to appreciate the AVMA's definition of the human-animal bond as a beneficial and dynamic relationship between people and animals that has social, emotional, psychological, and physical ramifications. That is a handy panoramic description. But when I am asked, "What is the human-animal bond?" my immediate response is to ask, "Which human, and which animal?" In spite of the physiology arising from shared genes and a shared evolution, our experiences and those of the animals that play a role in our lives will define the nature of the bond that forms between us.

A few years ago, I had the opportunity to write a chapter with Temple Grandin for my handbook. Many of you may be familiar with her work in the field of animal sciences; her work with animals has made a tremendous impact on how we view our interactions with cattle and other species. Dr. Grandin, as you may know, has been diagnosed with autism. However, she believes her autism has given her a unique perspective into the ways animals think and feel. She believes that "autistic people can think the way animals think," putting them in the perfect position to translate "animal talk." She notes that it took her a long time to realize her unique gift.

Being primarily a visual thinker, Grandin credits her distinctive insight into the minds of animals to this sensitivity to changes within an animal's environment. She notes that, like her, animals are sensory-based thinkers, not word thinkers. Once this is appreciated, we begin to understand animals very differently.

In her well-respected book, *Animals in Translation*, Grandin defines her perceptions of how animals perceive the world and the importance of animals in our lives. Early in the book, Grandin points out that "people and animals are supposed to be together" (p. 5), and she espouses how animals saved her life. During my talks with her about her perceptions of the bond, she explains that there is an unspoken human-animal bond that generally only those who have lived it can really understand. She notes that animals help us become more human for a variety of reasons. Thousands of years ago, humans who had domestic dogs had an advantage — the dogs protected and hunted for them, and as they both evolved, dogs were eventually bred so that they could be more attuned to human needs. Today this translates into one of the major ingredients of why the bond is so critical: companionship. People who attain more meaningful relationships with animals seem happier than those whose relationships are not complete. Grandin goes on to say that the bond is built on the mutual trust that neither one will hurt the other. In her book, she explains, "A good rider and his horse are a team — it's not just a one-way relationship where the human tells the horse what to do, and horses are super-sensitive to their riders and are constantly responding to [their] needs without being asked" (p. 6). She believes that the bond becomes more meaningful because we respect the animal's behavior and consider its point of view.

Dr. Alan Beck is a noted leader in studying human/animal relationships. He was the first director of the University of Pennsylvania's Center for the Interaction of Animals and Society and a founding member of the Delta Society, along with Leo Bustad and Michael McCulloch. Currently the director of Purdue University School of Veterinary Medicine's Center for the Human-Animal Bond, he gives great insight into how the concept of the bond was developed:

> The first "official" use of the term, "human-animal bond" appears in the *Proceedings of the Meeting of Group for the Study of Human–Companion Animal Bond* in Dundee, Scotland, March 23-25, 1979.
>
> The human-animal bond is not a discipline; it is a theoretic construct for observed behavioral events. The province of human-animal interaction is the behavioral, psychological, physiological, ecological, social, and

ethical consequences of the relationship between people and animals that is different than when either partner occurs independently.

Today, pet animals are pervasive in American society, as some 62 percent of all U.S. households have at least one pet animal. A vast majority of pet owners (76 percent) are found in the traditional family (parents, older adults, and siblings); 63 percent of owners are married.

The new commitment to animals stems not only from our general sensitivity to the welfare of animals but from a newer appreciation of the many roles animals play in our lives. The term "the human-animal bond" was unashamedly borrowed from the respected association found between parents and their offspring — the so-called "parent-infant bond."

To be a "bond," the effect on each partner has to be mutual and significant. The association between humans and their pet animals is, indeed, mutual and significant.

The human-animal bond involves complex psychological and physiological interactions between people and their pets that have profound influence on human and animal health and behavior. For the most part, the research was modeled after what was known about the effects humans had on each other — social support theory. Indeed, pets are often referred to as "members of the family," a metaphor to capture the feelings and intensity of the relationship, if not being biologically accurate. Family membership is a common way to elevate the importance of a person or object. Such is the nature of our relationship with our pets.

Perhaps another aspect of the definition of the bond could come from an ontological dimension of the relationship. By ontological, I [Dr. Alan Beck] refer particularly to the very nature of human existence and being. The bond between a loving human and loyal pet can transcend emotion and reach deep into our sense of what it means to be and feel human. Even the most emotionally hardened individuals (e.g., prison inmates) experience the bond in ways that can surface an almost primal awareness of self, of being in the moment, and of being in the absence of the social-psychological constructs that constrain learned behaviors (in this sense, there may be a liberating quality to the bond). There may also be a metacognitive dimension to the bond that engenders self-reflection and a heightened awareness of our core selves. For some, the bond may even take on an ethereal quality that lifts us out of our petty preoccupations and for a moment in time allows us to experience an almost spiritual connection with a pet. The bond is honest, without pretense, and is illuminative. For many of us, the bond brings out our very best selves.

REDEFINING THE BOND: STORGE—FAMILIAL LOVE

So what do we call our relationship with animals? A bond or kinship? *The Oxford English Dictionary* defines kinship as "the recognized ties of relationship, by descent, marriage, or ritual, that form the basis of social organization." Our "kinship" with animals is very much exactly that — a relationship we recognize that fits somewhere in our social organization — and it seems that what we feel for animals is often the same type of love we feel for family and close friends. Historically, the dog has become known as "man's best friend." When people, especially in Western cultures, describe a companion animal's place in their hearts, it seems most natural to use kinship terms like son, daughter, brother, and sister, or to say they are "best friends." But why do we do this?

The term "kinship" was created in order to describe familial relationships within a group of people, but it has come a long way. In Western society today the concept of kinship has changed and evolved to include people outside of the immediate and blood-related family circles. In sociocultural studies, where the term is most applied, anthropologists are beginning to recognize a need to update how kinship is talked about and used. David Schneider, in *A Critique of the Study of Kinship*, asserts that a distinction must now be made between "social or cultural kinship" and "physical kinship." Physical kinship relates more to reproduction and consanguinity, or being related by blood. Social kinship, on the other hand, relates to the idea that, in many cultures and societies, kinship terms are used for those outside of biological ties. Schneider cites an old debate between anthropologists in the late nineteenth century regarding Native American kinship terms. In the debate, Emil Durkheim argued that the "assertation [sic] that kinship terms mark true biological relations … cannot be so since, for in the case of the Omaha and Choctaw, a single term may be used for persons … who all stand in the same relation to ego so far as their totem" (p. 99). In other words, the Omaha and Choctaw people use the same "kin" term for people on the same social level as a person, rather than those who are blood related. Schneider goes on to argue, "It is therefore this social convention of their kinship, not their actual blood relationship, that defines them as kin and that therefore defines kinship" (p. 100).

Although Schneider was talking about Native Americans, I believe it is possible to apply this argument to our relationship with animals. When we invite animals into our families, we change our relationship to them in order to reflect the familial aspect of our feelings. We use terms that most accurately describe the feelings we have for them as surrogate members of our family, the same as we would a best friend or important figure in our lives.

Perhaps the reason we use kinship terms with our animals is because they describe a special relationship and have an immediate and definite connotation to which we can easily relate. Some might say this relationship is "the human-animal bond," assuming that "the bond" is enough of a description, and leave it at that. Yet, as we have seen, when we examine definitions of the bond, something is missing.

Let's again look closely at AVMA's definition: "a mutually beneficial and dynamic relationship between people and other animals that is influenced by behaviors that are essential to the health and well-being of both." This definition seeks to describe the benefits of the bond and acknowledges that it is indeed beneficial and relevant. The fact that it has been acknowledged at all indicates that there has been progress in the medical community to validate the "emotional" aspect of having an animal companion. While true, this is a very clinical and somewhat sterile description and does not quite capture what I believe are the most important aspects of our relationship with animals: namely, affection and love.

I propose we find a new way to describe the bond that incorporates these other aspects. Kinship isn't quite right, because it brings with it those other connotations that some might argue against; not everyone sees their pet as kin. However, I hope most people would agree that the same affection we have toward family members exists with these animals.

There is a word, *storge* (STOR-gay) that comes to us from Greece. It is one of six "types" of love and is well described by John Alan Lee in his book, *The Colours of Love*. Lee defines *storge* as "love without fever or folly, a feeling of natural affection such as you might have for a favourite brother or sister" (p. 77). A person who loves storgically has a "basic attitude of familiarity: 'I've known you a long time, seen you in many moods.' This familiarity breeds realistic candour and insight, not a probing, analytical kind, but quiet and stable" (pg. 87).

Surprisingly, Lee was not the only person to describe this type of affectionate, familial love. C.S. Lewis, author of the Chronicles of Narnia series, wrote a little-known book describing four of the main types of love. He says of *storge* (which he calls "Affection"), "Even in animal life, and still more in our own, Affection extends far beyond the relation of mother and young. This warm comfortableness, this satisfaction in being together, takes in all sorts of objects. It is indeed the least discriminating of loves" (p. 32). Lewis even recognized that this affection exists across species: "There need be no apparent fitness between those whom it unites . . . It ignores the barriers of age, sex, class, and education. It can exist between a clever young man from the university and an old nurse … It ignores even the barriers of species. We see it not only between dog and man but, more surprisingly, between dog and cat" (p. 32).

When we use this new word, *storge*, we immediately see that it encompasses both the AVMA concept of a having a beneficial nature as well as the kinship aspect of feeling deeply familial. *Storge* provides a perfect solution to the conundrum of finding a word that truly describes where our companion animals fall in our lives.

Tami Smith, a student at the Humane Society University, offers her perception of this unique contributing factor to our relationships. She describes an early experience helping raise piglets on her neighbor's farm and the way in which it changed her perception of animals and her relationship with them:

> Reflecting back on those years I would offer that the bond I formed allowed me to connect with other animals and to humans. I had to be gentle and quiet with the piglets, so I learned patience. The bond was an awakening of pure love. It was a bridge, a connection, to all other beings, which led to me attempting to be a blessing for all animals and humans. I would suggest that the most important aspect of the human-animal bond is the ability for it to allow for that awakening. When we treat our animals with love and respect, we open our hearts and minds to that pure love which allows for that connection to all. I imagine that the loving bonds that I have created with many companion animals over the years have been a constant reminder of that pure love.

From her description, it is clear Tami associates the concept of the bond with love, which goes deeper than any clinical definition we have come across so far. She clearly feels strongly that there is more to the bond than simple health benefits. What she feels for these animals is *storgic* love, because *storge* encompasses that purity she describes. As Tami has discovered, we have a particular love for animals that is not passionate or fleeting, but pure and simple and deep.

REDEFINING THE BOND: COMPANIONSHIP AND FRIENDSHIP

Recently, I was speaking to Marc Beckoff about his perceptions of the human-animal bond. Marc is an ethologist — a scientist who studies animal behavior — and a well-respected scholar in his field. When I asked him how he viewed the bond, he was quick to respond that it related to friendship. He didn't differentiate between friends who were human or nonhuman. I thought his response to be quite interesting, and he followed by saying that friends are kind to their friends, inferring the importance of compassion in any relationship.

In reality, how would many of us define friendship? In most cases, friends are beings (human and nonhuman) who enjoy spending time with one another and who are unconditional with their love. Friendship is a unique blend of affection, trust, respect, loyalty, and love. It also is a relationship that can never be one-sided. In the context of the given topic, I believe that animals can express their feelings and are extremely loyal. According to research, true friendship incorporates the two previously listed variables and seems to point out that the relationship is dependent on the importance of affection and a reciprocal alliance between the individuals. In most cases, friends usually are instrumental in providing emotional support. That being the case, it isn't illogical to assume that a companion animal could meet all of the above options. Consider the story of Hachiko, a golden brown Akita who waited nine years at a train station in Shibuya, Japan, for his master at precisely the same time every day when the train was due at the station. This appears to meet the test of feelings, loyalty, and friendship. And let us not forget the story of Argos, Odysseus's dog who waited twenty years for his master to return and died once he recognized Odysseus.

According to Townley (2010), there does seem to be a mutuality of affection between pets and people. When looking at friendships between people and their companions, one of the challenges often discussed is the terminology we use. Some believe, as Milligan (2009) does, that the terms "guardianship" and "companionship" are perhaps more appropriate than "friendship," because they more suitably identify the dependent relationships between animals and their human counterparts. Milligan states that, like friendship, companionship involves some kind of reciprocity and mutual appreciation. In his writing, he suggests human/animal relationships are deeply valuable and that the choice to modify the terminology and not utilize the term "friendship" does not imply a more resistant attitude.

Perhaps one of the most powerful aspects of our relationship with animals pertains to social supports. Many of us can speculate how our companions are supportive to our daily lives. Three researchers (Bonas, McNicholas, and Collis, 2000) at Warwick University in England developed a survey that they called the Network of Relationships Inventory. The inventory helped people to explain and evaluate the different kinds of supports they derived from both human and non-human relationships. Although their research seemed to indicate that human relationships scored higher overall in terms of major social supports, those who were surveyed seemed to indicate that pet dogs actually scored higher on certain areas such as reliance, nurturance, and companionship. Cats ranked lower than dogs in all of these areas. The researchers' study clearly points out that most animal guardians have no difficulty saying that their non-human companions are very important in their lives.

Again, I want bring the idea of *storge* and this new definition of contemporary kinship into the conversation. It seems that companionship and friendship can be used as words to readily describe aspects of *storge* and kinship, almost interchangeably. The relationship Beckoff mentions incorporates the aspects we see in *storge*: nurturing, reciprocity, and affection.

Molly Jenkins, a social worker for the American Humane Association, has no difficulty viewing her relationship with animals as friendships. She states, "Most of the animals I have known in my life have been among my dearest friends. I had an interesting experience a few years ago in which I referred to my cat, Loretta, as my friend. The person I was speaking with almost seemed to scoff or think it was somehow ridiculous to refer to Loretta as a friend of mine (rather than as my pet cat). I wish I had spent more time with this person to understand why the notion of human/animal friendship seemed wrong or, at the very least, inappropriate. Because for me, Loretta provides companionship, trust, cheer, comfort, and care. I am responsible for her well-being, but I also feel that she is attentive to my needs. Our relationship is mutually supportive and loving, which is something that I think marks meaningful friendships."

In a similar vein, I too believe that you can have a true friendship with an animal, as was the case when I met a dog who became a good friend. We used to take my oldest dog, Puppy, to a dog park, where we came across a friendly dog, Savannah. After a few encounters, she quickly adopted me as her human friend. Whenever I entered the park, she would run over to me quickly and wag her tail, waiting for a biscuit or two. As years went on, whenever I would walk around town and would bump into Savannah, she would look at me with those wonderful brown eyes, waiting for me to bend down and give her a belly rub and gentle pets. If she was lucky, I would have biscuits in my pocket to share as well. The end result was that we both left with warmth in our hearts.

As years went on, our relationship continued, although I didn't see Savannah all that often. In early 2008, I crossed paths with Diana (Savannah's adopted mom), and she shared with me that Savannah had been diagnosed with osteosarcoma. A few days later, Savannah had her front leg amputated, but the prognosis seemed quite positive; she went home thirty-six hours after her surgery. Once I heard the news, I asked her human family if they minded if I came to visit. Although I always got along with Diana and Wayne, we were mainly acquaintances, but they knew how concerned I was about their little girl and welcomed my visits. One visit turned into two, and for the next seven months, I would visit Savannah every Sunday. These became special afternoons for me. She really seemed to relish our visits. Whenever I arrived, she greeted me with tremendous enthusiasm. Through the years, it never ceases to amaze me that our friends, including dogs, can greet their loved ones with such exuberance.

Savannah had some canine siblings living with her, and when I visited I would always bring treats along for them as well, and though I would devote most of my attention to Savannah, I would try to share a bit of my attention with them. However, on one occasion, Savannah became very perturbed at sharing my attention, and she walked out of the room sulking. She didn't seem to want me to share that time with the others.

Our visits were special — just like spending time with my human friends. We periodically took walks. These were a challenge for her, but she moved with grace. I visited Savannah on New Years Eve in 2008. She looked tired but gave the appearance that she was happy to see me. That would be the last time I would see my dear friend. Shortly after my last visit, Savannah passed away.

Years ago, if you told me that I could have a friendship with a pet, I probably would have disagreed, but today I would concur with Molly's position that we can have that type of enjoyment with an animal companion; that they truly are friends and not subordinates. In retrospect, has my relationship with Savannah ever been repeated with other animals? It has not, but I think the possibility that these relationships can exist is something we all need to appreciate. Although Savannah passed away several years ago, I continue to think about her, and my friendship with her family has continued with periodic visits. Because of Savannah, I now have new friends with whom my newest puppies and I have play dates. However, whenever we're together, we still talk about our special relationship and my unique friendship with Savannah.

Now let me share with you the story of Daisy.

The stalking began early in the morning just as a hint of day began to lighten the gray California skies. She snuck into his bedroom, moved quietly toward his side of the bed, and began to whimper almost imperceptibly, but loud enough to carry. Soon he pushed the pillow off his face and opened one eye. "Good morning, Daisy. You'll just have to wait until I'm dressed and had my coffee. Now go back to bed." She padded softly out of the bedroom and went back to her pillow on the couch, knowing it wouldn't be too long before he staggered out of bed, groggy and in need of his morning coffee. Her job was done; all she had to do now was wait until he reached the kitchen table with his paper and coffee. Soon he appeared with his pants in hand and headed for the kitchen with her in lockstep. No letting go of him now — she had him right where she wanted him.

As he dropped into his chair at the table with paper and coffee before him, she sat patiently for about five minutes before she made her next move. Quickly, she went to his chair and placed her front paws on his arm, shaking his coffee cup. "Daisy, you'll have to give me a break. I'll be ready in a couple of minutes." She lay on the floor with her head between her paws, looking up at him with a fixed stare. Finally, unable to ignore her any longer, he went into the living room looking for his shoes. She began to race back and forth in the living room but never out of sight of the front door. It was time — time to charge outside, baying at the local squirrels and letting them know she was out and looking for prey. Not that she would ever do anything if she caught one. There was a flurry of activity at the front door, with the Beagle's dutiful barking and baying; the door opened and she was free but never out of his sight. If he wasn't behind her, she doubled back until she saw him and then charged off in search of new smells and tidbits only a dog could savor. Over the last nine years, they had become a fixture in the neighborhood, but how did this friendship begin? Where did she come from, or how did he find her? Who was this playful Beagle who loved people more than other dogs; what had brought them together? These are all good questions that deserve an answer, and you shall have one.

They met for the first time in the summer of 2003 when he had gone home to see his mother after a hiatus of twenty years. He had made the trip at the urging of his wife, who reminded him that he only had one mother and he needed to mend any broken fences with her before either of them died and it would be too late. It had been a memorable trip. He reconnected with his mother and found their differences were minor and few. They had a wonderful two weeks, just hanging out and reading in the evenings. The only disturbance in the house was his mother's new Beagle puppy that kept demanding attention and stole his blanket that first night. Finally, after repeated attempts to keep the puppy out, he surrendered and let her sleep with him.

That was their first meeting, and as the visit went on, they became even closer, especially in the evening after dinner. His mother was not a particularly good cook; in fact, everything she cooked was done in the microwave. So after dinner, he would grab Daisy's leash and take her for a walk to the nearest hamburger stand for something more palatable than corned-beef hash and pistachio pudding. When he and his mother would settle down after the evening walk to read, Daisy would jump in the recliner with him and nap. In retrospect, Daisy adopted him during that two-week period, and whenever he left the house to visit other relatives or play golf, Daisy would set up a howl of disappointment at being left behind.

After the visit was over and he returned to California, his mother told him how Daisy kept looking for him every day, and he admitted to his mother that he missed Daisy also, but there was no room in his life for another dog. Work and travel kept him on the go, and it would not be fair to a pet. He had also sworn after his last dog died that he wasn't going to take on another dog that in all fairness would become part of the family. He was too old and determined to make life simpler from here on.

However, soon after he was back in California, he received a call from his sister with terrible news. Their mother had stomach cancer and did not have long to live. Immediately, the whole family gathered at their mother's bedside and prepared for the worst. His mother did not have many requests, but the one she was most concerned with was the puppy. What would become of her? His sister and her daughter had three large dogs, so there was no room for Daisy with them. Would she go the Humane Society and hopefully be adopted? All eyes turned to him. He tried to avoid the obvious, but Daisy was there, also looking at him. There was no denying what fate had in store for the two of them — Daisy would go to California and become a part of his family. Shortly thereafter, Daisy began her trip west. Now, when he walks with Daisy and people ask him where Daisy came from, he always replies, "She's my inheritance."

There may be unintended consequences or unexpected aftereffects from our human/animal relationships. The relationship may yield more than just familial love; it may also serve as a link to others, just as Savannah was a link between her family and me. Often, pets serve as a bridge between others that can dissolve barriers and enhance friendships. If you think about it, Daisy is more than her owner's inheritance; she is a constant reminder of his mother. Sometimes, when they are walking and he talks to her, he kind of feels that he is talking to his mother at the same time. And perhaps he is, but one thing is certain: the two of them are one. She is his dog and he is her friend — faithful companions who enrich each other's lives.

—

One of the great mysteries in the evolution of our species is exactly when humans first encountered the dog, but that is lost in the shadows of time. We can assume, however, that somewhere along the way dogs began to travel with humans, and over decades, centuries, even eons, they developed a sense of belonging and an understanding that together they were a unit each dependent upon the other, not just for protection but also for comfort. From that early realization, the concept of *storge* came into being as a natural consequence of any relationship, including our very special relationships with companion animals. For those of us who have known the love of a family pet, especially a dog, we intuitively understand this kinship. As I have maintained throughout this chapter, our pets are not just pets; they are family. Just as we are there for them, they are there for us.

CHAPTER TWO

IT'S MORE THAN JUST PUPPY LOVE:
Relationships that Support Our Health and Well-Being

The little girl was quite young — too young to fully understand the situation — yet she had experienced it and now had no choice but to deal with it. She was so shaken she probably couldn't speak if she tried, but her embrace of Dutchess said what everybody there was thinking. Their embrace was so touching that a Yahoo.com photographer took their picture and featured it in a news story. She sat for a long time with Dutchess, and Dutchess never moved away, just leaned into the girl as if to hug her back. The moment resonated with Mark and everyone around them, and for a bit of time, they just fell silent and watched.

It wasn't a normal Saturday afternoon. It was a day of mourning in a town that had just experienced a horrific tragedy. The date was December 15, 2012. The town was Newtown, Connecticut. Just one morning earlier, twenty children and six adults had been shot and killed at Sandy Hook Elementary School. This normal community on the East Coast was dealing with unbelievable devastation and loss. Today all were grieving the loss of sons and daughters; some were adults but many were youngsters at the beginning of their lives. So many dreams and lives were left unfulfilled in a single moment of despair.

Many outsiders arrived in Newtown to lend support to this traumatized town, and among those responders were four-legged healers. Words were not part of their care. They lent support through their warmth, acceptance, reassurance, and physical presence.

The dogs were warmly accepted for what they brought to the town square. They offered a distraction of cheerfulness at a time when joy was hard to find. They also acted as comfort creatures for those who had lost their sense of faith in humanity and found evil staring directly at them.

When I first read the early reports from Newton, Connecticut, I felt great pain in my heart for all of those who had lost a beloved family member or friend, but I was pleased to witness an outpouring of support from strangers who wanted to help. I was equally pleased to see four-legged creatures who came to lend a helping paw. Thirty-five years ago, when my interest in the human-animal bond began to evolve, bringing comfort dogs would not have been an accepted practice. What has changed in the past several decades has been society's awareness of the value of this intangible connection to other species and how they contribute to our well-being. Next, an overview of our association with our faithful companions is presented. I also will discuss how animals improve our quality of life and explain why these relationships may flourish.

BOND 101: UNDERSTANDING THE PHYSIOLOGICAL AND PSYCHOSOCIAL BENEFITS OF ANIMALS

I have heard from many people over the years that they believe their pets help them feel better and that simply being in their presence lifts the spirits. Although these feelings may be intuitive, we now have scientific evidence that concurs with this position.

Headey (2007) notes that social science research from Germany, Australia, Britain, and the United States agrees that owning a pet has a positive impact on humans. These studies conclude that pet ownership is associated with better self-reported physical and psychological health as well as fewer medical visits. German and Australian surveys were administered to a large cross-sectional sample of citizens in both countries. These surveys asked questions about the role of pets in the lives of people and found that respondents who owned pets appeared to live healthier lives. The surveys led the researchers to assess why certain groups of people gained the greatest benefits from their interactions with pets. For example, older, shy, or lonely people appeared to benefit the most from the companionship they received, while those who traditionally lived more sedentary lives benefited more from the active lifestyles of their pets. The ultimate challenge for the researchers wasn't only documenting the health benefits of animals but also determining what causes these positive changes. This challenge presents one of the greatest questions left unanswered. Why do we have these unique connections with non-human companions? Later in this chapter we will discuss some of the reasons, ranging from our need to be closer to nature to our strong urge to be caregivers. For now, let's begin our discussion with an overview on the current research on the health benefits of pets in our lives.

It was in early 1980 when Erika Friedmann and her colleagues published a pioneering study that looked at pet ownership by seventy-eight adult patients who had been discharged from a coronary care unit. Their results revealed that, of the seventy-eight patients who were still alive one year post-discharge, fifty (64 percent) of them owned at least one pet. Of the patients who did not survive one year post-discharge, only three (21 percent) were pet owners. The results indicate that pet ownership promoted better health, but the reasons this occurred were not initially noted in the study. Later Dr. Friedmann proposed that pets help people relax and that calm interaction may lead to short-term, anti-arousal effects, including a decrease in blood pressure. Upcoming in this section of the chapter, we will discuss some of the current research suggesting there is a brain-chemistry "connection" with pet ownership that literally rewires how we think and feel. This new evidence emphasizes that positive emotions trigger the release of "feel-good" neural transmitters.

James Lynch, one of the co-investigators of this pioneering research in 1980, was a student of William Gannt (one of Pavlov's last students) at Johns Hopkins University. Lynch discovered that, when people pet a dog, they become more relaxed and calm. Lynch coined a term that he inferred was a vascular seesaw in human dialogue. He observed that blood pressure rises when people speak to each other, especially in emotional situations, yet blood pressure falls when people relate to animals. He believed this occurs because human-animal interactions, while limited in speech, are rich with tactile sensation. Touch helps people enter a state of hyper-relaxation.

These original findings ignited a flurry of new studies that looked at the health roles of animals in our lives. For example, Allen (2001) found that people with borderline hypertension lowered their blood pressure when they took their dogs to work. Similarly, findings from other studies demonstrated that petting an animal decreases blood pressure and heart rate. Friedmann and her associates (1980) found that, when children read aloud to a dog, their blood pressure was lower. It appeared that the presence of a dog reduced the psychological stressors for children.

The work of Serpell (1991), a leading anthrozoologist from the University of Pennsylvania, and that of Siegel (1990), indicated that pet owners have better physical health due to cardio exercise with their pets, especially dogs. Their studies also detected that seniors who adopted pets experienced a decrease in the frequency of minor health ailments, including headaches, painful joints, hay fever, inattention, and dizziness. It appears that pet companionship reduces negative responses to daily life activities.

Furthermore, we are now realizing that pets can reduce tension and increase the quality of daily life in a variety of settings. For example, research is clear in pointing out that people who brought their dogs to work were less anxious and more comfortable in the work environment. A 1987 National Institutes of Health (NIH) workshop entitled "The Health Benefits of Pets" laid the groundwork for recognition of the potential healing power of human-animal interactions. In fact, Beck and Glickaman (1987) at the meeting recommended, ". . . all future studies of human health should consider the presence or absence of a pet in the home. . . . No future study of human health should be considered comprehensive if animals with which they share their lives are not included" (p. 3).

Dog walking has always been considered a beneficial form of exercise. A professor at the University of Missouri and a friend of mine, Rebecca Johnson, developed a program in 1978 called "Walk a Hound, Lose a Pound," which paired overweight people with shelter dogs. Some research points to improved fitness and overall health as a positive consequence of dog walking. For example, in a study conducted by Coleman and his associates (2008), 53 percent of dog owners who walked their dogs met the national recommendations for daily minutes of moderate to vigorous physical activity, as opposed to non-dog owners. Furthermore, their research found that dog owners who walked their dogs were significantly less obese than owners who did not walk their dogs.

The human-animal relationship is beneficial to both pets and their owners. For example, petting and walking a pet decreases the heart rate and blood pressure not only of pet owners but also of the animal. In fact, physiological benefits, including lower blood pressure, can be gained simply from watching fish in an aquarium, a wildlife video, or a television program on Animal Planet. These findings were supported by the work of Beck and his associates (1981), who studied the impact on people who watched fish in tanks.

Beyond the plethora of research on the physiological benefits of companion animals, considerable research highlights psychological and social benefits of human-animal interactions. Such studies show that human relationships with animals decrease depression and stress and have a positive impact on loneliness and feelings of isolation. Various studies illustrate that the presence of a beloved pet acts as a buffer of protection against adversity. One such study was completed by Judith Siegel of the University of California–Los Angeles in 1993. Although it seems to be common sense, Siegel's research revealed that having an animal nearby significantly increased the chances of conversation, which indirectly encouraged social interaction. That is, strangers may verbally interact by beginning a conversation with questions about a pet's age, name, and breed. Many report that being around animals contributes to their feeling less isolated and more engaged with other individuals. Advertisers frequently use animals in ads and commercials because they elicit warmth and positive attitudes.

Deborah Wells (2009) highlighted that pet ownership may not only help the prevention of relatively minor ailments but may also reduce the chances of people developing more chronic conditions. There is a definite correlation between pet ownership and some of these chronic symptoms for elderly people.

In 1975 in England, Mugford and M'Comiskey conducted one of the pioneering studies that highlighted the importance of animals in the lives of the elderly. They found that older people who lived independently and were given a budgie (a small bird) for companionship had significantly improved social lives and appeared happier than the control group who did not receive a bird. Additionally, Dr. Raina of Guelph University in Canada conducted an insightful study in 1999 that found that seniors who had animals in their homes showed an increase in activities, such as getting out of bed, getting dressed, and acting more independently in their daily lives. In the study, Dr. Raina pointed out that these results were somehow related to the sense of responsibility and the feeling of being needed that seemed to encourage the seniors to be active and responsible for their pets.

Lynette Hart, a leading scholar in the field of human/animal interactions, had similar findings when she conducted a study of senior dog owners in 1995. In her research, she found that seniors who owned dogs took twice as many walks as non-owners, and that these individuals seemed to report less dissatisfaction with their social and emotional lives. Perhaps the most crucial piece of information reported in her research was the fact that seniors who had animals in their lives spoke more about their present lives than about events in their past. This insight suggests that having active lives and interacting with pets give people the impetus and strength to persevere in a positive manner and think of life in the present rather than only focusing on the past.

See page 32 for some highlights of the major studies over the years that have demonstrated how our relationships with animals provide many of us with unique health opportunities. I do want to confess that, although these benefits seem very dramatic, most pet owners wouldn't see them as the highlight of their human-animal relationship. "Love is what brings me back to my comfort creatures. These benefits are just the icing on the cake."

HEALTH AND PSYCHOSOCIAL BENEFITS OF PETS: WHAT DOES THE RESEARCH SAY?

- Petting an animal causes decreases in blood pressure and/or heart rate (Eddy, 1996; Friedmann, Beck, and Lynch, 1983; Shiloh, Sorek, and Terkel, 2003)
- Stroking a pet can lower heart rate (McGreevy, Righetti, and Thomson, 2005; Vormbrock and Grossberg, 1988)
- The presence of a pet dog or cat can lower levels of heart rate and blood pressure in stressful situations such as completing mental arithmetic (Allen, Blascovich, and Mendes, 2002)
- The risk factor for coronary heart disease was significantly lower for pet owners than non-owners, particularly for males (Anderson, Reid, and Jennings, 1992)
- Lower levels of serum triglycerides (high levels of which are associated with increased risk for heart attacks in elderly pet owners compared to non-owners) (Dembicki and Anderson, 1996)
- Pet owners had significantly lower systolic blood pressure; pet owners had significantly lower plasma triglycerides (Jennings, 1995)
- Walking with a dog increases and enhances the opportunities to initiate and sustain chance conversations with strangers than walking alone (McNicholas and Collis, 2000; McNicholas et al., 2001)
- Pets can reduce feelings of loneliness and isolation (e.g., Headey, 1998)
- Women living entirely alone were more lonely than those living with either pets or other people (Zasloff and Kidd, 1994)
- Elderly people with pets have also been shown to have fewer symptoms of depression than those without pets (Roberts et al., 1996)

PUPPY LOVE MAY BE CHEMICAL — HAVING A BIOLOGICAL SPA TREATMENT

The most interesting research being conducted today relates to the changes in our neurotransmitters and neuropeptides as a consequence of our physical interaction with animals.

The earliest research was done by a South African psychologist named Odendaal, who observed that, during patients' interactions with their dogs, their endorphin (oxytocin and dopamine) levels increased significantly, and that cortisol levels decreased significantly. In 2003, he and another South African researcher conducted a study that measured the levels of oxytocin in dogs and humans when they interacted with each other. They discovered that blood pressure levels decreased and oxytocin levels increased in both. Their findings are now leading new researchers to continue their work so that we can further understand the unique impact of our bond with other species. We could view petting a dog as a sort of "biological spa treatment." Petting and interacting with a calm species or our companion animals help us feel really good, which in turn helps us to relax. So what does that mean? Let's look for a moment at the chemical interactions that go on inside of us.

Oxytocin is a nonapeptide produced in the hypothalamus and released in the pituitary gland. Oxytocin makes us feel happy, calm, patient, trusting, and sensitive to nonverbal forms of communication. It also increases pain tolerance and helps wounds heal more rapidly.

In essence, oxytocin helps us feel happy and trusting, and we release it at very specific moments in life. It is involved in our social recognition. This neurotransmitter has a powerful effect on the body's ability to be in a state of readiness to heal and help grow cells. In women, it has been found that the more oxytocin flowing through their body, the more they are inclined to ask for and receive advice. These women are also more sensitive to nonverbal communication. The love a mother feels for her child and the love two people feel for each other is strongly affected by oxytocin.

An interesting study by Nagasawa and his associates (2009) found that people who stared at their dogs for extended periods of time reported feeling closest to their dogs over the course of the experiment. The study suggested that the social interaction of gazing into the eyes of their dog increased the owners' oxytocin levels. Perhaps this gives new meaning to the phrase "love at first sight."

Oxytocin-producing cells are found in every part of the brain that deals with behavior and emotion. Olmert, a researcher interested in the biology of the bond, suggests that "pets . . . make us feel generous, which may be their greatest contribution to our well-being" (2009, p. 229). She explains that we cannot care for a pet if we only cares for ourselves. Pets are "an antidote to narcissism and therefore a boon to the health of not just the owner, but the community" (2009, p. 229). Olmert believes this "unselfish quality is what others sense in a pet owner and what makes pet owners more approachable — more socially desirable."

WHY WE BOND WITH OUR COMPANION ANIMALS

Numerous established theories try to explain how this unique human-animal relationship is developed. The following represents a brief discussion of these theories and how they explain the evolving relationship of humans and animals. As you read the following passages, consider thinking about yourself and how each theory may or may not support your own desire to be with animals. The three theories are presented in no specific order. They are the social support theory, the attachment theory, and the biophilia hypothesis.

Animals as Social Supports

For some people, pets provide alternatives for emotional and physical support. But first, what is the *meaning* of social support? Lin and Dean (1986) believe that social support is a valuable measure of quality of life. They believe that positive social support includes numerous variables including having meaningful social contacts, confidants, and companionship.

Harvard professors Paul R. Lawrence and Nitkin Nohria devote an entire chapter of their book *Driven: How Human Nature Shapes Our Choices* (2002) to the topic of social bonding. They contend that the need for social relationships and to bond with others is deeply ingrained in the human psyche and is one of four fundamental "drives" that explain why humans behave the way they do. They state, "All humans share an innate drive to bond — and this drive is a primary one" (p. 76). Essentially, the human need (and ability) to join social groups is one reason why we are here and saber-toothed tigers aren't. Social relationships help to shield us against environmental threats. Social groups have a relative advantage over individuals in a number of ways (e.g., economic, evolutionary, organizational, health).

It is evident that an individual's quality of life cannot be enhanced in a vacuum or in isolation. Schalock (1996) suggests that the use of social support is an efficient and effective way to maximize a person's independence, productivity, and life satisfaction. Cobb (1976) believes that having solid social support helps people realize they belong to meaningful networks and that they are thought of and needed. Social support can include family members, other people, technology, in-home living assistance, and animal companionship. Although Schalock (1996) did not infer that animals and pet companions fit that role, many scholars have suggested that, for some people, they do. For example, Straub (2007) identifies various perceived social supports and highly recommends animals as one healthy alternative. However, there continues to be a void in the literature demonstrating the therapeutic role animals often play in social support, though what is known is generally positive.

One of the most valuable contributions of animal companionship is that it provides support in difficult times, particularly for children. According to Strand (2004), children who have pets in their home often turn to them for comfort during high-stress situations such as parental discord. Children who are able to use their pet interaction as a "buffer," or a self-calming technique, may exhibit fewer behavioral problems because they have an outlet to help them regulate reactions to environmental stressors. Pets may provide both children and adults with an emotional buffer to help them cope with stressful environments or emotional discord.

The narrative at the beginning of this chapter highlights how people might turn to animals in difficult times to find moments of solace. When Mark Condon brought Dutchess, a Golden Retriever, to the memorial site after the Sandy Hook Elementary shooting, he did not know what to expect. After arriving in Newton, he easily found the memorial site at a city park in the middle of town. There were flowers and candles and hundreds of people milling around, including reporters everywhere. Mark noticed how eerily quiet, even silent, the downtown area was. It was a surreal experience. He watched for a while as people waited in line at the gas station or walked up the sidewalk. It was difficult to know just what to do in such a situation, but he quickly realized the value of Dutchess's presence for this community in mourning.

In the midst of heartbreak sat Dutchess, a silent pillar of warmth and support and a refuge from having to know what to say or how to act. Dozens of people approached Dutchess that day. Some, relieved for a moment of reprieve from the tragedy, made small talk about what Dutchess and Mark do. Some were curious to understand how this dog, now blind, lived so happily after losing her sight. Perhaps they felt some inspiration in relating to the suffering of someone else. Most people, though, just sat with her, embraced her, petted her head, and cried. One young girl, clearly shaken by the event and likely in shock, embraced Dutchess and sobbed into her soft fur. Dutchess embraced her back, pressing her muzzle into her shoulder and absorbing her sadness.

The process of healing appears to be simple for Dutchess; she always seems to know what to do. When kids are happy and excited, Dutchess gladly reciprocates the joy. In times like the Newtown tragedy, she recognizes her role, and she doesn't need sight to tell her the mood of the people around her. People who see her at work just know she has a special knack for the job. As Mark and Dutchess walked down the street on their way home from the memorial, several surprising interactions with passersby took place. People called out of their car windows, "Thank you for coming." Dutchess brought comfort, support, and love to the memorial that day. She may not have known exactly what had happened, but she knew what was needed of her and was glad to give it.

Our connections to animals can help us navigate through difficult times, especially when we need someone to lean on or to help us open up. Pets are also often relied on by people of various ages as an outlet for feelings and emotional refuge (Fine and Eisen, 2008; Melson, 2001). It is not uncommon to hear that people who feel isolated turn to their animals for company as well as an excuse to leave the house. Let's look at Bill's story.

Bill has been battling AIDS for several years and has a devotion to the cats in his life because they have helped him cope with living in isolation:

> They pick up on my feelings of loneliness and comfort me in a way I could not imagine. When they know I am sad, they are more attentive to me; almost to the point of annoyance because they won't leave me alone. I somehow find a spiritual connection with them; the process of petting them and taking care of them allows me to take a break from my own mental anguish. Many times I sing with them and find this as an outlet to relieve some of my anxiety.

In many ways, Bill's cats inoculate him from his debilitation and give him an outlet of joy. It is not surprising that several researchers hypothesize that positive social supports may protect people from the negative impacts of stressors, such as loneliness.

Jerry Schubel's relationship with his dog while rehabilitating from a childhood illness provides another example of the positive effects of social support.

As a young boy in second grade, Jerry fell ill and was diagnosed with Bright's disease (a kidney disease). The disease is now much better understood and more manageable, but unfortunately, at the time of Jerry's diagnosis, Bright's disease was poorly understood and Jerry was not expected to live. Upon falling ill, Jerry was taken to the University of Michigan hospital; he was then discharged and allowed to go home, where he would spend the next year in bed. When Jerry got home from the hospital, he knew that something more serious was going on because, up until then, the family dog, Lee, had always been an outdoor pet. Suddenly Jerry's parents allowed Lee not only in the house but also in Jerry's own bed! This was the beginning of a relationship that would become a core part of Jerry's recovery. For the next year, Lee slept in Jerry's bed, seldom leaving his side.

Jerry's older brother, John, who was nine at the time, still had a very active childhood. Jerry and Lee would often look out of Jerry's bedroom window at John and others playing. Jerry understood why he couldn't play, but he became aware that Lee was also giving up his playtime for him; the dog seemed to sense that something was happening to Jerry, and he willingly forfeited playtime in order to hang out with him. Jerry remains convinced that Lee had a great deal to do with his getting well.

Jerry recalled one of the manifestations of Bright's disease: the person would become very puffy. Jerry would awaken each morning with his eyes swollen shut.

During those times, Lee was always there, just lying still by his side because Jerry was not able to be active at all. Lee was his constant companion; Jerry's mother taught and was gone much of the day, and his brother was either at school or outside playing. The dynamic between Jerry and Lee went from a relationship that took place in spurts of activity during the day to one of constant companionship twenty-four hours a day. Jerry agreed that his parents must have known there was something special between him and Lee, as they were the ones who wanted Lee to sleep in the bed with Jerry. When Jerry was asked what message he could tell others about this special relationship, he said, "You can live in a city in an apartment and be gone all day with your dog confined to your apartment, but when you get home, the dog is at the front door, wagging its tail."

Jerry was raised in a little town in Michigan, and an old German doctor who lived close to them believed that a diet of no salt would be Jerry's only chance of recovery — if there was one at all. Jerry's mother, willing to try anything, began to prepare only salt-free foods to see if this diet would be her son's cure. Miraculously, after the better part of a year, Jerry began to get better. While the no-salt diet was clearly a factor, Jerry is convinced that his partnership with Lee also helped in his recovery. When asked how his relationship with Lee changed his early perceptions of the value of pets, Jerry responded that it became very clear to him that "dogs don't care how you look; they don't care if you are having a bad day or a good day; they're always there, happy and wagging their tails. I know there were many days I certainly didn't feel very well and probably wasn't as nice as I should have been, but it never changed the relationship and constant support. Dogs are always there for you."

One last example of the social support animals can offer comes to us from Bob, whose experience with a dog allowed him to express feelings that had been locked in his heart for many years. Recently, he and his younger brother experienced some turbulence in their relationship. As children they were closer, perhaps because of their proximity in age, but as they grew older, they became more estranged. Bob grew increasingly disturbed by his brother's poor life choices, specifically his substance abuse. He was using methamphetamines and became HIV positive. He didn't take care of himself (often not taking his medications), and the ramifications of his actions were tearing the family apart. He was eventually hospitalized with a yeast infection and, after six weeks in the hospital, ended up developing pneumonia. Although the situation seemed initially surmountable, once he contracted pneumonia, his health declined significantly and rapidly. People who have immune-compromised disorders like HIV have a harder time fighting off illness. In this case, Bob's younger brother's body simply couldn't fight the fluids that filled his lungs. To make matters worse, one evening he had such a severe coughing fit that it injured his heart.

What started off as hospitalization for something minor grew into a much more challenging and life-threatening health crisis. As the brother's health turned for the worse, their mom called Bob, asking him to come home to say his last goodbyes.

Bob's brother was put into hospice care, and one of his final wishes was to have his Scottish Terrier visit him, as he deeply missed their companionship. Unfortunately, that reunion didn't occur, but the day they were moving him into hospice, a West Highland White Terrier therapy dog came to visit the hospital. A nurse inquired if the family would be interested in having the terrier visit the brother, and the family assented immediately. They placed the dog next to Bob's brother on the bed and gently moved his hand onto her body. Although there really wasn't any movement, the family noticed some fluttering in his eyes. It was at that moment, perhaps because of the emotions stirring up, that Bob moved closer to his brother and told him he loved him; this was the first time he had been able to utter these words in many years.

Looking back, Bob attributes the peaceful way his brother passed away to the presence of the Westie. His voice cracked as he reflected on his last moments with his brother: "In some ways, it was that Westie, or the presence of the dog, that allowed me to open up and to put aside my anger. Seeing my brother lying next to the dog allowed me the opportunity to tell him that I still cared for him."

The Attachment Theory

The attachment theory postulates that we internalize our social interactions with others as conscious and unconscious mental representations of self and relationship partners. In other words, " . . . interactions that we have with attachment figures who are available and supportive in times of need foster the development of both a sense of attachment security and an overall boost to one's mental health and sense of well being" (Zilcha-Mano, Mikulincer, and Shaver, 2011, p. 542). John Bowlby coined the concept of an attachment behavioral system, which describes any behavior that is displayed to achieve the goal of a child remaining close to his/her caregiver during moments of stress or danger.

Bowlby's attachment theory is ". . . one of the most influential theories in personality and developmental psychology and provides insights into adjustment and psychopathology across the lifespan" (Zilcha-Mano et al., 2011, p. 541). The overall goal of the attachment system is to seek protection by means of being close to an attachment figure. Attachment theory is an empirically supported framework that describes how close relationships (with people and/or animals) affect emotion regulation, mental health, and psychological development (Zilcha-Mano, Mikulincer, and Shaver, 2012).

In the attachment theory regarding parent-child relationships, the child takes on the dependent role while the parent serves as the caregiver, soothing the needy and distressed child.

Although Bowlby was first and foremost interested in the bond between mothers and their children, he did not restrict attachment theory to these relationships (Julius et al., 2013). Just as the concept of attachment can be used to analyze child-parent relationships, it can also be used to consider human-pet relationships. When we think about the connection we have with a pet, we likely don't think about much other than the warm, loving sensations that arise. Rather than contemplating the biochemical reactions that occur from the human-animal bond, we simply enjoy the benefits of these reactions. With regard to the human-animal bond, several studies have found that "physical or cognitive proximity to a pet can be a source of comfort" (Zilcha-Mano, Mikulincer, and Shaver, 2012, p. 572). The attachment theory suggests that we as humans have a need to take care of others. In essence, those that follow this orientation prioritize their need in being a caregiver to their pets.

McConnell (2011) documented the benefits pet owners gain from their relationship with their pets. McConnell's findings support the idea that we see our pets as attachment figures (Zilcha-Mano et al., 2011). Several measures of well-being were administered to both pet owners and non-pet owners; what was found was that pet owners displayed a fulfillment of social needs that non- pet owners did not. In conjunction with other findings regarding the benefits pets provide to their owners (i.e. comfort and relief), McConnell supports the concept of owners viewing pets as attachment figures (Zilcha-Mano et. al, 2012).

Living Testimonies of the Attachment Theory and Companion Animals

MaryAnn is a fifty-two-year-old woman who worked as a skilled wound-care nurse before being diagnosed with post-laminectomy syndrome, a spinal condition that causes severe pain. In MaryAnn's case, the condition has left her permanently disabled, but she was recently told that at some point she could regain her ability to walk. She has volunteered with PAWS as a foster owner and was happy to attest to the healing power animals bring.

Tara Whitefield from PAWS suggested that MaryAnn consider adopting a dog, especially because all of her pets had passed away. "When you're chronically ill, it's so important to do something for another being that's outside of yourself . . . and that's what I did. It became profoundly important for me to foster." MaryAnn fostered a couple of dogs for a while before Czach came to PAWS as a foster. She was a Miniature Pinscher, a breed MaryAnn had always loved. She initially fostered Czach and then eventually adopted her. "Perhaps I bonded quite quickly with her because she was supposed to be euthanized the day after they brought her to me. Her owner had died and there wasn't anyone else to take care of her. She also had some serious medical problems. But the more I got to know her, the more precious she became."

When she first started fostering, MaryAnn was concerned she wouldn't bond with dogs again because of her losses in the past. This was not the case with Czach; MaryAnn fell in love with her from the get-go, and her attachment only continued to grow. "It's the whole feeling of being responsible for someone besides yourself that helps with my connection to her. She needs me. I need to get out of the house to walk her. It's the feeling I need to take care of her . . . the greater purpose is her."

MaryAnn feels that Czach functions as more than just a pet: "She's kept me alive." The fact that MaryAnn is ill and yet able to still care for another living being (and is almost solely motivated by this caretaker role) truly exemplifies the essence of the attachment theory.

When researchers categorize human-pet relationships as attachments, they look at unique traits in each individual by analyzing "attachment style" or "attachment orientation." For the sake of continuity in this chapter, I will use "attachment style" when referring to individual differences.

Ainsworth (1979) and Mikulincer and Shaver (2007) found in their research that there are two distinct attachment styles — anxiety and avoidance. Someone who gravitates more toward anxiety attachment worries that a partner will not be there during times of need. As a result, the anxious person attempts to maximize proximity with the partner. For children, the most crucial factor accounting for the type of attachment to a caregiver is directly related to the child's experience with that person. Conversely, the quality of the caregiver's attention is directly influenced by his or her own personal attachment history and experiences with the child (Solomon and George, 1996, 1999, 2008).

Similar to what occurs in the caregiver-child relationship, according to the attachment theory, humans can get attached to animals as well. More often, humans take on the role of the caretaker. The effects of this attachment are greater than we may think. Julius et al. (2013), in their book *Attachment to Pets*, point out what we have already discussed in this chapter, that "animal contact or presence may be associated with better health, stimulation of social interaction, improvement of empathic skills, reduction of fear and anxiety, increased trust and calmness, improved mood and reduction of depression, better pain management, and reduction of aggression and anti-stress effects. Indeed, these effects are very similar to those observed in response to administration of oxytocin in both humans and animals and also in humans in situations where oxytocin is released by sensory stimulation from a trusted person" (Julius et al., 2013, p. 79).

Ainsworth described four criteria of a secure attachment figure: (1) the figure is a reliable source of comfort and reassurance; (2) the attachment figure is approached in the case of emotional stress in order to achieve a sense of safety; (3) being near the attachment figure is associated with positive emotions; and (4) separation from the attachment figure is associated with negative emotions (Zilcha-Mano et al., 2011, 2012). When taking these criteria into consideration, Zilcha-Mano et al. (2012) suggest that companion animals such as dogs, certainly can be considered as attachment figures to their owners.

Nagasawa, Mogi, and Kikusui (2009) maintain that the neuropsychological mechanisms of attachment are reciprocal . . . each species (humans and dogs) forms attachments with the other. In fact, over the centuries, dogs have acquired the ability to recognize and respond to facial cues from humans. The authors also describe "cross species empathy" — which, in part, might explain why Jerry Schubel's dog (highlighted earlier) was so responsive to his needs while Jerry suffered from a near-fatal kidney ailment.

During another occasion with PAWS clients, I had a chance to talk with Bruce, another individual receiving support from PAWS. Bruce is fifty-three and was homeless for a time after being a victim of domestic violence and escaping from his partner. He broke his neck in 2001 and consequently lost the use of his hands. Because he experienced reoccurring pain, Bruce turned to taking Tylenol as prescribed. Unfortunately, the large amounts he took to control his pain led to psoriasis of his liver. He is now on the waiting list for a liver transplant. While homeless, Bruce was fortunate enough to have the companionship of Bear, an English Setter/Labrador Retriever mix who became not only a pet but inadvertently a vital part of Bruce's medical treatment (from both an emotional and medical stance). Bear seems to recognize when Bruce's blood count becomes lower. This behavior has been proven and is trainable in medical-alert dogs, which we will discuss in Chapter 5.

Some scientists believe that, because dogs have a tremendous sense of smell, this unique talent can be used to detect even the smallest change in body odor. When Bear notices this change in Bruce, he puts his head on Bruce's abdomen. "He'll stand over me, and if something's going really wrong, he'll lick me awake and just stand there until I move on the bed."

On one particular occasion, Bruce's blood sugar went from 201 to over 827 in three days. Not knowing the exact levels of his blood sugar but aware that something was wrong (thanks to Bear's behavior), Bruce called his medical practitioners and told them he thought he needed to go to the hospital. When asked why, Bruce quickly replied, "My dog won't leave me alone." Sure enough, after Bruce arrived at the hospital and had blood work done, doctors were extremely alarmed at his outrageously high blood sugar level. If Bruce hadn't attended to his blood sugar, he could have fallen into a coma or possibly suffered from a stroke or heart attack.

Although Bruce's health is still slowly declining, he has a strong will to live. He keeps positive, although he worries about the future of his pal, Bear, and how he will be taken care of in the event of Bruce's passing. PAWS volunteers are very active in helping support Bruce and Bear. They help Bruce by walking Bear, providing foster care if needed, and delivering dog food. Bruce also uses the PAWS veterinary fund to get regular checkups and health care for Bear.

Bruce initially went out and found Bear at a local humane society. At the shelter, he called Bear over to come and sit on the bench with him and his partner. Bear sat and put his head in Bruce's partner's lap; they adopted Bear that afternoon. He became an integral member of the family and right away was in tune and protective of Bruce's needs. Bruce recalled one evening when he was taking Bear for his nightly walk, the dog stopped abruptly and sat directly in front of him for no apparent reason. Bruce then realized that a mountain lion (they lived in the hills of Sausalito, California) was sitting in the middle of the road. Luckily, having such a large dog next to him, the mountain lion chose to leave the duo alone.

When asked if his relationship with Bear has been more meaningful than with past pets, Bruce responded a resounding "yes" without hesitation. "My connection with Bear is like having a child. I feel like his parent and need to protect him. It is an amazing, deep relationship. He is constantly touching lives, and especially mine. Bear is my main reason why I am fighting for my life. Everyone knows that. His is the most important relationship in my life. As long as he stays happy, then I am going to try and do better."

Yet another amazing story of the benefits of attachment begins with an ad in a newspaper: "Free cat to good home." Alice McJohnson had always had a cat or two in her home and didn't have to read any further; she immediately decided to bring the adoptable cat into her home. Little did she know the impact this animal would have on her life.

Cinder the cat was about one year old when she joined the family. She shared the home with a variety of cats through the years, but from the start she was Alice's constant companion. She was an indoor cat but would try to sneak outside when Mittens (another adopted stray) went in and out, so Alice would keep a watchful eye on Cinder's movements. Like all good moms, Alice had to referee the sleeping arrangements on the bed at night and oversee the portioning of the special treat food. While Mittens was out patrolling the grounds, Cinder helped Alice with quilting and sewing by keeping track of the thread. As a good "sister," Cinder monitored Mittens's behavior by checking his breath when he returned home, then promptly found her place by Alice in bed.

As the years passed, Alice began looking for senior housing. However, not just any place would do. A primary concern was housing that would allow Cinder to share her apartment. Alice and her family located TigerPlace in Missouri, which not only allows pets to live with their owners in their apartments but also encourages their residents to maintain the human-animal bond they have enjoyed. The pets that reside at TigerPlace with their owners receive very special attention and care through the TigerPlace Pet Initiative (TiPPI) program. Rebecca Johnson, PhD, RN, FAAN, runs the program. She is also the director of the University of Missouri Research Center for Human-Animal Interaction, a collaborative center through the Sinclair School of Nursing and College of Veterinary Medicine. The TiPPI program includes a dedicated pet-care room where the pets can be bathed and groomed. A pet-care assistant, a University of Missouri undergraduate student, is hired to assist pet owners with any care they require with their pets. Some of these services include walking the dogs, cleaning litter boxes for cat owners, giving routine medication to pets, and providing transportation to local clinics for services that cannot be provided at TigerPlace.

Cinder and Alice moved to TigerPlace together. They both had adjustments to make in their new environment. Alice worried that, when she opened her door and took extra time to navigate through the doorway with her walker, Cinder would run out into the hallway and get lost. Several days after moving to TigerPlace, Cinder's curiosity got the better of her, and sure enough, as Alice opened the door, she ran out into the hallway. Alice alerted the TigerPlace staff, but despite thorough search efforts throughout the entire facility, they could not find Cinder. A pet-care assistant who was called later found Cinder asleep under a quilt display in the facility's living area. After her first rather wild adventure, Cinder never dashed out of the apartment again.

During the day, Cinder kept a watchful eye on Alice as she read her newspaper, cards, and letters sent from family and friends. When Alice would join the other residents at TigerPlace for meals, she would always bring back a glass of cold water to share with Cinder in her metal dish. As evening approached, they would both settle into the recliner to watch their favorite TV shows. Cinder always claimed her favorite spot on the right side of Alice's hip while Alice pet her and gave her an evening brushing. When the TV shows had ended, both Alice and Cinder headed to bed, and Cinder went to her preferred spot on the pillow next to Alice. Although Alice's hearing was declining, she was still able to feel Cinder's familiar purring as they fell asleep together. When morning came, they would greet each other with a "pat and kiss on the cheek" and head to the kitchen, where Alice prepared breakfast for Cinder before she joined the other residents in the dining hall.

Alice, at ninety-three years of age, and Cinder, nineteen, continued to age together at TigerPlace. One morning, when Cinder did not awaken as usual, Alice asked the TiPPI staff to come and check on her. Cinder was taken to visit the veterinarian and was diagnosed with diabetes. The treatment involved administering insulin twice a day. Thankfully, the TiPPI staff was able to assist with the regimen, and soon Cinder was able to be weaned off the insulin. Alice also had a responsibility to make sure Cinder received the correct amount of her special diet food.

As their lives continued together, Cinder was always watchful when people came into the apartment to check on Alice. She got up with Alice when she was up at night and only went back to sleep when Alice returned to bed. In the same manner, Alice always wanted to know where Cinder was when she didn't see her about. They developed what could be seen as a symbiotic relationship, each dependent on the other.

Alice became very concerned when Cinder stopped eating and began losing weight. She was diagnosed with renal failure. Alice faced a very difficult discussion: to consider euthanasia or to treat Cinder with fluids. Alice could not administer the fluids herself, but because she had the help of the TiPPI staff, she chose to treat Cinder. "I know Cinder continues to live to be with me, and I am trying to do the same for her."

The Biophilia Hypothesis

The concept of biophilia came out of the independent work of E.O. Wilson and Stephen R. Kellert. Wilson conducted his work at Harvard University, while Kellert was associated with the U.S. Fish and Wildlife Service. Both researchers were interested in discovering the basis of the human relationship with the natural world. Wilson, who first described the theory in 1984, suggested that all humans tend to bond and relate with other forms of life and nature (Kellert, 1997, p. 2). He believed that this innate propensity is what helps us survive. Without this in-tune relationship with nature, we would not know what is safe and what might be dangerous. Survival meant becoming more in sync with nature so that as a civilization we would know how to seek shelter and recognize what was safe to eat.

Earlier civilizations usually gathered cues from the animals around them. For example, they listened to birds. When songbirds were chirping or sounded somewhat cheerful, that may have indicated they were safe, but if the birds sent a more alarming message to each other or gathered around a single member of the flock, that could have signaled the presence of a larger predator. Our ancestors' attunement to the behavioral changes of other creatures that shared their environment helped them to use this information to adapt to their surroundings.

Our ancestors even coexisted with wolves. Even before dogs were domesticated and bred for various human activities such as hunting, guarding, and companionship, they played an important role. As with birds, dogs and other small mammals warned humans about the presence of larger animals or strangers. Wolves intuitively knew what to eat, and their keen sense of smell and ability to hunt without tools were traits humans did not have. Wolves, like people, were social animals, and this behavior may have attracted humans to them and led to the domestication of dogs as assistants and companions more than 15,000 years ago.

Our biophilia connects us to all animals and nature, which makes us a part of the world around us. Many of us have quietly sat in our yards or in a park or the woods to become part of our surroundings and have watched wild animals going about their normal activities. Perhaps we have seen deer walking through the woods. In moments like that, we have felt a sense of peace and community as the deer accept us as part of nature. The deers' calming presence communicates to us that we are safe. On the other hand, if suddenly we see a snake slither by our feet, we will feel alarm and maybe a moment of fear. That fear elicits a deep-rooted, primal/reptilian reaction in us to avoid a potentially poisonous snakebite. Both the tranquility we felt in the presence of the deer and the unease we experienced with the snake are thanks to our biophilia.

Similarly, the reasons we enjoy having pets are related to or because of biophilia. Having an animal or even a plant in the home simulates feelings of being one with nature. According to Wilson and Kellert, people have an innate drive to feel safe and content in nature. Even with our modern homes and conveniences, nature is as much a part of our instinct as it is for any other animal! Of course, the way we experience that desire is different for everyone. Some may enjoy having a pet but might hate camping. Some may prefer an urban lifestyle while enjoying the sounds of city birds, and others may feel the need for more green space. These differences are all accounted for in the biophilia hypothesis, but what is common for us all is our reliance on nature for our own well-being.

Without biophilia, our ancestors would not have survived and thrived. Their connection to animals and nature enabled their survival, but the benefits of biophilia go far beyond it. Great art, music, and writing have come out of our connection to nature. The strong emotions evoked by such relationships as those with our pets, or such experiences as being in nature in the presence of a wild animal, inspire great reflections and generally more positive emotions. This is why the study of biophilia is important; we understand that a connection to nature is important, and we understand that our survival is the greatest reason why. How and why we experience biophilia is different for everyone, and studying these differences is where the really interesting research is happening.

While Wilson and Kellert were studying what would become the field of biophilia, it became clear that biophilia is interpreted in different perspectives, has different purposes, and is expressed distinctly by every individual. They realized there is more than one biophilic approach. Kellert identified nine different values, or perspectives, that enable an individual to make decisions for safety or simply to feel enjoyment in nature. The root of all these values is our motivation for survival individually and as a species. Wilson (1984) lists the nine approaches as aesthetic (taking in the sights), negativistic (sensing danger), humanistic (feeling an emotional connection), naturalistic (enjoying recreation in nature), symbolic (language and metaphor), scientific (studying the details), utilitarian (taking what you need), dominionistic (conquering a challenge), and moralistic (doing what's right).

Almost like a personality profile, we all use every value in different ways and to different degrees. While we will draw from each value depending on the situation, we all tend to draw more readily from one value or another. Each biophilic profile is not better or worse than the other. Rather, the profiles give us a unique approach to our relationship with the world. Each value is like a lens, and each lens gives us a slightly altered view of what we see. We need different lenses for different situations. Depending on which lens we are looking through, we may utilize nature and our bond to it in many different ways. We may exploit nature for money, study it for understanding, explore it for entertainment, fear it for safety, use it for food or shelter, or interact with it for relaxation. Biophilia covers everything from a child wanting a pet dog to a businessman going into the logging industry. To begin considering each value, keep in mind that while negatives can come from some values, none are inherently bad, and all are necessary for our survival in different situations.

An Overview of Biophilic Values

Moralistic Value. Preserving nature for nature's sake and doing good are the motivating factors for a moralistic response. Some people derive a sense of belonging and safety from a healthy relationship with nature. This in turn gives them a sense of responsibility to care for nature, both for mutual benefits and with gratitude for what nature gives them in return. In essence, the moralistic value is one not driven by human gain but rather on the well-being of nature. A good example of applying moralistic values would be recycling. A growing number of people consider it a basic responsibility to conserve what we have and reduce the large footprint that modern life is leaving behind.

Animal shelters, rescue organizations, and animal-protection laws all stem from a moralistic value. This value can drive us to make small contributions and be the driving force behind big contributions and more significant decisions that benefit our environment, whether it is urban or rural. Choosing to give a large sum of money anonymously to an animal shelter has a strong moralistic value with the driving biophilic force behind it. People who rescue and rehabilitate animals are not likely to receive much back in terms of monetary compensation and possibly not in terms of a relationship with the animal they have saved; they, too, are driven by morals to make a difference.

Shawna, a school counselor from Minnesota, explains that one of the most moving experiences she had while on a trip to India was coming across a badly injured street dog whose life would certainly be in danger if he were left without help. "The pain he suffered from a paw ripped to the bone was clearly intense. I brought him home, stayed up all night with him, and took him to the emergency hospital in the morning. I realize those actions may seem extreme to someone who does not have a strong moralistic value. To some, the cost and risks of bringing in a strange dog — the missed night of sleep, the potential that the dog will die anyway, the idea that nature should run its course — may all be reasons not to have taken in that dog."

Humanistic Value. Anyone who has ever had a pet and considered it to be part the family has connected with that animal through their humanistic value. The humanistic response reflects our deep bonds with other beings in nature, such as our desire to have a pet or our craving to feel connected emotionally to a place and call it "home." Our humanistic value sparks an interest in bonding with another being. We often apply human qualities to animals or speak about them in anthropocentric terms, such as guessing their emotions or considering them to be friends. These are not "wrong" perspectives. In fact, as humans, we have no choice but to look at the world through a human's eyes. People with a strong humanistic value may not see animals as having any less value than people. They see a more fluid connection among species — a shared relationship and mutual respect — or at the least are able to develop a very close relationship with their own pets. Many times these are the pets we see safely harnessed in the front seat of a car or wearing a warm coat on a wintery day. They are not just pets; they are family.

People who volunteer at a shelter because they cannot have a dog and still want to have a relationship with dogs are looking through the lens of the humanistic value. People who take their pets on vacation or keep them indoors and treat them like family are likely viewing their relationships with animals through a humanistic lens. It is this value that enables us to feel empathy for animals and to feel sad when they are suffering, because we share their pain just as they share with us when we are in pain.

Naturalistic Value. This perspective of nature as a place to play is the value of those who feel better outside. Some can easily pass time or find something to do outdoors and feel happiest when they are surrounded by nature. This is obvious in children, especially those who anticipate the freedom of spending their weekends and summers out in the yard.

We all know or may even be that grown-up who never wanted to grow out of playing in the woods. Playing outside may have, over time, turned into hiking and camping trips as a teenager, and those may have even turned into a job with the forest service or as an outdoor guide. We may envy this carefree spirit who always seems happiest when he or she is active outside. For these nature lovers, the outside world is truly their oyster. While not everyone uses his or her naturalistic value to pursue a career as a park ranger, many of us still find solace in hiking or swimming in a lake or having a picnic outdoors.

Perhaps the best way to observe the naturalistic response is to watch children play outside. All they need is their imagination: trees are castles, rocks are cooking utensils, and sticks become everything imaginable from magical wands to walking canes. This indicates the risk we take with our children when they are denied adequate time outside for free play. We may be robbing them of the incredible power they have to develop their limitless imagination as well as a strong connection to nature.

Scientific Value. The scientific response has an obvious survival component. Scientific value encourages us to study the details of nature, to understand its patterns such as growth and the seasons. With the information we have acquired, we are able to advance everything from basic survival to every modern science. Much of responding to nature requires accurate interpretations of all the information we take in through our senses. We have a need to painstakingly record and understand things like weather patterns, color variations, and population fluctuations and how these specifically impact nature. Individuals with a high scientific value would be our science teachers, our geologists, and our naturalists. An example would be Jacob, the son of my good friend, who from a young age has had a keen interest in wildlife and the outdoors. Over the years, he has accrued a wealth of knowledge about natural resources and has become an avid outdoorsman. It wasn't surprising that, as he grew older, his vocational interests shaped his professional ones; he is now in graduate school studying natural resources.

Aesthetic Value. One of my favorite naturalists is a gentleman named Thomas Mangelsen. He is one of today's greatest animal and nature photographers. Mangelsen's youth took place in the beautiful outdoors of Nebraska and strongly contributed to his passion for photographing the Earth's wildlife and natural beauty. He has become one of the most prolific nature photographers of the twentieth century and has captured extraordinary moments in the wild while also contributing greatly to conservation efforts.

If one thing has blossomed in popularity with today's easily accessible cameras, it is nature photography. While photographers like Mangelsen truly have a knack and talent for capturing nature raw and undisturbed, nowadays almost everyone claims to be an amateur nature photographer. We love pictures or drawings of nature such as flowers, water, mountains, or forests. Specifically, we gravitate toward peaceful images, and through our aesthetic value we survey the land around us, taking in its overall sense. Free of any sense of danger, we might experience contentment and beauty around us. However, if we see a herd of deer run away or a thundercloud in the distance, we use that information to determine our next steps toward safety. It is this relationship between *Aesthetic Value* and our biophilia that sends us a sign "that God's safe in his heavens and all's right with the world."

Our aesthetic value is powerful and has a very direct impact on our moods. Imagine you are in a doctor's office. The furniture and walls are drab, everything feels cold, and you are nervous about your appointment. Then you notice a picture of a field of flowers and butterflies dancing throughout. You consider what the location of this picture might be. Have you been there before? Is it around here? What are those flowers? This is your aesthetic value coming to the rescue to distract you and calm your nerves. At the same time, if you look out the window and see thick, dark storm clouds approaching and notice the wind picking up and blowing the tree branches around, that may exacerbate your anxiety about the appointment. Our moods are often linked to our surroundings, and emotional problems like seasonal affective disorder (SAD) are more common in colder climates where there is less sunshine.

Symbolic Value. Myth and symbol are ways to imagine something we do not fully understand, so it makes sense that one way to perceive our relationship with nature is through mythic interpretation or symbolic representation. The symbolic response is visible in every cultural tradition such as the Chinese or Mayan calendars, religious stories, traditions around sacred animals, and national symbols.

For example, artists use strong symbolic values. Our symbolic value takes our basic observations and adds meaning to something we cannot otherwise fully understand. It is a way to communicate the meaning behind something and provides a way to record data that consist of our feelings and reactions. This value is innate and has been the key to our survival as a species. As such, this is one method we have used through centuries to assimilate an understanding of the vast, invaluable knowledge of information acquired by our ancestors.

Utilitarian Value. While all values seem to ask some version of "what's in it for me," the utilitarian response deals with what we take from nature and how we use it directly to fulfill our need for commodities. Our ancestors had a strong utilitarian value — they took only what they needed for survival, because taking too much meant that later there would not be enough. This may also be related to a *Symbolic Value* they attached to the land. They saw the land as a gift from the gods and, as such, it needed to be protected through practical stewardship. They hunted, fished, gathered, and later farmed with the utilitarian philosophy to take only what was needed.

Sustainability business practices come out of this value. Leadership in Energy and Environmental Design (LEED) certified homes, limits on fishing and hunting, and land preserves are all ways in which we attempt to balance what people take from nature with what nature needs in order to continue thriving.

As we learn more about biophilia, some of us may become interested in our own expression of the diverse biophilic values. Now that we are aware of these values, we can better understand how such an orientation may fit our personality style. Which ones do you think are expressed more persistently in your daily life? To help us better understand biophilia and our biophilic values, Terril L. Shorb and Yvette A. Schnoeker-Shorb (2013) created the *Kellert-Shorb Biophilic Values Indicator*[TM] (KSBVI). This indicator was based on Kellert's biophilic values typology. After completing the indicator, a profile can be created to show the relative expressiveness of each of the nine values at that moment in a person's life. Based on the person's experiences, social learning, and other factors, that profile is in constant flux. In an interview in January 2013, Shorb and Schnoeker-Shorb suggested that, "the natural world is quite literally our life-support system. This is true for our physical needs such as the air we breathe, the water we drink to slake our thirst, the food we eat to fill our bellies, and the raw materials we use to make our homes and tools. This dependency on the natural environment is true also for the psychological needs of our inner lives, where we turn for thought, reflection, language development and enhancement, a sense of belonging, and spiritual comfort." Shorb and Schnoeker-Shorb hope that we realize we are drawing from ancient capacities to respond to nature and that we truly appreciate what an enormous gift our relationship with the natural world is.

If you are curious about your own biophilic personality, consider the statements on page 51 and in what situations you might experience each value. It is important to note that these statements are not sufficient to determine a rank of your biophilic values. It is meant to offer an introduction to considering how you tend to express or use each value in your regular life and to better understand the meaning of each value. If you want more information about a full biophilic values profile, please contact Terril Shorb and Yvette Schnoeker-Shorb at nativewestpres@cableone.org.

———

In this chapter we've introduced the idea that a snuggle a day with "Doctor Fido" could keep the physician away. It is more commonly accepted today that our relationships and interactions with companion animals provide us with more than just love; they clearly can also have a positive impact on our health. Karen Allen (2001) calls this assumption the "pet effect" and discusses several of the benefits that can be derived from the relationship. On the other hand, others such as Hal Herzog (2011), a profes-

CONSIDERING YOUR BIOPHILIC VALUES IN YOUR OWN LIFE

Consider each question for your own values and lifestyle and answer with a "yes," "no," or maybe something in between.

1. I seem more aware than others of changes in my environment, such as changing weather or critters underfoot. I may not be afraid of potentially negative environmental factors, but I am always vigilant._____

2. I enjoy the idea of "conquering" something, like climbing a difficult mountain. I think it's interesting how we have learned to utilize the Earth through big feats like blasting tunnels to mine and building dams for power. _____

3. I believe it is our duty as humans to protect the Earth and reverse the damage we have done. It is wrong to exploit the planet's resources without protecting them. _____

4. I enjoy being in nature because I feel at ease, like I am among friends. I feel a relationship with animals and maybe even with plants, lakes, or mountains. _____

5. I enjoy analyzing nature objectively, understanding how and why things work. I tend to remember details about natural features.

    _____

6. I see mines, pipelines, hydroelectric dams, and nuclear power plants as necessary tools for our modern lifestyle, while I also see the risks and damages. Such use of nature is good overall if it is necessary for human societal development. Or, I enjoy fishing and hunting as a source for food and logging as a source for fuel and other supplies but believe we must ration these activities for future availability. _____

7. I've always liked to be in nature — playing, exploring, watching, and listening. I learn about myself when I'm outside in the elements and see my time in nature as fun. _____

8. I love scenery. I love wide expansions of nature such as views of an ocean or views from a mountaintop. Panoramic pictures are really interesting to me. I also like the ability to survey my surroundings — to see if a storm is coming or to see out over a field to find out what might be stirring in the grass. _____

9. I love hearing stories about ancient cultures and how they lived in nature. I like looking at pictures, am intrigued by mythology, and tend to be intrigued by the written or spoken language of other cultures.

    _____

KEY

If your response was "yes" to #1, you may have a strongly expressed negativistic biophilic value. This value is what keeps us from touching poisonous animals or staying outside in a lightning storm.

If your response was "yes" to #2, you may have a strongly expressed dominionistic biophilic value. This value motivates us to "conquer" nature or manage and control it.

If your response to #3 was "yes," you may have a strongly expressed moralistic biophilic value. This value causes us to consider nature's intrinsic value and feel obligated to protect it.

If your response to #4 was "yes," you may have a strongly expressed humanistic biophilic value. It is our feeling of connectedness to nature that often compels us to protect it — we see it as a part of us.

Statement #5 refers to the scientific biophilic value. If you agreed with this statement, you may strongly express an enjoyment of nature academically and objectively.

Statement #6 refers to the utilitarian biophilic value. This value enables us to utilize the Earth's resources and see nature for its extrinsic value, as in what is in it that can benefit us as individuals or humans.

If you agree with #7, you may have a strongly expressed naturalistic biophilic value. This is the value that enables us to feel at ease playing like a kid in nature, as natural as a fish in water.

If you agree with #8, you may have a strongly expressed aesthetic biophilic value. This value makes us appreciate the beauty on a calm day and gives us a general sense of safety by knowing what's on the horizon.

If you agree with #9, you may have a strongly expressed symbolic biophilic value. You may enjoy myth, story, languages, metaphors, and analogies. Our interpretation and communication about nature is just as critical as anything else. This value is what enables us to communicate and record what we see in nature.

sor at Western Carolina University, are a bit more skeptical and argue that the literature is inconsistent with its findings. According to Herzog, many studies have shown that pets benefit our health, but he also argues that he has a stack of articles that do not agree with these findings. He says that, in several articles, the media often sensationalizes findings that show positive outcomes, and results from studies that don't show significant outcomes often may not even get published. He suggests we be cautious in our explanation of these results and not over-exaggerate the outcomes. Although I agree with some of his comments, especially about over-exaggeration of implications in published research, I believe we shouldn't underestimate the benefit of cohabiting with companion animals.

In this chapter we also presented a few theoretical positions that explain the rationale for our desire to connect with other species, and each provides a different perspective for why we celebrate this unique bond.

Our relationships with animals can be captured in the moments of interactions with them. Especially intriguing is the connection homeless people seem to make with animals they find as companions; although they may have few fiscal resources, they have each other. In fact, Marc Beckoff (2013) shares that homeless people have told him "on more than one occasion that their animal companion is their best friend and oxygen, without whom life wouldn't be worth living."

I often think about an afternoon in Amsterdam when I watched a young homeless man interact with his dog. They clearly shared a special and deep relationship, and I noticed a distinct gleam in both the man's and the dog's eyes when they looked at each other. Apparently, Beckoff and I aren't the only people who've taken notice of homeless people and the animal population. The Veterinary Street Outreach Services, (otherwise known as Vet SOS) consists of a group of community-based, non-profit health clinics that recognize the important need of providing veterinary services to the pets of the needy in the San Francisco area. It is one of the projects instituted by the San Francisco Community Clinic Consortium, otherwise known as SFCCC, and was established in 1982.

Perhaps one of the greatest services Vet SOS provides is the opportunity for homeless persons to make sure their animals receive good care. Vet SOS gives wellness exams, trims nails and provides grooming services, and equips animals with food, leashes, collars, and halters. Ilana Strobel, who works for Vet SOS, has many endearing stories of her work for the organization, but one in particular stands out.

Bob had been homeless and living in a van for several years. He lived with his partner, Barbara, and they each had their own vans and their own two dogs. When he and Barbara were together, they would park their vans side by side. To support themselves, they received disability income and supplemented it by foraging and selling recycled scrap metal and cans. Sadly, Barbara was diagnosed with cancer and lost her battle for life. Even during this emotionally and financially difficult time for Bob, he adopted her two dogs.

On Thanksgiving Day, Bob arrived at the clinic with his brood of four. Ilana recognized him because he had been coming to clinics for the past ten years, but this visit was different; it was the first time he had been back without Barbara.

That day he arrived at the clinic to get the dogs booster vaccinations; he wanted to get them cleared so he could get an animal-control license. To make things easy, he brought one dog at a time from his van. In one of the exchanges, he brought a picture Ilana had taken of his family several years before, at a time when he and Barbara had first started their little family of adopted dogs. He reminisced with Ilana about that period of time when life was much happier. As he looked at the picture, tears gently rolled down his cheek. Not only was Barbara not with him any longer, but Skip, the last of those original four dogs, had just passed away. Bob felt alone. Although new dogs had joined his pack, he confessed it wasn't the same.

It was evident he was in mourning, so Ilana invited him to a Thanksgiving feast that was being organized at a local park. He refused the invitation, telling her it was too hard for him to interact with others and he just wanted to be alone. Although the new dogs were helping him keep busy, he was attempting to fill a great void in his life.

Ilana confided that she believes having pets brings meaning to the lives of homeless people, and I wholeheartedly agree! Their lives are more complete when they share with, care for, and protect another being. The relationship also provides them with companionship that enriches their daily life. It is now commonly understood that most people who are homeless will often sacrifice what they have and feed their companion animals before they feed themselves. This has not only been noted in personal observations but also in the existing literature. In fact, Leslie Irvine, in her new book with the telling title *My Dog Always Eats First* (2013), discusses several personal narratives that are poignant and powerful in exploring these unique reciprocal relationships.

Within this chapter we have highlighted the true benefits of our unique bond with all living creatures. Having a living creature to love not only provides joy and comfort but also may have many other life and health benefits. I believe we must celebrate these relationships, because the benefits are just the extra gains we derive. As Anatole France once stated, "Until one has loved an animal, a part of one's soul remains unawakened." We must celebrate and cherish this awakening!

THE ROLE OF
COMPANION ANIMALS IN THE FAMILY

L ife was good for Jane growing up in New England as a post-war child. From a young age, Jane started asking her parents for pets but was always told that pets were out of the question because of finances. As her family's business began to prosper, Jane's begging started again with more enthusiasm, but still the answer was an absolute "No." Her dad was pretty adamant about the responsibility and the time that was needed to have pets in a family, and he didn't want to deal with them. End of story!

Family life in the late 1940s and the 1950s with animals was much different. It was a different era. In Jane's small neighborhood, there were lots of dogs and many ran loose and participated in the kids' activities. It was not unusual to go swimming and have two or three dogs join in. Dogs didn't wear ID tags or collars, and they all seemed to get along. Amazingly, at the end of the day, they were all able to find their way home without difficulty. When Jane was a youngster, her favorite street dog was a Dalmatian named Jeff, who belonged to her back-door neighbors. He loved everyone and visited many of the neighbors daily. Often Jane would play with him for hours in her yard and then tell her dad how much she loved him. Her puppy eyes that glimmered with love didn't budge dad's position. No was no!

In 1959 the family moved into a gorgeous, big home on an acre of land. Jane's dad got involved in politics and was elected as the councilman in the ward. Nevertheless, there was no movement on having a pet in the family. Jane watched her wishes evaporate over the course of her childhood.

One Saturday when Jane was a young teen, her dad announced that the family was going to a fair. Although she was hesitant at first about going, she and her brother David were not given a choice. They were each given five dollars and told they needed to circulate at the fair and spend the money, as this was a fundraiser to help with a new ball field.

They began spending what seemed like a lot of money to them at that time. They played carnival games, bought raffle tickets, and had ice cream. When it got dark outside, the two of them discovered that they had twenty-five cents left. There was one last raffle on a big wheel near the entrance of the fair, so the two youngsters walked over and put a quarter down on a few numbers. They were hoping for a giant stuffed animal for their little sister. To their amazement, not only did they win — they also won the grand prize of the day. It was what Jane had dreamed for — a living, loving four-legged pal!

The prize was a ten-week-old female Beagle-mix puppy. The prize included a basket with the food and water bowls, a brush, and a toy. Jane's father was speechless and her mother just smiled. Her dad looked at both of them and said in a grouchy voice, "Well, it is what it is. Let's take her home and figure this mess out." What else could he say? They did what he asked of them and the result, in his view, had backfired.

When they arrived home and after the puppy had some time to acclimate, the family sat down to discuss their responsibilities. Jane eagerly wanted a name for the puppy, who was mostly black with a large, kidney-shaped white spot under her chin and white feet. Her father had the first suggestion. "How about Tennis Shoe?" he said. The kids laughed, but then David and Jane said, "How about Sneakers?" That evening the raffle prize was christened with a name, and life for this youngster changed forever.

So many things changed over the years with Sneakers. Within days, Sneakers was sitting with dad on the couch while he read the paper and following him in the yard while he gardened. She would hear him go into the shower in the morning and wait by the door for him to come out and then jump with sheer joy when he emerged from the room like he was a god. Dad would sneak table scraps to her when no one was looking, and soon she was in the bed with both mom and dad. Although the kids had needed to find a loophole to get Sneakers to join the family, hands down her favorite person in the house was the father.

The scenario you just read captures a life-changing event that happened to my dear friend many years ago. Sneakers not only blessed and enriched Jane's life but also impacted her destiny. Decades later, Jane is now a leading humane educator in the United States. She is also a mom and a grandmother who continues to integrate the value of pets in her own family. It is amazing that when we open our hearts to any being, human or nonhuman, the experience can have a tremendous impact on our lives. In a recent conversation that I had with Jane, she was able to articulate these thoughts through the words of her ten-year-old granddaughter, Eleanor. She has a mixed-breed dog (now maybe three years old) that the family rescued just before he was to be euthanized the following week. One evening when Eleanor was at her grandmother's house, she murmured, "Meme, I know we rescued him, but in a way he rescued us. Our family became complete the day he arrived. Now he sleeps in my bed and makes me feel safe in the dark. He is the very best!" Poignant words, uttered from the mouth of a babe. These words are similar to testimonials I hear almost daily from the families who engage with their animal companions. When we open our hearts, love and life usually come our way.

Although I didn't grow up with animals, I have witnessed the significance they have had on my boys and the family as a whole. They have been my boys' confidants, friends, and playmates. Visualize the following three scenarios. First, a young boy gently pushes a small Batmobile around the house with his Caped Crusader perched at the wheel. In this case, Batman is a Peach-faced Lovebird named Coshi. Or a Black Labrador named Hart playing defenseman in a daily bone hockey match. Hart was a true athlete, and no young Sidney Crosby (a hockey player with the Pittsburg Penguins) was going to stick-handle by her with a luscious bone puck. Finally, let your imagination go wild as you picture the daily ritual of a mom being followed by an entourage of critters putting her young son to bed. This entourage included a dog, a cat, and a Bare-eyed Cockatoo who would lead the pack in marching a young preschooler to his bedroom. Twenty-five years later, when that grown-up pre-schooler comes to see him, the cockatoo still views him as her little boy and coos and serenades him. In each case, what is felt is a tremendous amount of affection — a connection of souls. My life has been blessed (most of the time) with the creatures that have contributed to our household. They have helped etch within our house-hold the true meaning of a "home."

Today was Father's Day, and I received cards and gifts from both my boys and my daughter-in-law. Of course, Father's Day wouldn't be complete if I also didn't get a card from my four-legged and feathered children. In fact, on the cover of this year's card was a row of adorable Golden Retriever puppies, with one puppy looking the wrong way. My wife smiled as she asked me, "Who does that one remind you of?" We both giggled as I replied, "It sure reminds me of Ketzy" (our youngest Golden Retriever). Moments later, as I was placing the cards on the mantle, I was delighted to see Ketzy romping over with a bow on her neck. She was trailed by my wife and our oldest Golden, Magic, with their gift — a lovely golden coffee cup. Father's Day — or any day — wouldn't be the same in my family without our animal companions beside us. They make our family complete! Although we know intellectually that anthropomorphizing animals is silly, on a different level these little rituals reinforce feelings of affiliation with our pets while acknowledging the fact that we share an intangible quality, whether we call it a bond, an understanding, a connection, or love. The reality is that it really doesn't matter; we are family, and that says it all.

In our home, pets are as much members of the family as humans are. That means we have a moral obligation to ensure that each family member receives our love, respect, and support. I don't mean to conflate the values of animal and human lives, but I do believe that all are precious regardless of species and that humans are morally bound to support and nurture living creatures (big or small). Mahatma Gandhi once said, "The greatness of a nation and its moral progress can be judged by the way its animals are treated." I and many others believe that families should be judged in the same way.

While each family functions differently, companion animals impact members within each distinct family in unique ways. Although pets may have significant meaning to some members, there may not be such a strong affinity with others. What needs to be highlighted (as was discussed in Chapter 2) is the new awareness that companion animals contribute to our wellness both physiologically and psychologically. The deeper the connection, the more meaningful the animal's presence will be in our family constellation. Paul and Serpell (two well-known researchers studying human-animal interactions) (1996) found that living with a dog increased socialization, leisure activities together, and confidence in older children. Furthermore, McCullough (1986) found pet ownership to be enriching for families with disabled children. Companion animals boost children's well-being by giving them increased confidence and promoting independence and social engagement. While our children reap the benefits of social support and emotional and empathetic development, our older family members (the elderly) also benefit greatly. Research clearly suggests that the elderly may be more motivated to live a more engaged and a healthier lifestyle if they have companionship. A good friend of mine who is eighty walks his dog daily. Yes, the dog does need the exercise, but so does my friend; it is a mutually beneficial relationship as they wander the neighborhood visiting people and saying their morning hellos.

This raises the interesting point that many people are motivated by purpose. When we are younger, purpose is often affiliated with career advancement, academic or athletic accomplishment, raising a family, etc. When we get older (after climbing life's many mountains), such purposes can fade. For some elderly people, finding purpose in life can be significantly enriched through the love and care of a pet. There is a quiet and gentle dignity that often develops between elderly persons and their pets. Let me share a small example.

My friend Steve and his wife frequent the local Starbucks almost daily during the warmer months for a cup of chai tea. On most days they see several of the "regulars," Irene and her Fox Terrier, QT. Irene is elderly and lives alone, and QT is her best friend. There is an unspoken connection between Irene and QT that is quite lovely to see. With what appears to be a wave of the hand, a small whisper, or a nod of the head, Irene talks to QT, and QT responds immediately. In many cases, QT talks back, sometimes with movement, a bark, a lick, or a loving gaze. The repertoire of QT's behaviors is remarkable, but each is carried out as part of intimate riposte between the two. Their relationship is like watching two old friends who know each other's likes, dislikes, and moods rather than master and subject. In human terms, Irene may live alone, but she is never without her QT, and for her that is enough.

Over the years, I have spoken to many audiences worldwide about the roles that animals play in families, especially with young children. I often share in these talks one of my favorite photos I had seen taken outside a Parisian café. The photo captures a little toddler sitting next to his beloved dog with a cup of coffee resting on the table. It is an adorable picture that underscores how ingrained our pets are in our lifestyles. It is not uncommon today to see dogs joining families on daily excursions, whether they be walking around a mall or sitting at a coffee shop. These companion animals may act as friends, such as Lassie did with her beloved Timmy. As friends, they are confidants and a source of support and affection. In some cases, companion animals fill roles of other family members, members that have moved away or perhaps have died.

Although I view these relationships as extremely valuable, like any relationship, they can be misused and abused. We mustn't squander this free-spirited relationship and inadvertently place too much pressure on our four-legged companions to fulfill roles that they are not capable of realizing. Companion animals aren't surrogate humans but often are treated as our children. In *The New Work of Dogs* (2003), Jon Katz suggests that some people may be emotionally taking advantage of their relationship with animals and relying on them too much. Some see the new role of dogs as being the family's nurturer-in-chief. This role is an unfair expectation. As Katz elegantly writes in his Preface, dogs are "overwhelmed by the pressure put on them to fill complex emotional roles in their owners' lives" (p. xxii). Katz's book reminds us that dogs are voiceless, and that as guardians, we must respect their individual needs. Having companion animals means valuing that they are sentient beings who aren't human. Our companion animals have their own personal needs and desires that also must be considered. Respecting their needs only makes us more aware of their individual requirements and will allow us to coexist responsibly. As Katz states, " . . . we have to learn "how to understand them and, when necessary, to speak and act on their behalf" (p. xxii).

BENEFITS FROM LIVING WITH COMPANION ANIMALS

Companion animals provide stability in many peoples' homes. They offer a sense of continuity over the family life cycle and may serve especially important functions during major life events or critical life transitions such as divorce, marriage and remarriage, widowhood, and becoming an empty nester. It has been found, for example, that children do in fact fare better during their parents' divorce when they have a connection with a pet (Bennett, 2000). Another couple I know, Gary and Pam, have a companion dog named Mel. I am not sure what Mel's real capacity is as a companion, but she is always nestled in Pam's arms and seems to bring a warm sort of comfort to Pam, who would never think of going anyplace that would not welcome Mel. One thing is very clear, however: Mel provides comfort and a connection that are beneficial to all.

Many people perceive that their dogs or cats are wonderful listeners. As their companion animal sits loyally next to them, they spill out all of their emotions toward them. Although some may feel that it is silly to believe that our companion animals understand what we say, it is now recognized that dogs have been domesticated (over the past 10,000 years) to be excellent responders to our nonverbal communication. They have developed a keen sense to read our emotions. The more successful they are at this behavior, the more they are accepted into our pack. This is just one of the traits that connects us more tangibly with dogs than with other groups of animals.

Most of us would agree that companionship and friendship are crucial components to our growth during childhood. It makes sense, because the pets take on the roles of playmates and surrogate siblings. With the changes that we are witnessing in nuclear family structure, animals in the home may be providing needed consistency and social support. Pet owners often report feeling closest to their pets, with 85 percent (as discussed in Chapter 1) considering their animals as family members (Walsha, 2009). There is also the fact that 62 percent of homes have pets (American Pet Products Association, 2011).

It should be clearly stated, however, that there is a distinction between owning an animal and truly bonding with an animal. Obviously, the more time we spend with a companion animal, the more we will benefit from the relationship. It is critical for us to consider the degree of bonding when we try to understand the long-term impact of pet-child relationships. If we do not maintain a constant high degree of attachment, the results may not be the same. Studies show that the more emotionally involved a pet owner is, the more likely he or she will develop positive social bonds with lasting effects (Triebenbacher, 2000). One study suggested that 10 percent of high school youth in a tenth-grade sample reported that their animal-related activities were the most meaningful pursuits in which they were involved (Mueller, Geldhoff, and Lerner, 2013). On the other hand, researchers in Japan studied how having pets in childhood affected elderly Japanese men. The factors investigated included various health issues, companionship, life satisfaction, and loneliness. Their findings suggested that the men who owned a dog in the early stages of their lives rated companionship and social support quite high, because they viewed the importance of their pets in their lives. It seems that animal interaction at a young age may promote healthy companionship with others (human and nonhuman) later in life, which is an important component to overall happiness (Nagasawa and Ohta, 2010).

Recently, in May 2013, Dr. Megan Kiely Mueller completed her doctoral dissertation at Tufts University on the emotions and cognition of children from fifth grade to post–high school regarding animals. Fifty-five percent of her sample (7,000 youth and 3,500 adults from forty-two states) participated in 4-H at some point across the duration of the study. In discussing the results of her study, Mueller shared several critical points. Although most people believe that companionship with animals can make an important contribution to the growth of children, Mueller suggests that "We can't take a 'one size fits all' approach to understanding youth-animal relationships, and research has to do a better job of taking a nuanced approach to understanding human-animal interaction" (p. 101). For example, understanding the context of youth-animal relationships is important. Are the animals with which the child is engaged companion animals in the home or rather specific animals in activity settings (horseback riding, 4-H, volunteering in an animal shelter, or animals in therapeutic settings)? One outcome of her study is that "intensity" of involvement matters; that is to say, the more engaged the child is with the animal, the more of an impact the animal will have in shaping the child's character. She believes that, for families, it is important to think about the "goodness of fit" between the animal and the child/family in the service of promoting mutually beneficial human-animal relationships that are positive for the family, child, and the animal.

Regarding positive emotional influences from animals, unconditional acceptance is a large contributor; therefore, it is no surprise that the forgiving nature of animals causes children to rate them in their "top 5 important relationships" (Fine, 2012). Given the strong emotional attachments that are often formed by those who own pets, it may seem like second nature to consider their pet as a member of the family. As discussed in Chapter 2, attachment figures (as defined by Ainsworth, 1979) have four parts: proximity maintenance (residing nearby), separation distress (negative emotions when distanced), secure base (emotional security), and safe haven (feeling comforted in their presence). While there is little evidence to show that humans rely on dogs as a safe haven, the dependable nature of a dog may act as a buffer against social isolation. This buffer allows them to be considered attachment figures in certain cases. Daly and Morton (2006) report that children with high levels of attachment and engagement with their pets often point out that they are as close to their pet as they are to other members of their family. And, for those who maintain high levels of participation and attachment when caring for their pets, it is apparent that they place their relationship with them in high regard.

Probably one of the most enjoyable holidays that my children always loved was Halloween. Each year it was filled with decorating the house and, of course, going trick-or-treating together. I always smile when I think back to those days, when the boys would sleep with their candies because they worried I'd steal some of them. They knew me pretty well. In fact, I probably would have taken many of the small Snickers bars and candies if they had left them unguarded. My most memorable of the Halloweens was the time when the family was joined by our oldest dog, Puppy. We all went trick-or-treating and wore costumes. Sean was Dick Tracy, and Corey was He-Man. Several friends joined them, but probably the most comical was our dog, Puppy, who joined us for the first time. We dressed her as a reindeer. She had a sign on her that said, "I'm a reindeer. I don't speak human. Trick or treat. Can I get some treats, please?" At first she didn't seem very eager to be led around the neighborhood, but as she was rewarded with treats at the doors of various neighbors, her interest grew substantially. I will never forget one person who gave her a doggy Popsicle. This thrilled her to no end. Of course, we stopped for a couple of minutes as she devoured her treat. For the next thirty-five to forty-five minutes, Puppy was first to appear at every door. She sat attentively as she waited for her treat to go into a bucket. Halloween would never be the same again for the boys. Even now, we still smile as we reflect on that day.

Many child-development authorities assume that pets are an important part of a child's social and emotional development. Pets help children develop trust and self-esteem and learn responsibility and empathy. In fact, some research has found that not just the presence of pets, but maintaining a good relationship with them and having more than one increase empathy (Daly and Morton, 2006). These benefits are seen even in children as young as preschool (Meadan and Jegatheesan,

2010). There is no question that pets are social lubricants and often help children with communication and friendships. In my work with so many children who have pets, many emotions are expressed when they discuss their relationships. They mention the safe feelings they experience when they are with their animals. I always will remember one of my patients named Daniel who saw his dog as his best friend and little brother. He trusted his dog and seemed to deeply appreciate his unconditional love. As a child, his dog slept in his bed and even shared his pillow.

Perhaps a comment I hear the most often is how happy children feel (adults as well) when their companion animals greet them when they return home. Typically, their dog acts like they have been gone for months. The reaction is simply marvelous. In my home, Tikvah (the cockatoo) blows her trumpet of joy, welcoming me back. The dogs gather (and run) like it is the Calgary Stampede, wagging and shaking as the door opens. It is a greeting that makes me feel like everyone knows my name.

Let's face it — we set up our children to be animal lovers. We start during infancy when we decorate their rooms with animals and provide nursery rhymes that include animals. When the children begin to talk and make sounds, they almost always learn to say animal names and make animal sounds. In fact, many of the early songs they learn include animals, as do the infant and toddler books we share with them. As they age, they are gradually introduced to various species of companion animals and are taught to respect and be gentle with their four-legged companions.

There is no doubt in my mind that pets often defuse problems and conflicts in the home. When my boys were young and argued, it would upset our dogs. Their behavior would change, and either they would go over to the boys to try and calm the situation or they would retreat to a different room. Often, the dogs' reaction to the boys would help resolve the situation and cause the boys to change their behavior.

In this modern age of communication with social media, it is more apparent how beloved family pets are to all. Seeing pet photos shared on the Internet is now becoming the norm. My son's and daughter-in-law's new kittens, Hunter and Colby, are frequently showcased on their Facebook pages. My friend, Jane, shared with me that during a recent blizzard in New England, most of the posts depicted pets playing in the snow or paths carved out of the snow for the family dog. Photos of children on the web very often include the family pet. Most of the Christmas cards I receive have the family pets integrated. When our children were young, I was always amused when we took our family portrait. Can you imagine taking a picture with four humans (two of them young boys), three dogs, three birds, and a lizard? Just getting everyone to look in the same direction was a miracle. Nevertheless, the family photograph would never have been the same without everyone in it!

WHAT WE ALREADY KNOW OR SHOULD KNOW ABOUT ANIMALS, CHILDREN AND THEIR FAMILIES

We know from research that more than 150 million households in the United States have at least one pet. That means that six of every ten people in this country have at least one companion animal. According to a 2012 article and a national pet owners survey, there are more than 70 million dogs and as many as 85 million cats in American households (Reimer, 2012). Families spend about $51 billion annually on pet supplies, equipment, and care. Families with young children make up about 60 percent of pet owners in this country and feel that having a pet is healthy for the child in many ways, especially with regard to teaching responsibility and helping the child learn how to be kind. Research has proven repeatedly that simply having contact with a calm dog or cat can lower blood pressure and anxiety, thus proving that there are real health benefits in pet ownership. Often kids will share that their dog or cat sleeps with them at night and makes them feel safe. Children in single-parent households will often feel safer and more secure knowing the dog will alert them to an intruder, serve as a deterrent to a thief, and keep them company when they are alone. In fact, it is not uncommon for families to take their pets along on family vacations. We have done this for years, sometimes more successfully than others. The outcome is always great fun!

We have had many splendid adventures with our pack of dogs, cats, and birds. One trip stands out the most. It was our first trip we ever took with our first dog, Goldie, and our youngest cockatoo, Tikvah. It was early on a Saturday morning when my wife, the two boys, Goldie, and Tikvah hopped into the car to go on a weekend camping trip to Big Bear. We were all very excited about the trip, but unfortunately, on the way up our car broke down, and there was nothing we could do to fix it. We stood patiently, waiting for the AAA driver to come and rescue us — and what an odd group to see on the side of the freeway! Tikvah was chatting up a storm, and the kids were itching to get to the camping area (they were probably more wound up than the other family members). The tow-truck driver eventually showed up, and to his surprise, we asked for a lift. The driver drove in astonishment while Tikvah conversed and Goldie sat in the shotgun seat. Once we got to the shop, there were many curious and amazed faces as we waited for the car to get fixed. I guess they weren't used to seeing two kids hanging out with a bird who rested comfortably on the back of his Golden pal. Thankfully, we weren't there too long before we could return to the vacation. Traveling was always a richer experience with the whole family.

Each year, 175 million people in the United States visit zoos. That's more than the number of people who attend all of the sporting events combined. Kids are more engaged in schoolwork when the topic is animals, and many of the most popular programs coming into a classroom include animal topics and/or live animal presentations. Educators often consider those visits the most impactful and meaningful within the school year. Some teachers have classroom pets because they see the value as a calming mechanism for younger students and a teaching mechanism in science, language arts, and geography. I have seen good and not-so-good examples of animals in the classroom. In some special cases, teachers use the subject of animals and habitats as a launching pad for the entire year's lessons. One teacher told me that even the child who is least interested in school will be ignited by the incorporation of animal subjects.

Another example of how animals are appealing to many, and in particular to children, is through the media. All we need to do is look at the games, puzzles, and books on store shelves. The most popular ones are those that feature animals. Commercials that use a dog or cat, even for products that don't relate to the animals, seem to grab the attention of the viewer. We name cars after animals with great qualities, such as the Mustang and the Jaguar, and manufacturers of pharmaceutical products show healthy consumers walking dogs. Animals in a positive light sell goods!

In recent years there has been a rise in the number of movies and TV specials about animals. More and more programs focus on the lives, loves, and problems that animals face. No doubt, children today are exposed to animals in theaters and on the television. A particular favorite is the Animal Planet channel.

We also know that, throughout history, teaching children character lessons while incorporating animal responsibility as an example has been a successful technique. With younger children, encouraging tasks as simple as properly petting a dog or cat encourages kindness and care. Humane organizations throughout the United States boast that their missions include the need for humane education, and they often have a budget dedicated to these programs. Thousands of kids are learning about pet responsibility and compassion as a result of these professional programs. The view that talking to children about kindness to animals will translate into kindness toward people can be traced back in writings over hundreds of years. In the 1880s, Mr. De Sailly, an eminent and highly respected teacher in France, reported: "Ever since I introduced the subject of kindness to animals into my school, I have found the children less disorderly and more gentle and affectionate toward each other" (quoted in Eddy, 2004; original quotation in *Pennsylvania School Journal*, p. 335).

Finally, in recent years, the whole concept of disaster rescue of animals has become a household topic. With so many natural disasters being covered by the media around the world, we are realizing that the saving of a family pet can be one of the most meaningful of all. After hurricane Andrew hit central Florida, hundreds of accounts detailed children being reunited with family pets that had been lost. The reports shared how immeasurably powerful the reunification was on the family, and in particular for the child's recovery. In many accounts when owners are reunited with their pets, they feel that they can recover more readily from the loss of home and belongings because their family is intact.

ANIMALS ACTING AS SOCIAL BUFFERS FOR CHILDREN

Animals may also act as emotional buffers during stressful situations for children. Although research has often been brushed aside and regarded as anecdotal, more evidence is showing that animals help to regulate emotions. The affection from an animal while a person is feeling stressed is extremely important. The animal will bring a sense of stability when families are seeking transitional support, such as during a move (Walsha, 2009). The American Academy of Child and Adolescent Psychiatry states that "moving may be one of the most stress-producing experiences a family faces" (Steele and Sheppard, 2003). So where does the family dog come into the picture? An animal can bring joy and security to a new and unfamiliar environment. Pets provide "socio-emotional support that facilitates coping, recovery, and resilience. Bonds with pets can offer comfort, affection, and a sense of security" (Walsha, 2009, pp. 481–485). The flexible roles that an animal can assume to meet the family's emotional needs make them helpful figures during a difficult period.

Some scholarly research has documented the emotional impact that bonding with a pet has on a child. My friend Gail Melson from Purdue University conducted a review of the literature in 2000 and found that 79 percent of German fourth-graders sought out their pet when they were feeling sad. She also found that 75 percent of ten- to fourteen-year-olds in Michigan preferred to sit by their pets when they were upset and that 42 percent of five-year-olds turned to their pet when they were experiencing emotional upset (Melson, 2000).

McNicholas and Collis (2001) interviewed twenty-two elementary school-children who were seven and eight years old regarding their own model of an emotional and social support system. Children rated their support system of three outlets that included immediate family and pets, particularly cats and dogs. When presented with real-life stories, the children needed to choose which of the methods of support would best help them if they were the child in the story. At times, children chose their pets in situations that were more personally and emotionally challenging and embarrassing. Furthermore, their pets were reported to provide comfort and self-esteem and at times were more highly ranked than human interactions.

Although I, too, agree with this finding, I don't think the literature is conclusive about this outcome. Recently one of my graduate students conducted a study examining how students with learning disabilities (enrolled in special-education classes) versus students in general education would cope with stressful situations. Similar to the strategy discussed in the McNicholas and Collis paper, the children were read ten descriptions of a child engaged in a stressful situation. They were then asked to indicate for each situation which of six potential behavioral responses the child would utilize to cope with the stress when back home. The choices were talk to a friend, play an electronic device, pet or play with a pet, get something to eat, talk to a parent, or "other." Although it was assumed that many children would select the pet response, that was not the outcome. It is possible the subjects in the study didn't have a significant attachment to pets, but the results leave us with still more questions that need to be answered so that we can clearly understand the impact of pets as emotional buffers (McNicholas and Collis, 2001).

Finally, findings from a study conducted in 2004 by Elizabeth Strand, a professor of social work at the University of Tennessee, found that animals act as social buffers in times of distress. Her work suggested that children often turn to their pets in times of anxiety when they face emotional challenges at home, such as parents arguing. Many of us may be aware of soldiers who strike up relationships with stray dogs and other animals while on deployment. Both the soldiers and the animals seem to gain from these relationships. The dogs provide needed support for the soldiers during their deployment and perhaps act as social buffers for them from the stress of war (similar to what was discussed in Strand's work), while the dogs receive shelter, food, and companionship. These relationships are not new phenomena. I have come across many touching stories from World War II of how, in the heat of battle, a GI would find and adopt an abandoned and terrified dog, and together they would learn to survive the horrors of war. In some cases the dogs were trained by the soldiers to conduct dangerous tasks. These dogs not only provided comfort and support to the attending soldier but also to the soldiers in the particular unit. They became part of the family. One such story involved a German Shepherd–Collie–Siberian Husky mix named Chips. Chips was to become the only dog in military history to be awarded a Distinguished Service Cross, Silver Star, and Purple Heart for his gallantry and courage during the invasion of Italy. After the war, Chips came back to America to live with his handler, Edward Wren.

Stories like Chips and Edward Wren underscore the incredible power of the bond between humans and canines and the reciprocal benefits of these relationships, especially under highly stressful circumstances.

PETS AND CHILDREN WITH DISABILITIES

A family with two parents and three kids came into the shelter looking for a new pet. They were so excited and had their heart set on a wiggly, soft little puppy. The shelter didn't have any puppies, so instead they wandered through to visit the dogs. The staff gave them cookies and watched as they visited each dog one by one. A staff member noticed the family's son, the middle child, standing in front of one of the shelter's older dogs. He was silent but riveted. He and the dog had an instant chemistry, and it was palpable. The rest of the family was unaware of this connection and were ready to go to another shelter to look for puppies. But they just could not tear the boy away from the whining dog. Seeing an opportunity, a staff member offered to have them visit the dog outside. They insisted "no," they wanted a puppy. However, the staff member explained to the family all the costs, training, time, and responsibility involved in rearing a puppy. It was pointed out how each of these issues was already taken care of with this mature dog whose paw was reaching out to them. They looked at each other and shrugged. Within an hour, they were driving away with their new dog.

A few weeks later, the shelter received a thank-you card and photo of the dog and the little boy. As it turned out, he was not only the middle son and therefore felt a little left out at times—he also had Asperger's. The dog seemed to have an impact on his life. The boy was more social and happier, and they saw a significant improvement in his personality.

Lesson learned: sometimes it's not about what you want; sometimes it's about what you need.

Pets don't discriminate. If they're treated with kindness and love, their devotion is traditionally reciprocated with unconditional love and admiration. All families with children probably could benefit from the inclusion of pets, but proper preparation must be made for successful adoptions. (This topic is discussed in more detail in the upcoming chapter.)

The belief that families with children benefit from including pets is no different for those who have children with disabilities. Children with special needs may relish and benefit from pets, just like any other child. The most important goal is for parents to *make plans before specific pets are properly integrated into a family. This includes considering the species of animal, the age, the gender, and the size.* Although this suggestion is similar for all families, parents who have children with special needs may need to consider a few other factors, such as the child's behavioral and developmental levels, before they jump into adding a new family member.

Over the years, I have worked with children with various special needs, and I have witnessed firsthand the significance of pets in many of my clients' lives. For example, when I initially met Alfred (a boy with whom I worked many years ago), he was very lonely and was an outcast with his peers. Alfred was diagnosed with a learning disability, and our major goal in therapy was to help him with his social skills. When we first met, Alfred and his family didn't have any pets. When he was at my office, however, he interacted with my therapy animals. He especially loved my birds, and eventually his family adopted a cockatiel for him. They became friends quickly, and over the course of a few years, Alfred became more social, competent, and outgoing. I have witnessed many similar scenarios over the years with very positive outcomes. Although the benefits for children with special needs may seem similar to those for any other child, children with disabilities may profit even more. Many children with whom I have worked had dogs that provided wonderful company, love, and devotion. In some cases, the family pet became the catalyst for social opportunities with other children, while in other situations the pets acted as an external barometer to help children gauge their excitement, frustration, and/or anger.

This past March, while lecturing in Spain, I had the opportunity to meet Nuala Gardner, who authored a book called *A Friend Like Henry* (2008). The book captures the life of a family whose child (Dale) had autism. At the age of five, Henry, a Golden Retriever, joined the family and their lives were changed forever. Shortly after Henry's arrival, Dale's behavior and expressive language greatly changed. He became more engaged with the world around him as Henry helped unlock some of the barriers created by autism. Nuala attributes her son's growth to Henry and believes that the dog was a strong contributor to Dale's life. She shared with me videos of Dale's behavior before the arrival of Henry as well as videos today of him training his new dog. You would be amazed to see his growth! Henry died in April 2006, but his legacy and his imprint on Dale still live on.

As I noted, although I strongly recommend that families consider having pets for their children with disabilities, I do believe that *planning must occur* to make sure that the transition involved in integrating the pet is successful. I also believe that integration needs to be slow. The right set of precautions must be built in for the safety of both the animal and the child. It is also important to think through how the child will engage with the pet and what will be the child's responsibilities.

Children who have developmental disabilities may need to be supervised somewhat closer in their early interactions with their pets to find out how they will interact with one another. They may need instruction on proper interaction, and boundaries may have to be established. Furthermore, if children are highly impulsive (such as children with ADHD) or easily agitated, parents must consider the animal's safety. I always caution that pets should never be used as perpetual babysitters.

Families who have children with developmental disabilities such as Asperger's or autism will benefit from knowing how to select a pet that fits their child's way of

processing information. George Eliot (1857) in her novel *Mr. Gilfil's Love Story,
Scenes of Clerical Life*, once stated that "animals are such agreeable friends — they ask
no questions, they pass no criticisms" (p. 332). Eliot's comments are very apropos. In
a couple of articles I've written on the roles that animals have in the lives of children
with autism (including a chapter I prepared with Temple Grandin), I suggested several reasons why pets and service animals may be appropriate companions to persons with autism spectrum disorder (ASD), including how unconditionally accepting animals are. I also discussed why some of these children might react indifferent-
ly. It's important for parents to recognize that some children may respond negative-
ly to their interactions with their pets, not because they don't like them but because
their senses are overstimulated. For example, some children with ASD may not be
able to tolerate the smell of a dog, and this may cause them to react harshly. Others
may have auditory oversensitivity, and the sound of a dog barking may not be tolerable. The impact of sensory oversensitivity varies and can have a strong effect on an
interaction. In my work with children, I sometimes have to determine why they
might not want to interact with the animal. Simply put, some people with various
levels of ASD may avoid animals only because they have extreme sensitivity to either
sound or smell (it may not have anything to do with the animal specifically).

On the other hand, some believe that persons with ASD may respond well to
animals because these individuals are visual thinkers and solve problems differently. For example, Temple Grandin believes that some children with ASD might relate
well to animals because these children are sensory-based thinkers. In essence, animals do not think in words. Grandin believes that dogs' cognitions are filled with
detailed sensory information and their world is filled with pictures, smells, sounds,
and physical sensations. This may be the same manner in which children with ASD
solve problems, and this may make them ideal candidates for having dogs.

THE ROLES OF PETS WITH TWEENS AND TEENS

It's amazing that we spend so much energy talking about the roles that animals
have in the lives of children who are younger than the ages of eleven or twelve, but I
feel that animals fill an important role in the lives of teenagers as well. In the years that
I have worked therapeutically with animals and teens, I have witnessed firsthand how
many of them are willing to take down some of their barriers and guards because they
just feel much more relaxed having their pets with them. Although a teen may project
the need to be adult-like, many teens seem to still really appreciate the free spirit of an
animal in their lives. Think of Sami and Chloe that we discussed in Chapter 1. Chloe
was Sami's service dog and was very involved in her life. However, when Sami was out

with her friends, many treated Chloe as "one of the girls." Many teens may allow an animal within their life circle much more than they would an adult.

THE ROLES OF PETS WITH YOUNG ADULTS AND ADULTS

Adults, especially those in special circumstances such as newlyweds, empty nesters, single adults, and widowers, may have added advantages for their relationships with their pets. The presence of an animal may give clarity to their life and provide them with more purpose. For some, these relationships may help to alleviate their perceived sense of emptiness and provide them with continuity from their earlier life of living at home.

I think of one of my college students named Krista. Recently I learned that her roommate moved out, and Krista was not used to living alone. Consequently, one night at about 2 A.M., she drove to her parents' house (about five minutes away) and picked up her dog, Tika, to keep her company. Her apartment complex did not allow pets, so she had to be very discreet. Krista shared with me that although Tika was excited to see her, she didn't seem very comfortable in her apartment. This was the first time Tika had been there. She acted timid and curious with the new surroundings and followed Krista's every step like she was her shadow. When it was time to go to sleep, Krista let her climb into bed with her. It was like the good old days again. Her closing comment still resonates in my mind. She said, "I finally wasn't alone." Tika's visit illustrated how valuable companion animals can be in the lives of many young adults.

Companion animals also have specific roles with newlyweds and young couples. Having an animal in the life of a young couple often gives them the chance to co-parent and see what it's like to bring up another being.

A couple of weeks ago, my son and daughter-in-law decided to get a kitten. They were simply elated! They did all their homework and looked hard to find a reputable shelter from which to adopt him. For the past ten days, their lives have been totally altered as they share in the responsibilities and care of little Hunter. They're learning co-parenting while bringing up this lovely little cat. They're also learning the responsibility of raising another being and seemingly have enjoyed what they're doing. My phone is filled with messages describing Hunter's antics. Having a kitten in their lives allows them to think about what it might be like to have a child, but equally as important, it teaches them how to be selfless and share their love with a dependent being. Many young couples admit that having a pet was like having their first child. Six weeks after Hunter entered their lives, they adopted a new playmate for Hunter. The kitten's name is Colby.

PETS AND OLDER FAMILY MEMBERS

We can't underestimate the importance of animals throughout life, not only for children and young adults, but of course for the elderly. Research has identified that seniors who are pet owners seem to live in the here and now, rather than reminiscing about their yesterdays. A senior citizen who has a companion animal allows that individual to be a giver rather than only a receiver. It gives them a purpose to wake up in the morning—to cook, to walk, and to shop. Much research over the years (some of which we'll discuss later on) shows that companion animals can even bring life into an environment that may not be as stimulating. Birds chirping or cats meowing can bring vibrancy into a living environment. It's like my eighty-year-old friend who is awakened every morning by his dog. If she doesn't get the response she wants, the dog puts her cold, wet nose in his ear to say, "It's time to get up."

Definitive research shows the positive impact pet ownership has on the elderly. In my textbook *The Handbook on Animal-Assisted Therapy* (2010), Mara Baun and Rebecca Johnson report many physical benefits of pet companionship, including exercise. Minor health problems are also less common among those who own dogs and cats, and those who have companion animals reported fewer doctor visits when compared to those who do not have pets. Some believe that this finding could be attributed to the healthy distraction pets provide, making the elderly less focused on their own ailments. Finally, social interaction is one of the secondary benefits for elderly persons who have pets. Deborah L. Wells explains that the elderly are less likely to feel isolated and lonely when they have a pet.

SAFE INTEGRATION OF PETS AND KIDS: FROM INFANCY THROUGH CHILDHOOD

Francois Martin, an animal behaviorist at Nestle Purina Food, suggests how we can successfully incorporate a new animal into a family (2013). He explains the importance of research and lifestyle considerations prior to adoption. The American Kennel Club has a website that delivers detailed information about each dog breed so that potential owners can find the best fit for themselves. Allergies, temperament, and size all influence a dog's overall disposition. With this being said, Martin stresses the importance of personal interaction. He suggests going to a dog park or a dog show in order to meet the type of dog ahead of time. Each animal has a different temperament, but the basic profile of a breed remains somewhat constant. These suggestions are important to think about before we bring an animal into our family life.

Infants

Infants learn about animals very early in their lives. We decorate their rooms with animals; often their first gifts are stuffed animals. We teach them nursery rhymes that include animals. Researchers have discovered that toddlers often make animal sounds before they can speak and will have a pet's name or identification (dog, cat, bird) included in their first words. Many of the first songs that children learn include animals, and many of the early learning books we provide to children feature animals. This begins, for many children, a lifelong interest in animals.

We must be especially attentive if we have an infant at home. We must NEVER, EVER leave infants and pets together alone or unattended. Newborns and infants are overwhelmingly the victims of fatal dog bites, and very few ever involve serious aggression. Rather, a single investigatory "pick up" with a dog's mouth can be fatal to a delicate newborn.

We also must be careful to never fall asleep while the child and pet are together. We can never, ever take our eyes off them. Dogs simply don't realize that a newborn is a human. To them, the baby is an unusual toy or perhaps a wounded animal. If we think of our child as an injured bunny that we've brought into our home to rehabilitate, we would never think of leaving an injured bunny on the floor unattended with a dog, right? We should apply the same thought process to a newborn. It might be helpful to think of our pet as a sharp corner of a coffee table, or a knife, or a wall outlet. Such things do not need to be removed from our home, but they must be monitored at all times. Supervision is the most important key to safe interactions between babies and pets.

I strongly recommend making a child-free zone for the pet. This could be a crate or a special room, or a perch for kitty. The pet needs somewhere to go that is always off-limits to the child. This place should never be used as punishment, only as a safe haven. Likewise, it's helpful to have a pet-free zone for the child. This is often the bedroom. Baby gates and screen doors are wonderful ways to keep interested cats and dogs out of baby's room (at least unless a parent is available to supervise or until the child is older than eight or nine years of age). The insert on page 74 synthesizes the critical information that families need to consider.

If we already have a pet and are adding a child to the mix, the above information still applies. One additional recommendation, however, is to obtain a piece of clothing from the child. We should avoid choosing the cap or blankets used immediately after the birth of a newborn. Instead, a cap, a blanket, or clothing that the baby wore after receiving his or her first bath is a good option. We can show the item to our pet and encourage him to sniff and investigate. We then reward, praise, and treat the pet as he does this.

Safety tips for babies and pets:

- Never leave pets and children unattended
- Create a pet-free child zone
- Create a child-free pet zone
- Feed dogs separately
- Teach child to touch gently
- Any aggression, fear, or anxiety requires help from a professional

We must not let the pet take the item in his mouth, play with it, or lie on it. If the pet growls or hisses or displays anxious or fearful behavior, we should never punish or correct him! The pet is telling telling us that he is uncomfortable. Instead, we ought to remove the item from the pet and call a professional right away (see resources). It is wise to never handle fear or aggression toward a child on our own. A professional can help resolve the problem entirely or let us know if it simply isn't going to work out.

Another helpful activity is to get a recording of baby cries and coos. These can be downloaded online for free. We can play the sounds at a very low volume and reward our pet with praise, petting, play, or treats — whatever his favorite thing is. If the pet is relaxed and ignoring the sounds from the infant, we may increase the volume, but if he is tense or nervous, fearful, or aggressive, we should turn the volume down even lower and keep it at that volume. It is important that we play these sounds as often as we can until the pet ignores them and is relaxed. We should continue this process until we can blast that screaming baby recording throughout the house!

When we bring a baby home, we are adding not only the baby but the baby's "stuff"—items to which the pet is not accustomed. If we set up these objects well in advance, the pet can investigate them. This helps us avoid our pet associating "those weird things" with the arrival of the "weird creature" (the baby!). To pets, unusual things are just weird. They need time to adapt, investigate, and become familiarized with everything — strollers being pushed around, toys making noise, bouncy chairs, vibrating seats, baby carriers, cribs, and rocking chairs. When our pet is allowed to investigate and get his smell on these items, he has only one major change to make when the baby comes home.

To summarize, it is not uncommon for dogs to respond differently to babies than older children and adults. In essence, babies do smell and move differently, and they are initially somewhat of an anomaly for dogs. Recently I spoke with my friend Fernando Silva, who is a leading dog trainer in Portugal, about how to introduce existing companion animals to new arrivals. Fernando often gives lectures to new parents; the following six points briefly highlight his suggestions.

- The key for successful integration is preparation. Parents who are expecting can do this by simulating baby experiences — for example, placing a car seat in the vehicle with a baby doll and taking a drive with the dog in the car. The dog can practice sitting or lying down next to the car seat. When the dog cooperates, he should be reinforced generously to encourage the positive response.
- A month before the baby's arrival, the dog should be trained not to enter the baby's room without being called in. This way, once the baby does arrive, the dog will already have experience of not entering the room unless asked.
- Parents should record a baby crying so that their dog will get used to hearing the new sound. This will help acclimate the dog to the baby sounds when the baby arrives.
- It is helpful for the parents to bring home the first soiled diaper. On arrival, the diaper can be placed next to the baby doll (which was used in the practice sessions). The dog is allowed to come over and smell and sniff. Most dogs are curious, and they will want to smell and "discover" the new odor.
- When parents are ready to introduce their dog to the new infant, they should do it in a neutral place. The dog can be allowed to sniff and smell the baby while the baby is in the arms of a parent. Of course, parents should liberally reinforce the dog's behavior and response.
- Early on in the interactions between the infant and the dog, parents must remember to give their dog attention as well. This will help foster a smoother transition.

Although I recommend caution during the introduction of a dog or cat to an infant, I know that many parents have experienced and witnessed remarkable outcomes with their pets and infants. Although the suggestions discussed are conservative, I do think that many people underestimate the intelligence and compassion of our four-legged friends.

Years ago, a friend of mine took in a stray that a student of his asked to shelter for a little while. The student had found the dog and wanted to keep him but needed some time so he could talk to his parents and see about keeping the dog himself. Temporary turned into permanent, and the stray settled down to spend twelve years with his adopted family. They named him Buffis. He was a medium-size animal and weighed about thirty-five or forty pounds (depending what came off the table that week), and he was fearsome to behold. When he barked, the fur on his back stood up and his fangs came out, giving him a wolflike appearance. Although he looked fearless, he never bit anyone, but he certainly frightened many strangers who dared to venture near the gate.

For the first few years of his life with the family, he was the only other resident other than my friend and his wife. One fateful day that all changed when their daughter was born. At first Buffis hid from the little stranger, but gradually he began to take up a position near the baby's bassinet. He remained on guard when mom and dad were not in the room. He seemed to sense that this little stranger was his responsibility, and whenever the baby coughed or made a sound, Buffis would stand up on his hind legs and look in to see if everything was all right.

As the baby grew, Buffis was always there, allowing the little stranger to pull his ears or take his ball. They became friends, and he left the big folks' bedroom to sleep with the baby. If the baby's parents stopped in at night to check up on the baby, they could count on finding Buffis lying on the floor with his head between his paws, watching his darling angel. If the baby cried at night, Buffis was there with his paws on the crib or bed, looking to see what was wrong, and sometimes his presence was enough to calm her down and allow her to fall back to sleep.

This stray with no pedigree and little formal training found his way into a family who loved him and was willing to give him a chance. He repaid that love by watching over a helpless member of the family. Buffis had a great life, and his little friend was happy with him by her side or swimming in the pool with her. Yes, Buffis loved the pool, and when the baby was in the pool, so was he. He gave his loyalty and love to his family, and they returned it until he took his last lap around the pool and left behind a wonderful memory.

Buffis's story makes us realize how valuable a pet can be as an infant grows up. My boys were around creatures great and small most of their lives, and they were blessed with the presence of animals. Each one made a unique contribution to the family dynamic. I wouldn't change those moments for anything.

Before we leave our discussion on introducing infants to pets, let me highlight a few helpful references. The following resources will provide more information for parents with babies on how to integrate their dog with their new child.

- Pet Meets Baby (American Humane Association); free download: www.americanhumane.org/interaction/programs/humane-education/pet-meets-baby.html
- familypaws.com/introduce-your-dog-and-baby
- familypaws.com/our-programs

Warning signs your pet is uncomfortable:

- Moving away from the child
- Tense body
- Panting
- Ears pulled back or out to the sides
- Wide eyes
- Lip licking or drooling
- Hissing, growling, or swatting
- Eyes looking away from the child
- Shrinking, lowered head, cowering

If you see any of these, remove the child from the pet, reward your pet for telling you in an appropriate manner they are uncomfortable, and contact a professional.

Toddlers and Children

Once children are toddling, they are much less at risk for confusion or misidentification from your dog. This is the stage, however, where parents have to really be on their toes! Everything is being grabbed, pulled on, going into the mouth or bitten, banged on, and more. The child is developing motor control and also investigating the world, but this is where toys come in. It is just not appropriate — or safe — to allow your child to do such things to your pet. Nor is it appropriate or safe to expect your pet to tolerate it. I often see photographs and videos of inappropriate interactions between children and pets. What may appear "cute" is actually an incident waiting to happen. If a pet is giving warning signals that he is not comfortable, the parent must intervene and remove the child from the situation. A pet should never be punished for communicating his discomfort — if this happens, the pet may not communicate next time, and this can easily result in a bite or swat "without warning." Instead, parents should reward the pet by removing the child and telling the pet he is a good boy. It may feel counterintuitive — like aggression is being rewarded, but, in fact, the pet is being told that the parents saw the warning signs and respected his good, clear communication. The pet understands that he doesn't have to go any further with the warning signs. Parents need to listen to their pet, and if they see warning signs, it is important to contact a professional right away. Table 3.2 synthesizes the critical information that families need to consider.

Tables 3.1 through 3.3 list suggestions on how to deal with undesirable behaviors of pets, as well as what can realistically be expected from a well-mannered cat or dog within the family. In Table 3.4, we present commonsense ideas to help integrate dogs within an existing family.

TABLE 3.1 WHAT FAMILIES SHOULD EXPECT IN WELL-TRAINED PETS

The following represent the basic behaviors that all pets should know to be safe and well behaved around your family, especially the children.

Dogs:
- Does your dog sit and stay when you tell him?
- Does your dog come when called?
- Does your dog not jump up on kids, or does he get down when told?
- Does your dog not get on furniture, or does he get down when told?
- Is your dog non-aggressive toward men, women, children, and other dogs in your home?
- Is your dog non-aggressive toward men, women, children, and other dogs outside your home?
- Does your dog have nice leash manners?
- Does your dog go to the bathroom outside?
- Does your dog adapt to new places and things in a calm, confident manner?
- Does your dog back away from his food on command?
- Does your dog drop toys and chews on command?

Cats:
- Does your cat use the litter box?
- Does your cat get off of counters or tabletops when told, or stay off altogether?
- Is your cat non-aggressive toward male, female, and child houseguests?
- Does your cat walk away from people when she is irritated or frustrated?
- Does your cat never scratch furniture, screens, etc.?

CATS, KIDS, AND SAFETY

If a family with children is thinking of getting a new cat, it is best to stick with a juvenile or young adult (six to eight months of age or older). Young kittens, although they are irresistibly adorable, are very fragile and easy to carry. Children can accidently scare, drop, or injure a kitten through play. Additionally, kitten nails and teeth are very sharp, which means that play (or self-defense!) can quite easily result in injury to the child. Further, by adopting older cats, parents can assess the animal's innate personality, rather than getting a kitten only to find out its personality isn't compatible with the family. Parents can visit a local shelter and ask for cats that have

TABLE 3.2 TIPS FOR DEALING WITH UNDESIRABLE BEHAVIORS OF PETS

- Rule out any physical or medical causes for unwanted behavior with your veterinarian. Is your kitty peeing outside of the box because she's sick? Probably!

- Pets are more trusting, productive, and happy in environments where they are clearly shown what to do, and when they are properly trained and then rewarded for the correct behavior.

- Instead of just scolding an unwanted behavior, try the following:

  – Provide a behavior the pet will enjoy that is an alternative to the behavior you don't want. If the behavior is natural (like chewing), make sure the alternative is an outlet for that behavior. Example: Instead of scolding kitty for scratching furniture, provide a scratching post in the spot where she is scratching.

  – Praise the pet as soon as he engages in the alternative behavior. Example: Yes! Good boy! Thank you for dropping that shoe and taking that toy!

  – Manage the situation to prevent the behavior from happening, and be prepared with everything you will need to deal with it should it arise. Example: You know your dog is a sleeve-grabber on walks. So before you leave for a walk, have something handy to put in his mouth instead of the sleeve.

TABLE 3.3 CAUTIONS FOR PARENTS INTEGRATING PETS WITH CHILDREN

The following list suggests ways that parents can handle potential unsafe situations with pets.

- If your pet has any aggressive behaviors, contact a professional right away! It is important to teach children when and why to stay away. Aggression toward children is typically based in fear for the pet's personal safety or a threat to their resources (e.g., bed, food, toys). This applies to both cats and dogs.

- Children should never be involved with training an aggressive dog. Consult a professional trained in handling such cases ASAP.

- Parents must realize that pregnant or nursing pets can act unpredictably — and understandably so! The pet that was previously your child's best friend is now a mom protecting her own babies or her hormones may be raging.

Solutions:

- Spay or neuter your pets so that heats and pregnancy are never a risk.

- If your pet is pregnant or in heat, keep your children away from her or always find yourself supervising their interactions. Children have no business around dogs under these conditions — it's simply not safe.

- If you have multiple pets in the house, recognize that the pet that is expecting or has given birth may have a significant impact on the behavior of other pets, regardless of species and gender. I suggest that parents consider waiting until the babies are eating on their own to allow children to visit, and then only if mom is in the other room.

- Sick, injured, and elderly pets have much less tolerance than they previously had. Be aware of these possible changes and supervise the interactions.

lived with children in the past. Seek a cat that is mellow, confident, and playful — a cat that enjoys being held, is not shy, seeks affection, and is a gentle player.

It is critical to teach children how to interact appropriately with a cat. Swishing tails are tempting to grab, but this is not acceptable. Soft bodies make

TABLE 3.4 COMMONSENSE SUGGESTIONS FOR INTEGRATING DOGS WITHIN THE HOME

- To optimize socialization experiences for a puppy, it is important to get the puppy out of the home early in his life (after the vaccinations have all been given). The puppy can be held and walked around to experience various types of stimulus such as noises from cars, ongoing traffic, other animals, and people talking.
- At home, there must be a designated space for the dog. This space will help set boundaries for the puppy. Crates are usually excellent alternatives and will help limit damage to furniture and personal objects.
- Guardians of puppies should buy appropriate toys for their pet for stimulation and chewing. Products such as Kong toys and chew bones are excellent options. These items can typically be filled with pet food, yogurt, and cheese, which can be used to motivate the puppy to play with them.
- When families start early puppy training, they should consider utilizing a harness — an "easy-walk" harness in which the leash is attached at the chest is a good choice. The harness promotes smoother walking and discourages the puppy from pulling.
- Only positive approaches to dog training are strongly recommended. Find trainers and schools that follow this philosophy. Clicker training methods are viable alternatives.
- Supervision is necessary when a family's dog plays with other dogs or children. Following this precept will avoid potential problems.
- An exercised and engaged dog is a happy and balanced dog. Exercise will prevent potential behavioral problems and promote health.

wonderful pillows and feel snuggly to hug, but few cats enjoy (nor should they be expected to tolerate) such interactions. Parents must teach their children to pet the cat gently and to stick to the top of the head and the back. They should never carry the cat under the arm like a football, grab any part of a cat, or pull the fur.

Parents may instinctively want to declaw a new kitty to keep their children safe from scratches. Unfortunately, this more often than not backfires. Declawed cats can easily wind up developing litter-box avoidance issues, chronic pain, aggression, fear, and other behavioral issues. Instead, parents need to teach their children how to interact appropriately with cats so that scratching never becomes an issue. Also, remember that declawing is a nice way of saying, "amputate." A declaw actually involves the amputation of every toe at the first joint.

Family members need to scoop litter boxes daily and do a complete litter change weekly. The box itself should be washed with dish soap and hot water. And it is best to keep kitties inside. Dirty boxes harbor bacteria, and outside cats are exposed to parasites. Unfortunately, curious children can find their way into a litter box, and well…

Cats should visit the veterinarian annually. Especially as they age, cats can be very stoic. It is easy not realize that the cat is ill or in pain, which tends to be the underlying cause of many aggressive behaviors.

CONSIDERATIONS FOR POTENTIAL PET OWNERSHIP

"The decision requires a reality check!"

Families should be asking themselves questions to prepare for a pet adoption or purchase. Having these discussions should never be as a result of a heart-tugging puppy in the window or a free kitten at the flea market. Pets are a huge commitment of time, money, and love. Preparation starts with a conversation. It should always begin with the adults in the household talking about the many aspects of pet responsibility. Each day in America, 1.24 million animals are sitting in shelters waiting to find a forever home. Many are there because of mistakes or, more significantly, their previous family's realization that their decision to acquire a pet was not well thought out. They were ill-equipped to deal with the many pressures of an addition to the family that had not only the basic needs of food and water, but also required attention, medical care, exercise, training, and grooming. In some cases, people see that the novelty of a new pet that Johnny had to have has already worn off, and they are on to other interests.

Additionally, for many families there is the ideal of Suzy having a pet and caring for the animal to learn responsibility. They create lists of what needs to be done, and Suzy swears that she will give up everything if she can just have the puppy that the family down the street has to offer for free. What we forget to consider is that Suzy will soon be older and her interests will change to sports or cheerleading or clubs, and soon the pet will be insignificant in terms of what needs to be taken care of. Now the adults are taking Suzy to events and meetings and no one is home most of the time. Pet chores and time get put on the back burner, and the pet suffers.

When my children were younger, they had responsibilities with our pets. Their jobs were to help with the feeding, grooming, and picking up after the pets. I am not going to lie and say it was always easy. There were times when they may not have wanted to pitch in, especially in what I called "poop patrol." However, we were relentless and didn't allow them to shirk their portion of the responsibility. Loving an animal isn't only when you want to get or give "loving." It also includes times when the pet's needs have to be met.

Jane shared an excellent example that occurred in her family many years ago when they argued about which person had to feed the dog. She shares, "When our kids were young, they begged us to take the last German Shepherd puppy of a litter from our friends up the street. With a full house and a full-time job, I couldn't imagine taking on any more work, but little by little the kids chipped away at us. At their age, most kids had a dog. Well, we gave in. They were in orbit over this new girl, at least for the first four months, after which the responsibility was becoming a task and the novelty was surely wearing off.

"One night after dinner they were arguing about whose turn it was to feed her. I was down the hall helping the youngest get ready for bed. I watched as the dog sat and watched them argue but wasn't getting her meal. After about twenty minutes, I went in and fed the hungry dog that was in the habit of eating at dinnertime like everyone else.

"So the next night at dinnertime, I fed the dog and set the table but didn't make dinner. The kids waited around the table and finally asked what we were doing about dinner. My husband and I ignored them and just kept talking. Finally, we had to answer them because they were getting out of control. We simply asked them how they thought the dog had felt the night before when no one was willing to give in and feed her. Suddenly you could see the lights going off in their brains.

"We told them, 'Now you know how your dog felt last night. She was so hungry but had no way to tell you. She sat patiently waiting for someone to get her something to eat and you guys just argued. We need to always keep in mind that she is a member of this family with feelings. When you start to feel hungry at dinnertime, you need to remember that so does she.' They were all speechless, and although there were still occasional problems with tasks, for the most part they were much more aware of the dog's needs and much better pet caregivers. Now they are adults with children, and all of them have pets and always consider what their pets need as a priority. Most importantly, they are great, caring, and considerate adults and parents!" Jane often looks back at her children's upbringing with the animals and credits their experiences as the greatest influence on their kindness and compassionate personalities.

On the other hand, it is equally as important to find jobs for your companion animal. Dogs love routines and respond wonderfully to human direction, especially for purposeful activities. For example, my friend's gardener takes his dog to work with him every day. His dog loves to ride shotgun in the pickup truck and dutifully accompanies him as he goes about his various yard-work tasks. Zip (the dog) takes his job very seriously and is almost never distracted by other dogs, cats, bunnies, or a cool place to take a nap. Instead, he is a steady companion. Jobs don't have to be so noble and specified. They can be simple daily routines such as going for a walk, preparing for dinner, or playing Frisbee. The point is that, just like humans, dogs thrive when life is purposeful and meaningful. It must be understood that, just like humans, dogs left alone are much more likely to be unhappy and ill behaved.

COMMON QUESTIONS ABOUT GETTING A PET

Should We Wait Until Our Kids Are Older?

This is an individual choice. Families need to be aware of what they are getting themselves into before they leap into getting a pet. They shouldn't be coerced by their children into making an irrational choice. Sometimes families decide to wait on having a pet, and that decision should be congratulated. People who are willing to admit they are not ready or that the time is not right are making a quality choice. They are so much more likely to do a better job when they are ready for a pet. The Buddhist proverb that says, "when the mind is ready, the teacher comes," seems to fit this position.

For Whom Are We Getting the Pet (the Kids or the Parents)?

Earlier we discussed getting pets for the kids, but the fact is, parents are getting the pet for themselves as well. Moms and dads will definitely be involved! Children will need to be reminded to feed the dog, they may lose interest in taking the dog for walks, and they may even be resistant and do whatever it takes to get out of cleaning the poop in the yard. That is the reality. They all say they will do anything if mom and dad will just say yes. Remember how I begged for my first dog Goldie! Invariably, a few weeks later the novelty has worn off, and in some cases the pet is lucky if the youngsters spend a little time throwing the ball. Kids are kids, and they are often preoccupied with many other activities. As the years pass, parents will find themselves with the dog or cat while the kids are at school, participating in sports, and attending parties. To be realistic, parents should simply get a dog or cat for themselves, because the lion's share of the work and all of the expenses fall on the grown-ups in the house. Parents need to think about when they are tired at the end of the day and the dog sits next to the couch, looking at them with that wistful look that says, "Let's go for a walk."

Also, as parents, we should consider how the pet will be trained and by whom. Katenna Jones, an animal behaviorist, explains that having a companion animal join the family is a big step for most people, and fortunately, good information is abundant to help families make a good choice. Deciding who should train the family dog is another matter. Katenna says, "Unless you have lots of experience training dogs yourself, you probably have not even considered who should train your dog." Table 3.5 synthesizes our interview in March 2013, in which she helped me understand the important variables to consider when finding a trainer. Her book, *Fetching the Perfect Dog Trainer* (2012), is a great resource for more information.

TABLE 3.5 QUESTIONS TO CONSIDER ABOUT DOG TRAINING

1. Do we need to get a professional trainer?

	Yes	No	Unsure
Do we need a trainer?			
Have we received conflicting advice from TV, friends, books, magazines, websites, etc.?			
Is anyone in the house frustrated with, afraid of, or wants to "get rid of" the pet?			
Have we tried training with no success?			
Is our pet displaying severe issues like anxiety, aggression, and phobias?			

If answers to any of the above questions are "Yes" or "Unsure," a professional trainer is definitely needed!

Where to Find Reliable Resources

Internet searches; advice from friends, family, neighbors, and coworkers; and local animal professionals (groomers, shelters, veterinarians) may all be good resources. Families should ask these individuals about their own personal experiences with trainers, their reputations, and their successes.

2. What should we ask while interviewing potential trainers?

Question	Possible Answers
Do you use primarily reward-based training?	Yes? Proceed. No? Walk away.
May I contact past clients who experienced problems similar to mine?	Yes? Proceed. No? Walk away.
May I watch you train?	Yes? Proceed. No? Walk away.
Can you guarantee results?	Yes? Walk away.
Do you pursue continuing education? Are you a member of any professional organizations? What certifications do you have?	No to all three? Walk away.

3. What should we expect from training?

Service	Details	Pros	Cons
Private Training	Typically for specific goals, such as house-training or anxiety. An option when relevant group classes are not available in your area, such as agility or dog-dog reactivity.	Often at your home or at an agreed-upon location; tailored to your needs.	Typically costs more than a group class.
Group Classes	Typically for multiple dogs and families with the same goals (puppy socialization, manners, sports, etc.)	Often cheaper than private classes; socialization for pet.	Often not as convenient for schedule and location; less tailored to the customer.

Who Will Care for the Pet? Are the Kids Really Going to Take Responsibility for the Pet Without Oversight and Being Reminded?

The fact is, the children will do everything the first few weeks. If more than one child is involved, they will likely fight over caring for the pet during this time. Setting up a schedule and keeping the kids plugged into the care plan for the pet is important to the future of kids. Teaching responsibility and respect are important character lessons for the children, and it is easier to use pet-care examples than human-care ones when trying to teach them.

Parents cannot just assume they are doing what is expected. Many of our children will try and cut corners or will conveniently forget. They are kids after all, and we can't expect perfection when it comes to pet care or cleaning up their room. It is so important to set a good example in terms of pet care by demonstrating the proper behavior. Most importantly, it is important to remind kids that pets are living things that have needs and that they are completely reliant on us for many of their necessities. If pets are hungry or afraid, it is hard to know what the problem is. They will wait patiently, but they will still be hungry or sad or afraid, just like our children. When children begin to realize how important they are in their pets' lives, they become more plugged in about pet care and responsibility.

When asked what degree of involvement children should have in taking care of a pet, Francois Martin (the behavior specialist at Purina mentioned earlier) emphasizes the well-being of the animal. He doesn't believe that young children should be given full responsibility to care for an animal. Instead, they can do as much as possible under parental supervision. Having a healthy and happy dog or cat can be achieved through multiple caregivers in the family.

For families with teens at home, it is important to set realistic expectations when it comes to pet care. Of course, some children will be incredibly helpful long-term and actively involved in the pet's life and daily care. However, such cases are often the exception rather the rule. In most situations, parents can expect a honeymoon phase where the child is completely infatuated with the pet for a period of weeks or even months, but it is completely natural and normal for some tweens to outgrow their interest as they mature into teenagers. Some teens find other interests, and they quickly lose interest in one thing and move on to something else. Be patient and set realistic expectations. Fighting with teenagers and forcing them to take care of the pet is not healthy for the parent-child relationship, and it will not benefit the pet either. It is not at all uncommon for animal shelters to receive a pet after a child "stopped taking care of it." Remember, the adult in the household is always responsible for caring for a pet. Most children cannot be expected to be accountable for a pet's care long-term. Therefore, parents should set themselves up for success when choosing a pet and when encountering their maturing teenager.

Another consideration is when the children move on with his or her life. It's scary, I know! But college, work, their first apartment, and so many other adventures await, and the kids may soon not live at home. In most cases, they can't take the pet with them, or it just may not be appropriate. Parents need to be prepared to care for the pet on their own, without the child. If they can't fulfill that obligation, bringing home a pet may not be the best option right now. (Of course, there is always the exceptional child who is fully responsible for all care of their pet throughout its lifetime.)

Some excellent resources that can help parents get their children more involved in pet care and training are listed at the end of this chapter. For a list of suggested

EVERYDAY PET ACTIVITIES FOR CHILDREN

Walking the dog: For smaller kids, clip a second leash to your dog so an adult has control but the kid has fun!

Feeding: Teach your child to prepare the food, ask the pet to sit, and deliver the food. This can help your pets to view the child as a resource provider.

Veterinarian visits: Though it may be more work to shuffle and schedule, take the kids along to veterinarian visits. It is important for them to see and understand what goes into pet care and that pets get shots too.

Training: Enroll your pet in a group class that welcomes kids, or hire a trainer to work with your kids. Involving them in the training is key to good communication and having dogs see kids as respected members of the family. Your trainer can help you decide, based on your child's age, maturity, physical size, and specific personality, what activities are appropriate for them and which should probably be avoided for now.

Dog park visits: Use caution at dog parks with both kids and dogs. Stick to small parks where there are only a few dogs that are matched for age, size, and play style. Kids should stick to the perimeter and never run and yell. Check out Sue Sternberg's Dog Park Assistant app on iTunes; it is a must-have to learn proper dog-park etiquette and safety.

Visiting friends: When kids' friends come to visit, they all get very excited and rowdy. The more kids and the more excitement, the more these factors will impact your pets. Shy, elderly, or sick pets should be provided a child-free zone that is respected. Don't take your eye off interactions with kids whom your pets don't know well. Just because your pets are okay with YOUR child doesn't mean they will be okay with another child. Also, you don't know that child's behavior around pets. If you see your pets being treated in any way that is inappropriate, be their advocate and take them to a quiet, child-free zone anytime that child is around until they learn appropriate behavior.

Parties and holidays: These are stressful for you and, as a result, are also stressful for pets. With more than a very small number of calm, older kids who are familiar to your pet, it's best to provide a quiet space to keep pets away from the noise and risks of eating unsafe human food, escaping out an open door, and having stress-induced nips or scratches.

activities that will be enjoyable for children to do with their pets see page 89. As the old saying goes, the family that plays together, usually stays together.

THE NEGATIVE SIDE

Pet Loss

On the down side of this topic, we know that the child's first experience with death may be that of a pet. How the loss is handled at that time can really influence how a child views and deals with death in the future. In recent years, many books have been written for children to help them understand and to assist parents in the proper handling of the subject. How the event is handled and how the death is acknowledged will be critical to how the child recovers from the loss. Chapter 7 delves deeply into how families can cope with such loss. Integrated into the chapter are suggested resources on this topic. In the PAWS for Thoughts appendix, families will find a wonderful memorial booklet that can be completed by family members to help them express their loss. Humane education websites can also provide guidance to parents or teachers on how to handle questions and disclosures of feelings and loss.

Dog Bites

Animals are emotional beings just as humans are, so with our interactions with them comes a risk of injury. According to Colleen Lynn (2013), 50 percent of dog-attack victims in 2012 were adults (twenty-one years of age and older), while the other half were children (eight years of age and younger). The majority of children killed by dogs in 2012 were aged two and younger. The simple fact that a pet caused a death is heartbreaking; however, it is helpful to keep the total fatalities in perspective. The amount of reported deaths in America from dog attacks in 2012 was only thirty-eight. These numbers suggest that the potential for owning a hostile dog is slim and may be avoided by considering the breed and background of a companion animal. In some of these cases, the dog's behavior can be attributed to irresponsible or careless owners. Well-trained, socialized, and cared-for dogs generally don't kill people regardless of breed.

Taking precautions around an animal may prevent injury. Francois Martin encourages constant supervision for children under the age of five when they are near a pet. Even though a dog may seem "childproof" because of its age, breed, or previous interaction, it is still important to remain cautious. Puppies and kittens that were socialized around children from early in their lives are more likely to have an agreeable temperament around children as they age. Fatality statistics should be no reason to avoid getting a companion animal, he explains, but finding the right companion requires some work. Martin's questions for families who plan to incorporate a new animal into the mix are, "What's your situation? What's your lifestyle? What are you willing and ready to do? Go from there and find your best match."

We know from the CDC that dogs bite about 3.5 million children each year and that the younger victims experience the worst injuries. Interestingly, the lion's share of those incidents occur as a result of a family pet. Too often, we read of accounts where children have been left unattended with the family dog and tragedy strikes, and often with the owner saying, "The dog never misbehaved like that before." It seems that, although we teach our kids to be careful around strange dogs, we forget to teach them to respect certain boundaries of our family dogs. These injuries cost the insurance industry more than $1 billion a year in claims and account for one in seven hospital and emergency room visits for kids. Reducing these statistics comes down to teaching children simple rules about respecting animals, their feelings, and their space. There is no question that teaching children the rules when they are young and preparing pets for the addition of a child will both work to reduce injuries and keep pets and families together. There is no need to relinquish a pet because a new member of the family is expected. By doing a bit of homework, preparing for the changes, and teaching both the pet and the child boundaries, many tragedies can be avoided.

Financial Issues

Despite the emotional and physical benefits of having a companion animal, finances are an essential consideration prior to adoption. According the ASPCA, the average cost to own a dog is between $580 and $875 per year. In the first year alone, however, expenses can reach between $1,300 and $1,800. According to Hal Herzog, pet ownership can be quite expensive, averaging about $8,000 for a medium-size dog and about $10,000 for a cat. Beginning with the initial purchase, a future owner must make the decision to adopt a shelter animal or purchase one from a breeder. Adoption fees are generally much less costly, with no definite price. Purchasing an animal from a breeder averages $500 and can reach much higher depending on the breed (John, 2012). After taking an animal home, spay/neuter charges range from $190 to $220 depending on the size of an animal, and veterinary visits range from $210 to $260 per year. Add on an extra $70 for any de-worming, blood tests, and microchip costs. In addition, the price to feed a dog can range from $55 to $235 per year (depending on the dog's size). Expenses for an animal can add up quickly, so this important decision requires thought ahead of time (ASPCA, 2013).

Furthermore, families who live in a detached single-family home are more likely to have pets than families who live in a multiple-family dwelling. Like humans, pets require ongoing medical care, and those expenses are often unpredictable and very costly. For example, over the life of a dog or cat, routine vaccinations and office visits for relatively minor ailments will run into the hundreds of dollars. Add the unfortunate but often-necessary treatments for various cancer surgeries, cuts, and broken bones and the total will run into the thousands. All too many pet owners fail to account for such costs before making the decision to buy or adopt an animal. Animal shelters are full of pets requiring medical attention that owners are either unprepared for or are unwilling to provide. More attention to the subject will be given in Chapter 4.

Health Issues: Allergies

Allergic reactions are a common concern when families are thinking about adding an animal to the family. There is good news for those who are worried about their health while living with an animal. Recent exploration on this topic explains how having an animal in the house doesn't increase the risk for allergy development but may reduce the risk instead! This is because exposure to bacteria from a dog (through licking or interaction) leads to immunity development (Leigh, 2011). More intensive studies have found no correlation between the development of allergies and respiratory symptoms in children exposed to dogs in their first year of life (Lombardi, 2010).

Similarly, asthma is less likely to develop when children have pets and older siblings. Those with severe asthma have much thicker base membranes in their airways than those without asthma, which has been discovered to develop at an early age. A combination of environmental factors and genetics will alter development, according to the hygiene hypothesis. It promotes the idea that exposure to germs as an infant will encourage an immunity protection response. With this research, it has been concluded that exposure to dogs at an early age is a contributing factor to allergy and asthma prevention (Almqvist, 2003).

While this research is promising, the Humane Society puts allergy risk in perspective. "Any and all cats and dogs may cause reactions for people who are allergic to animals," the organization explains. "There are no 'non-allergenic' breeds of dogs or cats." Even though certain breeds may not cause as much of an impact on allergies, a combination of factors contribute to an individual's risk. By creating an "allergy-free zone" where animals aren't allowed, using air purifiers, and keeping animals groomed/bathed, allergies can be avoided and treated more effectively (Humane Society, 2012).

Domestic Violence in the Home

It's important for us to recognize that the environment in which a pet lives is usually the same environment in which our children live. And we can learn a lot about a household just by looking at the way an animal responds. Both children and animals are at risk in homes where there is domestic violence, and when animals are abused, children are also more likely to be abused. Children who are exposed to domestic violence are almost three times more likely to be cruel to animals than non-exposed children.

One of my colleagues, Frank Ascione, has found that children who have been physically or sexually abused traditionally have a higher incidence of abusive behavior toward animals, for several reasons. One is the lack of boundaries in relating to their peers, which can transcend to human-animal relationships. Sometimes, the behavior occurs because it is what they've witnessed, and they're imitating violence toward animals. The cause could also be a desire for revenge, because children are angry about what they have seen.

I suspect that some children who are subjected to a violent and abusive home environment will often withdraw (or deviate) from the customary feelings and empathic sensitivities possessed by children who live in healthy family environments. In an effort to cope with the pain of a dysfunctional home environment, some children become anesthetized to the traumas and stresses of that environment. As a consequence, they shut themselves off from thinking, feeling, or caring about others. Under such circumstances, it is little wonder that children might either objectify or mistreat animals. In severe cases, the animal becomes a surrogate for an abusive parent, sibling, or other abusive adult and a convenient target at which to direct one's inner rage.

Violence Toward Animals

Finally, we know that in many parts of the country, animal fighting is a way of life and that tens of thousands of children are exposed to blood sports as a typical experience. Many children see this as income generating, like any job in a household. Family members rely on their dogs or roosters to put food on the table and pay the bills. These children are often exposed to violence from an early age and see no harm in the practices. One child told me that his father taught him that pit bulls have no feeling in their heads and necks and that this is the job they were bred to do in life. Apparently, that father never saw the old Spanky and Our Gang, whose loyal companion and protector was a pit bull. Another boy told me his father was arrested for fighting dogs and he was glad because he secretly felt so bad for the dogs and was happy that they didn't have to fight anymore.

Blood sports attract a subculture that includes gambling, drugs, and prostitution, to name a few illegal activities to which young children are also exposed. These practices are polar opposites of the character education that school systems and religious groups try to share with kids to make them better, kinder, and more productive citizens. Desensitizing young children to cruelty of any kind conversely teaches all of the worst social messages and encourages crime and criminal behavior. Again, we should take to heart the words of Gandhi when he noted that our sense of morality should be judged by the way we treat animals.

The Solutions

It is overwhelming when we look at all of the issues facing animals in our society, from cruelty, to overpopulation, to endangered species. Teaching children to appreciate and understand animals and their world, and demonstrating empathy and acts of kindness, are a way of working toward a kinder and more compassionate world. Humane education, whether it is from a parent, a teacher, a humane educator, or a friend, will help build on a child's quality of character and contribute to that child becoming a kinder and more caring adult. Humane education contributes to a kinder society one child at a time and is good for the future of our country. I encourage everyone to begin teaching early and to continue to encourage character values throughout a child's life.

—

I will never forget the day Puppy gave birth to her litter of pups. We had just rescued her (she was actually my first therapy dog) a month earlier, and the family was not prepared for what we were about to experience. We weren't aware that Puppy was pregnant until the very day we brought her into the veterinarian's office. We were concerned about some swelling we felt. "Not only is she pregnant, the pups should be on their way," the veterinarian said to us. Boy was he right. By the time we got home, she had gone into labor, and over the course of the next several hours, our family grew incrementally. Nine puppies were born that day. If you have never witnessed puppies being birthed, it is a magnificent experience. My boys were able to not only view the birth of life, they were able to help in the process. One of the pups, the runt of the litter, was struggling to stay alive because he had limited oxygen. I immediately brought him to the veterinarian to see what could be done. The veterinarian quickly put the puppy on some oxygen. After examining the puppy, he also confirmed that the puppy would need to be tube-fed if there was any hope for his survival. "He is too small to battle his big siblings for the food. The only way we are going to keep him alive is through tube-feeding him. We could do it for you for the next couple of weeks, or we could teach you how to do it yourself," he went on to say. I decided I wanted to do it. By the time I got home, my life was about to change. I named the new puppy Shrimp.

Shrimp was at my side for the next three weeks. He went everywhere with me, including hockey rinks, my work, and even to a commencement speech that I was giving for young adults with developmental disabilities. His life challenge was actually the theme of my commencement speech.

As we began to adopt out all the puppies, it was hard for my boys to give them up. They became so attached to each of the pups and seemed to find specific qualities they loved in each of them. But as the days went on, the pups were all adopted out except for my little buddy Shrimp. I was worse than the kids. We became so inseparable that it was incomprehensible to see life without him. No discussion was to be had. Shrimp would become a permanent fixture in our family. He ended up living with us for the next fifteen years and he was the sweetest soul.

Yes, I have to admit that family life is definitely enriched with companion animals in them. In most cases, with proper planning and a strong willingness to share the love in your heart, family pets can enrich our homes. They contribute to our well-being and help us become more selfless and caring.

Companion animals can become core members of our family only if we allow them the opportunity to be fully integrated into our lifestyle. When this principle is followed, the outcome can be miraculous. In his book *Marley and Me*, John Grogan (2005) writes that, although our pets have shorter lives, "They spend most of it waiting for us to come home each day. It is amazing how much love and laughter they bring into our lives and even how much closer we become with each other because of them."

Becoming closer as a family is perhaps one of the greatest benefits of having pets. Families who embrace this position not only understand this but also lay these foundations for their children so they will embrace and value this belief in their own future families. We must have done something right in our family. My first grandchildren are kittens. The existence of Hunter and Colby in Sean's and Nelli's newly formed family continues a legacy demonstrating the importance that companion animals have in our lives and homes.

DOG TRAINING RESOURCES FOR CHILDREN

1. American Kennel Club. *The Dog Listener*. Raleigh, N.C.: AKC. http://www.akc.org/dog_listener/ A short video from the American Kennel Club that teaches children how to stay safe around dogs by becoming a "Dog Listener."

2. Benjamin, Carol L. 1988. *Dog Training for Kids*. Hobokin, N.J.: Howell Book House. A humorous, illustrated "home-study course" to teach children how to train their dogs in seven common problem areas.

3. Dahan, JoAnn. 2004. *Kids Training Puppies in 5 Minutes*. CreateSpace Independent Publishing Platform. Puppy training in 5 minutes with step-by-step photos; also a DVD for instruction.

4. Dunbar, I. (2006). *Dog Training for Children* (DVD). James and Kenneth. Children's tendency to approach a dog with a positive attitude gives them an advantage to training dogs. *Dog Training for Children* covers topics from house-training to playing with toys. For more information: http://www.jamesandkenneth.com/store/show/DV803.

5. Gunter and Newcomb. 2006. *Pet Science: 50 Purr-fectly Woof-Worthy Activities for You and Your Pets*. Asheville, N.C.: Lark Books. A discovery book for children to understand dog behavior through imitation and activities.

6. Pelar, Colleen. 2005. *Living with Kids and Dogs Without Losing Your Mind*. Woodbridge, Va: Dream Dog Productions. This 176-page book provides information and pointers for parents who are raising children with animals. Each stage of the life is covered.

7. Pelar, Colleen. 2012. *Puppy Training for Kids: Teaching Children the Responsibility and Joys of Puppy Care, Training, and Companionship*. Hauppauge, N.Y.. Barron's Educational Series. A ninety-six-page paperback book directed toward young readers with advice on how to care for, train, and keep their puppy out of trouble.

8. Tucker, Michael. 1998. *Dog Training for Children and Parents*. Hoboken, N.J.: Howell Book House. Easy-to-read instructions that children and parents can follow to implement commands that will build bonds with their dog.

CHAPTER FOUR

RELATIONSHIPS ARE AN INDIVIDUAL CHOICE:
The Baskin-Robbins Phenomenon

In the 1994 film *Forrest Gump*, one of the most noted quotes shared by Forrest was, "Mama always said, life was like a box of chocolates — you never know what you're going to get." Forrest's comment highlights many of the mysteries we find in life, where we never really know what will occur. However, over the past few decades, confectionaries have made our choices simpler by taking the mystery out of choices and providing consumers with a key that unearths the layer under the chocolate coating. This key provides us with more information about our choices but in essence still never guarantees our satisfaction. On occasion, many of us just enjoy making a serendipitous choice and being surprised at what we encounter. We may experience feelings ranging from delight or disappointment, but we are willing to take a chance, because we want to have the opportunity to have this unique relationship. The advantage to having more knowledge about our selection is that the outcome of our choice may turn out more satisfactorily.

So how does this example relate to matching the best pet for us? The answer is simple. With some preparation and guidelines, we can take the mystery out of the selection and ultimately become more satisfied with our final choice. Of course, as with anything in life, there are no guarantees, but educating ourselves in advance can help increase the likelihood that we will select a suitable furry friend for ourselves and our families.

I remember when my wife and I got our first dog, Goldie. I was so excited! I had never had a four-legged buddy, and I desperately wanted one to join our newly minted family. While neither of us was as educated (as we should have been) in what steps we needed to consider to select the best dog for a family, we were ready to invest a strong commitment to make this process work. Looking back on our selection, Goldie was a terrific dog. Sure, we experienced growing pains with the addition of a puppy to our family, but because we were determined to establish a loving relationship, we had wonderful years with our buddy, Goldie.

As I started writing this chapter, I was strongly reminded of what ice cream was like when I was a child. Those were such special times; having ice cream when I was a kid was definitely a superb treat, but the choices were so limited (still yummy, of course). We really only had four choices: chocolate, strawberry, vanilla, or Neapolitan. However, even then, it was sometimes hard to narrow down the choices. Then along came ice-cream shops like Baskin-Robbins, where ice-cream choices exploded and mouth-watering, gooey, frozen concoctions such as Rocky Road and Fudge Brownie were available. In fact, Irv Robbins once said, "Not everyone likes all our flavors, but each flavor is someone's favorite."

The same holds true for our beloved pets. The personal bond between people and their companion animals is a unique connection. Some people may like large animals while others prefer small and portable ones. Ultimately, many variables may come into play both consciously and unconsciously when these choices are being made. How people reach their final decision regarding the best selection for them remains a mystery to many, but one thing remains constant — the choice that is made can produce elation or, unfortunately, disappointment at times. However, even when the outcome is not a desired outcome, it is our commitment to our pet that will be the final factor in determining a happy relationship.

A friend of mine has never carefully selected any of his pets. Instead, he has taken in strays and dogs that were unloved or left without owners. He has never regretted these choices. Though the dogs have all been good and faithful friends to him and his family, some of us may not find the same fortune if we randomly take in pets with unknown backgrounds. We need to consider all of these factors when we choose a pet.

Over the years, my wife and I have had the wonderful opportunity to adopt a series of companion animals into our family. In most cases, we never made the choices spontaneously, and we always tried to make informed decisions. We have been fortunate, and all of our companion animals have blended seamlessly into our family. In the next several pages are some guided insights on how best to select a pet, with the understanding that this is not a perfect science. Only with hard work, commitment, and the acceptance that life at times can throw you a curve, the outcome, perhaps, will work well. We all must be flexible and recognize that sometimes we won't get the perfect companion — yet we can *make* that companion perfect for us. Too often, we have unrealistically high expectations of relationships with our companion animals, and then animals fail to live up to these expectations. Consequently, far too many animals are relinquished or abandoned every year.

The following insights will hopefully help to alleviate this situation. I will apply Irv Robbins' philosophy in helping to match families with the best companion animal and will provide a framework for realistic choices as they relate to variables in lifestyle (e.g., finances, age, and family dynamics) and health concerns.

During my research to create a rationale for pet selection, I spent a great amount of time speaking to dozens of people who had ideas of what should be considered when getting a pet. These contributions are incorporated as well.

KNOWING THE DOGS YOU SELECT

Two Critical Variables: Activity Level and Size

Dr. Stanley Coren, professor emeritus at the University of British Columbia, is well known for his contributions to understanding dogs and their behaviors. I therefore reached out to Dr. Coren for his opinion. We discussed numerous issues that he felt were critical. He believes that the most important variables to consider when selecting a companion animal (particularly a dog) are the size and activity level of the breed of dog. He suggests that smaller and less active dogs seemed to relate well to people who are not very active themselves. His point makes great sense. We need to match the physical needs of a dog to our own personal lifestyle.

Dr. Coren also believes that we need to understand the characteristics of specific breeds when we choose a dog. When we adopt a dog, we are adopting a being that is roughly equivalent to a two-year-old child. Superdogs, like Border Collies, are about the cognitive age of two and a half. We need to grasp this concept and recognize that our beloved companions will often behave like perpetual toddlers.

Hare and Woods published a new book called *The Genius of Dogs* (2013), and their work at Duke Canine Research Center suggests that dogs are much brighter than we realize. They believe that the intelligence of an animal should be viewed differently and imply that assessing how successfully the animal manages to survive is one way to consider his intelligence. They explain that, although many people view the evolutionary process of domestication as making dogs dumber and more dependent, they actually believe the opposite has occurred. They note, "The genius of dogs is their ability to understand human communication and their motivation to cooperate with us. Their genius is probably why they are so easy to train…. A cognitive approach works so well with dogs (in training), not because they have no mind, but precisely because they do" (p. 234). Based on their work at Duke Canine Cognition Center, they believe that dogs may be at a very advanced level when compared with other nonhuman mammals in comprehending visual gestures and perhaps learning new words. They also have an exceptional ability to copy the behavior of others and find ways to get others to help them. For example, my now twenty-month-old Golden Retriever has learned that when she loses her ball behind couches or the television, she will bark, get my attention, and then point with her snout where the ball is resting. She may not be able to communicate in English, but nonetheless, she gets her point across.

Over the years, Dr. Coren has written several well-respected books informing the public about pet matching. In his book, *Why We Love the Dogs We Do* (1998), he has done an exceptional job articulating his perceptions. In the book he explores how we can find a dog that contains a desired set of characteristics within a breed that may be the best match for us. Some of the highlighted areas include the dog's friendliness, intelligence, and activity level. Coren places various breeds of dogs into seven distinct groups representing various types of personalities and attributes. Future human owners are grouped into four distinct clusters and a rationale is given on how those specific traits may also influence the possible match. Once future owners have considered both dimensions, this information will be helpful in selecting a dog that best matches their present way of living.

Why We Love the Dogs We Do is an outstanding resource for helping us select a pedigree dog. Table 4.1 synthesizes some of the major findings that Coren highlights. The characteristic in Table 4.1 tend to be true as they apply to well-bred examples of the various breeds. And remember — it is important to work only with a reputable breeder to avoid unwanted qualities that may occur among poorly bred dogs.

In addition to Coren's book, Benjamin and Lynette Hart prepared an excellent volume entitled *The Perfect Puppy* (1998) in which readers gain valuable information about specific traits and behaviors of various breeds. The Harts discuss the differences between male and female dogs and break down the overt temperament styles of various purebred dogs into thirteen key characteristics. They also believe that when we are deciding upon the best puppy for our family, we need to think of our own personal lifestyle (e.g., family makeup, living arrangements, yard space, and specific expectations of a companion animal). Matching this information to specific factors about the animal (such as the breed and the gender of the puppy)

TABLE 4.1 COREN'S SEVEN PERSONALITY TYPES OF DOGS

Personality Characteristic	Traits	Examples of Breed
Friendly (Affectionate and Genial)	• Like people and seek them out. • Good companions, but probably wouldn't make a good guard dog. • Benefit from exercise. • Can live inside.	• Bichon Frise • Cavalier King Charles • Golden Retriever • Portuguese Water Dog
Protective (Territorial)	• Good watchdog/guard dog. • Generally only socialize with people they know. • Strong and muscular, so need experienced owner. • Quick learners, dependable, and obedient	• Boxer • Gordon Setter • Schnauzer
Independent (Personable and Strong Willed)	• Do well with people, but don't seek them out. • Try to be the leader around other dogs. • Selfish and spontaneous behavior. • Strong will can make them hard to train. • Active and love to be outdoors.	• Airedale Terrier • Irish Setter • Siberian Husky
Self-Assured (Spontaneous and Audacious)	• Small and confident. • Good watchdogs. • Active and can be difficult to train. • Entertainers.	• Fox Terrier (Smooth and Wire Coat) • Scottish Terrier • Shih Tzu
Consistent (Self-contained and Home Loving)	• Predictable and repetitive. • Like being in a family or social environment. • Accepting and like people. • Mostly smaller.	• Dachshund • Whippet • Pekingese
Steady (Good Natured and Tolerant)	• Quiet inside. • Easygoing and can handle being alone all day. • Can tolerate roughhousing. • Consistent behavior • Can be distractible but have good memory once trained.	• Bernese Mountain Dog • Great Pyrenees • Saint Bernard
Clever (Observant and Trainable)	• Smart with a strong will to work. • Easy to train. • Somewhat spontaneous and distractible. • Good watchdogs. • Love people and dedicate themselves to their people. • Can adapt to living inside.	• Australian Shepherd • German Shepherd • Papillion • Poodle (Standard, Miniature, and Toy)

will help create an ideal fit. The Harts also add to the equation other specific factors, such as where the puppy will be obtained, if the puppy is spayed or neutered (or will it be), as well as the plans of the future family for integrating the puppy into the family (which includes training methods). We as potential owners should strongly consider the thirteen characteristics discussed in the book in order to help us make more reliable decisions.

Table 4.2 highlights these thirteen characteristics and summarizes their meaning. The Harts also grouped the thirteen characteristics into four major categories: reactivity, aggression, trainability, and investigation. In Table 4.2, I have also identified the alignments of the four groupings with each of the characteristics.

Complimenting what has already been noted about dog selection, Francois Martin, Ph.D., a senior leader of the Behavior Group at Nestlé Purina, also agrees that it is important for potential guardians to strongly consider their lifestyle before making a selection. In our recent interview (2013), he pointed out that there is as much variation between breeds as there is within a breed. That's why we also need to select a potential pet based on the individual animal and his temperament.

Dr. Patricia McConnell is a well-known ethologist and animal behaviorist who has considerable knowledge of dog behavior. She authored one of my favorite books on the subject entitled *The Other End of the Leash* (2002). She also believes that it's important to consider the dog as an individual. As she told me, "We need to understand the dog's personality, rather than just looking at the breed. We must spend time with a potential pet to see how he behaves in different situations."

Many informal scales are available to help assess a dog's temperament. Jack and Wendy Volhard have developed a useful, well-respected instrument called the Puppy Aptitude Test, which allows us to rate ten very specific variables. We are also encouraged to use this scale to evaluate younger dogs. Two other instruments, used by some shelters to evaluate dogs, are Sue Sternberg's Assess-A-Pet and Emily Weiss' Safer/Meet Your Match Program sponsored by the ASPCA. These instruments evaluate a dog's readiness for a good adoption as well as the candidate's lifestyle. Although there are some concerns about utilizing tests such as these, at least they can be good starting points for potential pet owners

"Know Thyself" Before Making Choices

In addition to her recommendation about knowing an individual dog's personality before choosing an animal companion, Dr. Patricia McConnell also believes that one of the most crucial aspects in pet selection is for us to be open-minded and consider many species of dogs before we make a selection. We also need

TABLE 4.2 **HARTS' 13 CHARACTERISTICS FOR PUPPY CONSIDERATION**

Characteristic	Definition	Grouping	Predictive Value
Excitability	How easy it is to "set off" a dog with a novel stimulus.	Reactive	High
General Activity	How active a dog is (running, playing, etc.).	Reactive	High
Snapping at Children	Used as a warning sign toward unwanted interaction. Commonly directed at children because of curiosity height (with adults, the hand usually gets snapped at).	Reactive	Moderate
Excessive Barking	Can bother neighbors and the owner.	Reactive	Moderate
Playfulness	Contributes toward success as a child's pet. May continue into adulthood in some breeds.	Investigation	Moderate
Obedience Training	All dogs can be obedience trained with enough time and effort.	Trainability	Moderate
Watchdog Barking	Sounds the alarm when an unfamiliar person is around but does not tend to attack.	Aggression	Moderate
Aggression Toward Other Dogs	Needs to be kept on a short leash or away from other dogs completely.	Aggression	Moderate
Dominance Over Owner	Females are less prone to this. Important aspect to consider for family dogs.	Aggression	Moderate
Territorial Defense	May attack an unfamiliar intruder (take size into account).	Aggression	Moderate
Demand for Affection	Tends to be stronger in females.	Reactive	Low
Destructiveness	A necessary evil of puppyhood, and usually subsides into adulthood.	Investigation	Low
Ease of Housebreaking	The dog realizes the entire house is its den and learns habitual behavior of where and when to eliminate.	Trainability	Low

to ask a lot of questions before making a decision. One of them might be what characteristics we are looking for in a dog.

Dr. McConnell adamantly believes that the first step to pet selection is thinking about how we live our lives rather than considering a specific species or breed of animal. We need to know ourselves before we add another being to the equation. If we are by nature sedentary, should we adopt an active breed such as a Beagle? Probably not! It wouldn't be fair to either us or to our prospective pet.

Many of us have false expectations of how and what an animal will contribute to our lives. This is NOT why we should get a pet. We can't fantasize that an animal will change our lives, because we cannot count on the fact that the new pet will change our lives FOR THE BETTER. We can count on the fact that the animal will contribute to our lifestyle, but our livestyle probably won't change tremendously.

In many ways, acquiring a pet can be compared to building a marriage, or even to buying shoes. For example, we may want to get an exotic-looking pair of shoes, but if they don't fit at that moment, they may not be the best choice at that given time. Similarly, too often we rush into decisions that lead to disappointing outcomes. This is one reason why so many animals are abandoned every year.

As we continued our discussion, Dr. McConnell and I listed more questions that we should ask ourselves so that we can understand our situation better. For example, what do we like to do when we come home? And what other obligations do we have in our daily life? We may assume that a new pet will motivate us to do things, like getting out to exercise. The fact is, if we haven't already found the motivation, rarely will a dog provide it either. If we don't like to walk, we shouldn't expect any tremendous change in our exercise routine, even if we add a dog to our family. Such wishful thinking typically doesn't work out and may produce an adverse outcome. If we adopt an active dog that requires a lot of walking and stimulation, yet we are not active ourselves, we'll eventually feel guilty that we're unable to meet the dog's physical and mental needs. Bringing an animal into our family requires a real commitment not only to the dog but to ourselves as well. We must ask ourselves if we're willing to make that commitment.

Knowing our lifestyle also includes what we do on a daily basis as well as on the weekend. If we travel a lot, is it fair to have a companion animal, especially one that will often be left at home? How will we deal with our downtime? Do we enjoy going to sporting events, or do we like being outside?

In my conversation with Dr. McConnell, she also noted the importance of always trying to make an adoption decision away from the animal. We need to go home and think about it. This way, we can make such an important decision objectively rather than running on ethos and making a rash, emotional decision that we may regret later on. Many other professionals in the animal-welfare realm will agree and tell most potential buyers that we should ignore our initial feelings and use our head rather than our heart when we choose a new pet. When emotions guide our decision, we will ignore the signs of a non-ideal match.

We obviously can't expect an ideal match every time, and even if we do find the perfect dog or puppy, there are bound to be a few bumps in the road. However, if we feel bonded to our pet, we're much more likely to commit to working through any short-term challenges. Love is a factor that must be considered, but we cannot always expect love at first sight.

According to Abbie Moore, executive director of Adopt-a-Pet.com (North America's largest non-profit pet-adoption web service), "There is a wealth of advice to be found out there about how to choose the perfect companion for you." She also believes that we need to look at our lifestyle and find a companion animal that best fits our activity level and the size of our home and yard. Also, we need to know whether we prefer an independent, slightly aloof dog or one that will smother us with sloppy kisses. We all get companion animals for a variety of reasons — for companionship, perhaps as playmates for our children, or perhaps for protection and security.

In our conversation, Abbie used a wonderful metaphor in describing the entire process of adopting and integrating a new pet into a home. She believes that matching is only the first step. She explains "that although making a good match is important, it is only part of the equation." The equation is a multi-step process. Similar to going swimming in a pool, matching could be compared to getting onto a diving board. It is the first step in the process of entering the pool and swimming. Abbie believes that we also need to take into account what occurs after we dive into the pool and begin swimming. Similarly, there are other steps that occur after we acquire a pet and bring him home, such as bonding, training, and meshing our lives together. The last component in this equation are the waves that will be generated in the pool once we enter. There will be times when we'll swim when we'd rather just tread water. The same holds true in our relationship with our pet. However, with proper preparation, we will eventually be swimming together with our dog.

Theresa Patton (owner of James, winner of Best in Show at the 2007 Westminster Kennel Club's 131st Annual Dog Show at Madison Square Garden in New York) also agrees that we must know ourselves before we add to the equation. In a personal communication she said, "You need to do your research first and look at your lifestyle." She recommends that we consider the interaction time we will have with our dogs so that we can honestly make the correct decision. We too often think only about getting a puppy. Unfortunately, that period lasts for about six months. The small, cute puppy grows up and becomes a mature dog. That cute puppy (or any species in its youth) will be an adult for a much longer period of time. We should think of the inconsiderate people who adopt small alligators and then release them into the environment once they outgrow their aquariums. Responsibility comes with a price.

We must reflect before we act. If we do, it will save us (and our companion animal) from unintentional heartaches. And we need to remember that relationships are often developed rather than just found. Having a strong commitment to engaging with a companion animal and a strong desire to make things work usually trump the negative situations, even when a match is not made in heaven. Good matches are made, not pre-destined. Preparation simply makes it easier for the match to work. Perhaps this is why the friend I mentioned earlier has always had such good luck with randomly chosen pets. Preparations made within the family enabled both the animals and the humans to bond and become a single unit.

Several other questions and answers to consider are discussed below. In a recent conversation with my friend Jane Deming, a respected humane educator, and with Katenna Jones, an animal behaviorist, we discussed these scenarios. This additional information is meant to compliment the information that Dr. McConnell and I initially introduced.

Do we want a puppy or a dog, a kitten or a cat?

This important question needs to be examined carefully. If we get a puppy, we'll need to spend a lot of time shaping his behaviors and developing the relationship. And remember — a cute puppy grows up quickly. If the puppy is left in a crate or a gated area all day, proper training and behavioral growth can and will most likely be delayed. An older dog comes with many benefits. What we see is often what we get. Older dogs often tend to not have the chewing issues or the problems that very young puppies pose. Also, let's keep in mind that a one-year-old dog is still a juvenile and was a puppy just a short time ago.

Sometimes older dogs or cats are great additions. They require less time and can be less active. Older pets spend much longer in shelters waiting for a new home. Yet many are loving pets that would be great companions.

The American Veterinary Medical Association (AVMA) published several brochures in 2010 about what we should know when we're considering the purchase or adoption of various species of animals. Table 4.3 highlights some of this information. AVMA's website (www.avma.org) allows us to review these documents in more detail.

Dr. Elizabeth Shull, a faculty member at the University of Tennessee for sixteen years and veterinary practice owner in Knoxville, developed a wonderful, unpublished handout that provided guidance on pet selection. In this handout, she presented a simple species comparison between cats and dogs that may be helpful to

TABLE 4.3 SELECTING A SPECIFIC PET: CONSIDERATIONS AND GUIDELINES
AVMA Brochures (2010) on How to Select a Pet

Dogs	Friendly, affectionate, smart, and entertaining. Easily socialized. Tremendous diversity in breeds of dogs. Many issues to consider such as size, haircoat length, temperament, and activity level. Certain breeds of dogs are at greater risk for certain medical conditions. Smaller dogs tend to have longer lifespans. Need to prepare an appropriate place for the dog to sleep, eat, and play.
Cats	Affectionate. Easily housetrained. Can live in small spaces. Variety of breeds. Need mental stimulation. Need routine veterinary care.
Ferrets	Affectionate and social. Need specialized attention due to special needs. Love to chew and crawl into spaces. Need constant monitoring while out of enclosure. Need a lot of attention and exercise. Have a strong scent. Illegal in some states.
Fish	Can add variety and decoration. Observing fish lowers stress levels. Tank maintenance can be simple or complicated depending on types of fish and their needs. Startup cost is usually expensive. Special considerations need to be taken when adding new fish.
Rodents (Hamsters, Gerbils, Mice, Rats, Guinea Pigs)	Make great "first pets" with appropriate adult supervision. Very short life span. Cage sizing is important based on size of animal. Must be supervised while out of enclosure. Bedding is important and must be changed often. Heterosexual pairs will breed often if housed together.
Rabbits	Clean and affectionate. Tame when properly socialized. Must be handled carefully because very fragile. Love to chew on things. Must be supervised when out of enclosure. Live 5-15 years. Do not need routine veterinary care, but checkups are advised. Overall cost of maintenance is relatively low. Can be housetrained.

Reptiles	Usually only eat about once a week. Each species has many different requirements. May need special lighting and food. Great for those who are allergic to pet dander. Cost can vary greatly depending on species.
Amphibians	Great for those who are allergic to pet dander. Most require live food. Each species has many different requirements. May need special lighting and food. Risk of salmonella, so proper handling is important.

those of us who are not committed to a particular species for our new pet. Dr. Shull says that most cats are traditionally smaller, utilize litter boxes, and seem to adjust well to solitary living. On the other hand, dogs come in various sizes, need more housetraining, and appear to be less tolerant to solitary living. They seem to thrive on attention and contact.

Do we have the time?

We need to be honest with ourselves: how much time do we really have? How often are we at home, and how much time do we really have to devote to our new companion? Do we have time to properly interact with our new companion and provide him with the exercise that is needed for a healthy lifestyle (at least for the pet)? In other words, will we have time for exercise, grooming, training, play, etc.? If we have families, we need to consider the children's ages and involvement. For example, right now we may have young children who might be home all the time. In the future, though, that may (and likely will) change. As they get older, they may become more involved in extracurricular activities like sports teams or gymnastics. How much will this alter our commitment to our pet? How much time will the family be out of the home, and how long will the pet be left alone? And, if we travel, can the pet go with us on vacations? If not, who will care for him?

If dogs are part of our future, they are dependent on us to have their needs fulfilled. Who will be there to walk the dog or to let him out? For the bond to flourish, their needs have to be met! Cats, on the other hand, do better by themselves and often sleep for hours on end. However, they still need attention and support. Cats need to be protected from both man-made dangers (e.g., cars) and wild predators. And cats that get lost are the least likely to be reunited with the family. Shelter statistics show that a cat that gets lost is returned to the owner only about 2 percent of the time. Like dogs, cats also need ID tags. It is best if dogs and cats are microchipped to increase the possibility of their return.

Do we have the finances?

Unfortunately, the love for a puppy or kitten does come with a price — not just for his acquisition but also for a lifetime of continued care, which may include veterinary support during illness. Of course, there are other expenses such as food that can range in price depending on brand and quality. If our pet has allergies, he may require a special diet, which can be more expensive. If we choose a non-traditional pet such as a parrot or lizard, we'll need to find a veterinarian who has an expertise in that field of care. Also, for unique species or large animals, the care could be more costly. While insurance is an available option, it is still expensive. Are we prepared to accept this additional expense?

One other expense that we may not consider initially is the training — for both ourselves and our companion animal. Proper training can prevent challenges in the future and enhance the bond. If issues such as the dog growling at family members, the parrot screeching beyond control, or the cat spraying in the house are left unattended, they will probably lead to other problems. Shelters are filled with negative stories of pets whose families have given up. We owe it to the pet to be prepared, and training is just another investment that needs to be taken seriously. Often, a simple correction and dedicating time to working through the challenge are all that are needed. On a lighter note, when we do consider training, whom is to be trained — the animal or the human? (Probably both!)

Finally, we need to think about what might change in our life. Is our job secure? Can we stay where we are living? What changes might there be in the future? We may be able to afford the pet now, but do we feel fairly secure about the future? There is no way that a family can completely predict what might happen in the months or years to come. We do, however, need to do be as realistic as possible about all that we can control. In the end, if we are thoughtful about the decision to get a pet, we reduce the likelihood of making a mistake. We must remember that pets are living beings.

The responsibility that comes with being a guardian for companion animals cannot be underestimated. Pet responsibility is a major life decision, and it is different than dealing with non-living tangibles. When we purchase a bike that doesn't work out, nothing is lost other than the money we spent for it. That is not the case with pets. When we get a pet and it doesn't work out, the pet can go from sleeping at the foot of our bed to a far less desirable environment (and one that may potentially result in euthanasia).

Do we have the space?

It is amazing how many of us relinquish a pet because it got too big or we ran out of space. If we live in an apartment, then a Great Dane is probably not the best dog breed for us! Dogs need room to run, and if we want a dog but have no yard, we need to think what size of dog would work for us. And if we want a more active dog, we must decide whether or not we'll REALLY get off the couch and provide the dog with enough mental and physical stimulation so that he stays healthy and happy. If our home is large enough yet doesn't have a yard, maybe a small breed of dog can exercise inside.

Then there is the question about small pets that always seem to get underfoot inside the home. We may decide that we can't have a dog, but we CAN have a guinea pig in a cage. Remember that cages for small pets that spend the lion's share of their lives in wire enclosures need to provide enough space for exercise, and they must have room where the animal can hide and sleep. Most of us don't realize that being in a cage on the floor is terrifying for small mammals; it is important for cages to be elevated on a shelf or table. If our child has a small room, a small mammal will need his cage to be on a desk or shelf so that he can feel safe. We often forget, too, that small animals such as guinea pigs and hamsters tend to be nocturnal and spend a lot of time on their treadmills at night creating a lot of noise, or night music.

Finally, we need to think about where we'll keep the animal's food and how often we'll need to clean and handle him. For caged animals (like birds), keeping everything clean can also be a task. We must have something in which to keep the pet while we're cleaning, and that, too, may require space. We'll also need a dry environment for the pet's food. This means that every aspect of the pet and his care will require space for the items he needs.

Does anyone have allergies?

There are options for children who have allergies and asthma. In recent years, as many as 40 percent of kids have some sort of allergy. Some pets are hyper-allergenic, and that might be a good place for us to start our research. Children who have fur or dander allergies often react to cats, dogs, chinchillas, ferrets, and some birds (to name a few). There are breeds of dogs and cats that are less of an allergy trigger than others. For that reason, we need to do quality research in advance to eliminate the possibility of a bad reaction. This is a much better option than being forced to re-home a pet.

Some studies indicate that if pets are in the house early in a child's life, that child may end up with immunity. However, if the entire family wants a cat but dad is allergic, the family may eventually be forced to relinquish the pet. It's best to consider other options right from the start. For example, my wife has significant asthma, so when we tried to have a guinea pig, its presence seemed to trigger an allergic reaction in her. Fortunately, we were able to adapt some of our living arrangements so that our guinea pig could live with us throughout her entire lifetime. However, because my wife is quite allergic, we don't have guinea pigs in our home today — but this does not preclude many other species.

Some families may already have a pet before they have a child. What if the baby is allergic to the pet? If we have any concerns that a pet might compromise our family with regard to allergies, we need to check with our primary-care physician as part of our information-gathering process. We don't have to discard the idea of having a pet just because of the "allergy" reasons. Some suggest that if we are determined to have a pet in our family, we should get the person tested to try to identify what the reaction is being caused by. We shouldn't just assume it's an allergy to the cat or the dog.

Are we prepared to invest time and resources into training that will teach us how to coexist with a pet?

Over the course of a pet's lifetime, we often may find changes in his behavior. Some may be wonderful and some may be completely unacceptable. For example, a cat might take a while to get used to the different litter in his box, and the solution to that situation can be easily solved. On the other hand, a dog might get more anxious with age and become quite destructive when left alone. Resolving this predicament may be challenging and time consuming and may require securing professional support that can be expensive. As potential pet owners, we need to consider the extraneous costs that we may have to assume to have a pet in our family. I have strong feelings about quality training and feel that we should all have this opportunity. Unfortunately, pet ownership (just like parenting) doesn't come with a manual. We need to do our due diligence to make sure we are prepared for our roles. Many communities have a number of pet-adoption programs that are reasonably priced, which can help us get started.

We should not consider giving up as an option. With time and patience, most pets will respond to training. Often, a qualified trainer or behaviorist can provide great guidance and help us resolve any issues fairly quickly. Negative behavior typically is triggered by something, and with an extra set of eyes examining the problem, solutions can be found. Veterinarians may also be able to give us insight into the problem. Some changes in behaviors such as nipping or missing the litter box can actually be linked to health issues.

Living arrangements: Do we have the landlord's permission?

When we rent a house, a condo, or an apartment, we often sign a lease agreement that lists the rules for the rental. If a landlord says no pets, that is the rule. We need to know these rules before we acquire a pet. Again, this is where we can apply the bicycle analogy — no harm for new, non-living purchases, but great pain and anger when it is a living and loyal companion that had no say in the outcome of his adoption. We cannot blame the landlord if that is the agreement we signed.

On a positive note, the landlord's perception could change over time. If we live in a home with a no-pet policy and the landlord sees that we pay the rent on time and keep the property in good order, he may be willing to compromise or make an exception if the pet is suitable. The owner may ask for an additional damage deposit, but that could be negotiated. A friend of mine rented a house that had a no-pet rule, but when her mother brought her dog to visit and the owner met the dog, he relented and allowed her to keep her pet. Things are always changing, but we can't count on it as a certainty when dealing with landlords.

If we tend to move from apartment to apartment, we can never be 100 percent sure that the next place will allow our pet. If we might not be able to secure a pet-friendly apartment or house next time, then it is wise and much kinder to wait until we are more settled than to take a chance that we'll break a pet's heart or our own.

What will we do if we go on vacation?

This is the age-old discussion for pet owners. Will the pet be safe, happy, and well cared for? Can we vacation where pets are allowed? If we take frequent vacations and the pet will have to be left alone, is that fair to the animal? Will our absence cause some anxiety and sadness? Some pets stop eating while their owners are gone, and this a major concern. Traveling with our family is important, but we need to make plans so that our companion animals are safe and comfortable. Over the years, we've had many sitters stay with our pack of four-leggers so that it was easier for them to adjust to our absence. The key is finding pet hotels or sitters whom we can trust and who will treat the pets like they are their own.

We must do our due diligence when it comes to pet sitters or lodging. A great way to accomplish this is by talking to others in the animal-welfare field. Veterinarians, groomers, staff at animal shelters, and pet-food suppliers seem to have their finger on the pulse within a community and often have wonderful references. We should never be afraid to ask for references. It's important that we meet them in person to be sure our pet will like them as much as we do. We should always ask if they are insured and bonded! And we need to always keep a copy of our pet's medical records and veterinarian information for emergencies. Finally, we should be sure our pet has an ID tag or is microchipped.

If we want to take our pet with us, the AAA and some travel agencies offer information about pet-friendly vacation areas and hotels. We should never consider vacationing with our pet if we haven't already made arrangements that are pet-friendly. We'll need a quality crate, a leash, a collar, and disposable bags for cleanups along the route. Airlines do allow pets on board. Small animals can go under the seat in front of us in a carrier and larger animals in baggage in a secured crate. We should always speak to airline representatives to be sure the pets that are not seated with us are in pressurized cabins and are kept free from extreme changes in temperatures. It is also better if we take a direct flight so the pet is not stressed by being moved from plane to plane or ends up sitting on the tarmac for extended periods. We might want to check with our veterinarian to see if a sedative is appropriate for our pet.

Also, large venue attractions often have places for pets to stay while we are at their facilities. Disney, for example, has gorgeous air-conditioned kennels that are clean and cheery with lots of fresh food and water (so that if we are driving there, we don't need to leave pets in the car).

Is this going to be a safe pet? How big will he get? How long will this pet live? Could he be dangerous?

I believe it is obvious that lions, tigers, bears, venomous snakes, alligators, monkeys, and the like do not make great pets. In fact, in some states, it is against the law to own them. Personally, I see no benefit in having an animal that can kill you or do damage to anyone you love. With approximately 5 million companion animals being euthanized every year because there are not enough homes, why on earth would we keep an apex predator as a pet, knowing full well that no good can come of the decision either for us or for the animal. Rain forests are robbed annually of many species such as lizards, birds, and small mammals for the pet trade. These animals belong in the wild and are not meant for domestication.

When we decide to acquire a new pet, we need to be sure that the pet will be safe with our family and with any other pets we have. Therefore, we should research where the pet came from to be sure it was legally acquired; *this is very important*. Making sure that the pet is free of diseases and/or parasites that could harm us, our family, or our pets is critical.

Many of the cute little snakes that we see in pet stores will soon outgrow their enclosures. Iguanas will grow to the point where they can be a danger to family members. Some reptiles carry salmonella, which can be deadly for babies, the elderly, and those who are immune-compromised. Sadly, it is almost impossible to re-home many of these animals. Many rescues are full or even overfull, while others can't afford to add animals to their already overstretched budget. We must do the right thing and get a pet that is safe and appropriate for our family and personal circumstances.

One variable that we must consider is the longevity of the pet. Gerbils live for two years, while some turtles and parrots can live up to 100 years or more. Dogs and cats can and do live long past their life expectancy, so it is not outside the realm of possibility that we could have a dog or cat for fifteen to eighteen years.

Lastly, even bringing home a new cat to live out his life with our other cat can be risky and may require some special skills; or even adding a dog to a house with a cat. Working with shelters and adoption counselors will help, as will reading up on how the introduction should take place.

Do we adopt, go to a pet store, find a breeder, or find a pet in an ad or online?

Of course it is always recommended that we adopt from a reputable shelter and rescue a pet. The shelters and rescue groups around this country are packed with unwanted, homeless animals. Giving one a good home is the ultimate in good deeds. There are wonderful pets that deserve a second chance. We should check in our own communities, as many of the shelters spay and neuter pets and vaccinate them before they can be adopted. Having that work done first can save us much time and money, and when we bring the pet home, he will be completely ready to join the family.

If we want a purebred dog or cat, we actually can find the breed of our choice in a shelter or through a breed-specific rescue organization. Some shelters report that up to 30 percent of the pets that come into the shelter are purebred. If we can't find a specific breed of dog and are struggling to find one, we can ask the local shelter or humane group for a list of breed-rescue groups or check with breed clubs through the American Kennel Club website. For the most part, it is not recommended that we purchase from a pet store. Most of them purchase their pets from puppy mills, and these puppies often have physical and emotional issues. Seldom is there any concern for lineage, and many of the females spend their entire lives in cages, pumping out as many puppies as possible. If we want a purebred puppy, we should ask around to find a quality local breeder who has the parents on the property. This way we can see the conditions for ourselves and observe the temperament of the mother dog. Good breeders care about their puppies and are more than willing to answer any of our questions.

PUTTING IT ALL TOGETHER

This chapter identifies a number of variables that we must consider when we think about having a new pet join our family. Each of these variables should have some impact on our selection, with some of the variables being more important than others. At the end of the chapter, I have included a simple survey called

CAPTURE THE MOMENT

David Sax's photography captures the emotional connections that are formed in our relationships with animals. This collection of pictures captures the bond that bears witness to the significance of these moments.

Lifestyle Attributes for Pet Selection (LAPS). This is a helpful guide to assist us in analyzing our lifestyles for the best match possible. Although there are no guarantees, planning for the best match is highly suggested.

⸺

I just came home tonight after having dinner at one of my favorite Mexican restaurants (another story for another day). While at the Cantina, I recognized an acquaintance of mine munching on some chips and salsa. I went over to him and he introduced me to his wife. We spoke about random things for a few moments before his wife disclosed that their thirteen-year-old dog had just passed away two days ago. Once she found out I was a dog lover, she opened her heart to many emotions that were locked within. They did not have any children, and this was the first loss they had experienced as a couple. It only took a few moments for her eyes to fill up with tears. She tried to compose herself and felt genuinely embarrassed about her unbridled emotions, but I reassured her that there was no need to feel ashamed. Love has no boundaries, and when a life is gone, emptiness will be felt. She reminisced for a while, but throughout her tribute, it was evident that she was letting me know that he was the best dog in the world! Just like the words of Irv Robbins quoted earlier in this chapter, "each flavor is someone's favorite." I cannot agree more wholeheartedly.

Relationships of many individuals to their companion animals would include words like the "greatest" or "best." On the other hand, I also hear from others who tell me their pets are the dumbest or wildest in the world, but they wouldn't trade them in for anything. The concept of "not trading them in" is the premise that I have highlighted in this chapter. There are no guarantees in life. Even when we prepare and plan, sometimes the outcomes aren't what we had hoped for. What we can only hope for is that, in the end, we get the best out of it. I have learned to understand this concept even more clearly in my work with families who have children with disabilities. I often find myself talking to parents who are bringing up children with various needs, and they share with me their challenges and joys.

Years ago I became acquainted with a poem, "Welcome to Holland" (1987), written by Emily Perl Kingsley. The poem (which some call an essay) was written to help others understand what families may be feeling when they have a different and/or unexpected parenting experience. Kingsley uses the metaphor of a planned journey (initially wanting to go to Italy but the journey takes the couple to Holland) to clarify the unexpected detour that people may feel, if what they expected in the parenting process doesn't come to fruition. She writes, "For the rest of your life, you will say, 'Yes, that's where I was supposed to go. That's what I had planned.' But there's been a change in the flight plan. They've landed in Holland and there you must stay…. It's just a different place. It's slower-paced than Italy, less flashy than Italy. But after you've been there for a while and you catch your breath, you look around…. and you begin to notice that Holland has windmills and Holland has tulips."

Although the intention of the poem wasn't directed to the theme covered in this chapter, the message found within does fit its objective. To be satisfied with our choice, we need to go beyond our desired match and work on doing what it takes to make it work. Good marriages and strong families are nurtured and developed. The same holds true with our partnerships with our animal companions.

I don't want to underestimate the topics highlighted within this chapter nor the strong insights elicited by our panel of experts. We need to make the best decisions and plans we possibly can when we plan to adopt an animal companion, but in the end, it is what we do with our lives *together* that will make our relationships rich with fulfillment or empty without sentiments. We will be able to judge our outcome by understanding the efforts that we put in to making our lives sounder and more intertwined. Those of us who can find these ingredients will also find more meaning in our relationships and will be able to live the motto espoused by Roger Caras (president of the SPCA) when he once said, "Dogs (but in our case any species of animals) are not our whole life, but they make our lives whole."

Lifestyle Attributes for Pet Selection (LAPS)

The following Lifestyle Attributes for Pet Selection (LAPS) survey is a tool I have developed to help us get a better understanding of the specific needs and circumstances of our unique lives and families. While the LAPS has not been validated, I believe it can help us learn the type(s) of companion animals that may be best suited for us and our life situations. We must answer honestly, because we are the only ones who will ever see this, and the more honest we are, the better we will be able to select which companion animal may be a great fit for us!

LIFESTYLE ATTRIBUTES FOR PET SELECTION (LAPS)

———————————— **Time** ————————————

I work long hours.

I	2	3	4	5
Never		Sometimes		Usually

I travel a lot for work or pleasure.

I	2	3	4	5
Never		Sometimes		Usually

I have time to exercise my companion animal.

5	4	3	2	I
Never		Sometimes		Usually

I have time to train my companion animal.

5	4	3	2	I
Never		Sometimes		Usually

I have time to play with my companion animal.

5	4	3	2	I
Never		Sometimes		Usually

I have time to socialize my companion animal.

5	4	3	2	I
Never		Sometimes		Usually

I have other family members who need a lot of time and attention as well.

I	2	3	4	5
Never		Sometimes		Usually

A score greater than 18 indicates that you are a very active person! A companion animal that does not take up as much time (such as a cat, rabbit, or rodent) may be a better fit for you.

———————————— **Finances** ————————————

I can afford all the things needed to first bring my companion animal home.

I	2	3	4	5
Never		Sometimes		Usually

I can afford the routine/preventative care my companion animal would require.

1	2	3	4	5
Never		Sometimes		Usually

I can afford to provide care for my companion animal in an emergency.

1	2	3	4	5
Never		Sometimes		Usually

I can afford day-to-day expenses for my companion animal.

1	2	3	4	5
Never		Sometimes		Usually

I can afford to have someone care for my animal if I am away.

1	2	3	4	5
Never		Sometimes		Usually

I can afford to care for my animal for several years.

1	2	3	4	5
Never		Sometimes		Usually

I can afford the pet deposit my landlord requires.

1	2	3	4	5
Never		Sometimes		Usually

A score greater than 18 indicates that you can probably afford an animal that might have more start-up and long-term expenses. Examples of animals that can be more expensive to maintain are dogs, horses, and certain species of birds.

Space

I have a large enough backyard for the companion animal I am considering.

5	4	3	2	1
Never		Sometimes		Usually

I have a large indoor living area for the companion animal I am considering.

5	4	3	2	1
Never		Sometimes		Usually

I have enough space to contain all of the things my companion animal requires.

5	4	3	2	1
Never		Sometimes		Usually

I know my landlord will be okay with my companion animal living with me.

5	4	3	2	1
Never		Sometimes		Usually

A score of greater than 11 indicates that a smaller animal may be more appropriate for you. You may want to consider a cat, fish in an aquarium, or a rodent.

——————————— **Family Considerations** ———————————

I live with people who have allergies to certain animals.

1	2	3	4	5
Never		Sometimes		Usually

I live with people whose other health concerns need to be considered.

1	2	3	4	5
Never		Sometimes		Usually

Small children or elderly people live with me.

1	2	3	4	5
Never		Sometimes		Usually

Small children or elderly people may be living with me in the future.

1	2	3	4	5
Never		Sometimes		Usually

My family is always on the go or not home very often.

1	2	3	4	5
Never		Sometimes		Usually

I have other companion animals in my family that will need to be introduced.

1	2	3	4	5
Never		Sometimes		Usually

A score greater than 15 indicates that you have many people in your life who will need to be considered when adding a new companion animal to the family. You may want to research hypoallergenic animals or see if any animals are not recommended for people with certain health conditions. Dogs, cats, and rodents can make great companion animals for the children and elderly, but size and energy need to be taken into account.

_____ **Pet Care** _____

I have enough time to contribute to care for this companion animal.

5	4	3	2	1
Never		Sometimes		Usually

I will be the primary person who is responsible for looking after this companion animal.

5	4	3	2	1
Never		Sometimes		Usually

I have someone who will take care of this companion animal when I am gone.

5	4	3	2	1
Never		Sometimes		Usually

I will provide training for this companion animal.

5	4	3	2	1
Never		Sometimes		Usually

A score of greater than 11 indicates that you do many things with your time. A companion animal that does not require as much constant care may be something for you to consider. Examples of animals that are more content to be alone for long hours include cats, reptiles, amphibians, and fish.

MUCH MORE THAN PUPPY LOVE:
How Some Companions
Become Therapy and Service Animals

Matthew came for his biweekly visit. He was quite groggy when he first entered the office, but that all changed quickly when a zealous Ketzy greeted him. As she bounded toward him, he began to smile and giggle, which made Ketzy even more excited. Her body moved with her doggy samba swagger. Her tail took on a life of its own, shaking and thumping wildly. Matt chuckled and grinned widely as she snuggled by him and began to whimper as he pet her in a loving manner.

Ketzy is one of my current therapy dogs. Over the past fifteen years, Matthew has known all the therapy dogs in my office, and each one has had a special relationship with him. He often reminisces about their lives and how they have all had a special impact in his life and on our relationship. His favorite now is Ketzy, but every time he visits, he continues to recall a different story.

Matthew and I first met when he was about twelve years old. He came to see me because of difficulties that he was having at home and at school. His initial diagnosis was a developmental disability. At his local school, Matthew was in a Special Ed classroom and displayed some obsessive behaviors that interfered with his participation in school activities; compared to his peers, he seemed to have more difficulty adjusting to everyday life. Early in our therapeutic relationship, I quickly realized that Matthew had not only a developmental disability but a psychiatric disorder as well. This is known as a dual diagnosis. In Matt's case, his psychiatric challenges impeded his psychological well-being. During the course of a few years, he made some progress but also struggled with bouts of regression, resulting in pervasive challenges across his life.

Matthew was hospitalized a couple of times because he became unresponsive to others or, on occasion, acted out physically toward others. During this period, he also lost his mother, which seemed to be the proverbial "straw that broke the camel's back." When looking back on this period, it is evident that his connection to me has always been supported by his relationship with the therapy dogs. He had always eagerly looked forward to our visits, especially when he was able to walk and interact with them. The dogs seemed to bring out a genuine warmth in Matthew.

On many occasions, the dogs supported Matthew during difficult times. I recall a period when his family contacted me because Matthew had become socially mute and wouldn't talk for days. When his family arrived for a visit, Matthew initially sat in my office, unresponsive despite my urging him to talk. On that given day, the two therapy dogs in my office helped ease the tension and allowed him to open up. The "girls," as he liked to call the therapy dogs, tried persistently to communicate with him. But he was insistent on refusing to speak. In fact, by the middle of our visit, he mimed his words, which seemed to confuse the dogs even more (as they sat vigilantly by his side). Eventually, I just looked into Matthew's eyes and told him that I knew he was having a hard time, but he might consider recognizing it was hard for the dogs to understand why their friend wasn't verbalizing or laughing with them. My comment seemed to turn a switch on in his mind. During that time, Matthew began to talk to them, first in a low voice that tried to assure them that he was okay and wasn't mad at them. They became the vessel on which he allowed his voice to be carried and heard once again.

Ketzy, his new friend, is slightly older than one year now and often shows her youthfulness and excitement. Her response to Matthew always seems to get him more engaged than during their last visit — he perks up immediately when the dogs are around. He reminisces about his favorite experiences with them. For example, a time many years ago, Puppy — the oldest canine matriarch in my office — pulled an entire pizza from a table and ate it from topping to crust! He always talks about how amusing it was to catch her in the act. Her paws were crossed, cheese and sauce all over her face, but she didn't seem to mind to share what was left over.

Years later, I told Matthew about a past incident where my younger therapy dog, PJ, suddenly grabbed my wife's tostada bowl and ran off to devour it. Rather than call PJ back, my wife (who is very good with the dogs) began chasing her. You can only imagine the comedy that ensued. Matthew always laughs about that episode.

It's amazing to watch Matthew surrounded by the dogs, most recently Ketzy. They seem to bring out of him his best self. More importantly, they get him to respond and he becomes more grounded during our sessions when they accompany us. He is clearly more comfortable communicating when they are around and he opens up more readily; perhaps it is because he feels safe and is among friends.

There's an old saying, "There is no greater psychiatrist in the world than a puppy licking your face." In many ways, that statement is very true. Those of us who have ever received the tender love of a puppy can easily imagine how therapeutic it can be. I came upon this approach of animal therapy completely by accident and long before its potency was recognized in the field. It was my first pet, Sasha (a young gerbil), that allowed me to witness firsthand how an animal can have an impact in a therapeutic setting. I simply brought her to a social-skills training program to share her with the children. To my amazement, children who were usually active and impulsive instead sat patiently, waiting their turn to hold her gently. Once I recognized the great effect this small creature had, she became a regular guest to our program and a catalyst for my pursuit to learn how to incorporate a wide array of animals into my therapy.

Over the last fifty years, animal-assisted interventions have grown from strategies explained primarily by anecdotal comments to outcomes now being investigated with more sound empirical inquiry. Findings from these studies are beginning to provide the evidence needed to help establish animal-assisted interventions (AAIs) as an upcoming and complementary, alternative form of medicine. Historically, AAIs can be traced back hundreds of years. In fact, Florence Nightingale in 1859 once said, "A small pet is often an excellent companion for the sick. For the long, chronic cases especially, a pet bird in a cage, sometimes the only pleasure of an invalid confined for years to the same room" (p. 58). It's amazing that the comment of Florence Nightingale influenced many clinicians to look at how they could apply animal-assisted therapy (AAT) in their environments. Although AAT was used in a variety of settings, it wasn't until the 1960s that Boris Levinson (1969) identified the activity as a practice. In fact, Coren (2010) pointed out that Freud even brought his Chow Chow, Jofi, to several of his psychotherapy sessions. Freud noticed that the dog seemed to make his patients feel more comfortable.

AAIs are considered the umbrella term that encompasses both animal-assisted activities (AAAs) and AAT. AAIs are the most frequently used by professionals. The significant difference between the term "activity" versus "therapy" really is about the person or animal who delivers the intervention. According to Pet Partners, AAT is a type of human-animal interaction with the aim of helping people meet specific treatment goals. It is usually designed by a therapist, teacher, clinician, or other health-care provider, depending on the clinical setting. In contrast, AAAs are more widely utilized but are often much less formal. For example, an AAA could be a brief therapy-animal visit in a hospital without a therapeutic plan or goal or regularity in the frequency of sessions. It is important to note, however, that while these AAAs are more spontaneous in nature, they may be equally as valuable.

For example, Amy McCullough from the American Humane Association describes a time when her therapy dog was asked to fill a tremendous need for a patient. She recounts:

> A few years ago I received an urgent call from a local hospice for a patient who had no family but had loved dogs all her life. The hospice worker told me the patient was near death and wanted to see a dog before she passed. I loaded Bailey, my therapy dog, in the car, and we immediately headed to the facility. As Bailey and I entered her room, we could see the elderly woman hooked up to machines to monitor her heart rate and breathing. She appeared to be asleep, but when we approached, she opened her eyes and the hospice worker softly introduced Bailey and me. I had Bailey sit in a chair next to the bed so the patient could see her. She reached out her hand, gently stroked Bailey's head, and thanked her for coming. She then drifted back to sleep.
>
> Bailey patiently watched over this dying woman from the chair. Every so often, the woman would wake up and call out, "Bailey?" I would tell her Bailey was right here. She would stay awake just long enough to make eye contact with Bailey before she would fall back to sleep. After an hour or so, Bailey and I told her goodbye and headed home. We later learned that she passed that same night.

A colleague of mine who volunteers with his Boxer named Mia experienced a similar situation at a nursing home. One of the patients who was terminally ill had developed a strong relationship with Mia over the course of several months. Even during the agonizing aftereffects of chemotherapy, Dianne would always smile and laugh whenever Mia came to visit. Mia likes to gently lick her friends when she arrives, and Dianne used to say, "Mia's licking kept her ticking." One day, only hours away from death, Dianne's family asked if Steve (my colleague) could bring Mia in for a final visit. Although Dianne had been in and out of consciousness for several days, her daughter felt that Mia's presence would still be a comfort to her mother during her final moments. When Mia arrived at Dianne's bedside, she silently surveyed the family members standing by, looked lovingly at her friend Dianne, and without warning, gently jumped on the bed and lay down next to her. Dianne stirred, opened her eyes slightly, and reached for Mia with her left hand. Upon finding Mia's furry head, Dianne smiled weakly and called out, "Oh Mia, Mia, Mia." There wasn't a dry eye in the room. What is so remarkable about this situation is how Mia, who is normally quite animated, seemed to know that something wasn't right with Dianne. As Dianne lay near death, Mia instinctively knew what to do. She was gentle, calm, and quietly loving. There was no doubt that Mia and Dianne shared an intimate moment that brought great comfort, not just to Dianne but to everyone in the room.

EARLY HISTORY OF ANIMALS IN THERAPY

By the mid 1970s, Boris Levinson's work with animals in psychotherapy acted as an impetus for several others interested in channeling some of this development in human-animal interactions into other therapy environments. Dr. Levinson was a child psychologist who discovered quite serendipitously that he could incorporate a therapy dog during his sessions with children. He noticed that Jingles, his therapy dog, often softened the children's defense mechanisms as Dr. Levinson began to relate more easily with them. He was the first person to coin the term "pet therapy" in the mid-1960s. Dr. Levinson once stated, "A pet is an island of sanity in what appears to be an insane world" (1962, p. 59). He went on to elaborate that our friendship with companion animals retains its traditional values and securities in our relationship with our pets. I once commented that the relationship with therapy dogs seems to help care providers to go under the radar of children's defense mechanisms. The children begin to feel more comfortable and at ease and therefore are more willing to open up and be more responsive to therapy. This is likely what occurred in Dr. Levinson's sessions.

Early in the development of AAI, there were many skeptics about Levinson's insights; his first major lecture on pet therapy at the American Psychological Association's Conference in New York City (in September 1961) was poorly received. Another early pioneer of pet therapy was Dr. Samuel Corson, a professor of psychiatry and biophysics at Ohio State University. Dr. Corson was very interested in understanding the roles that animals could have in therapy and how animals could act as a social lubricant to this process. Dr. Corson noticed, as did Boris Levinson, that when a client visited with a therapist accompanied by an enthusiastic and calm animal, the client immediately communicated more and was less resistant to the interaction. Corson was known to say that, "A dog was man's best friend because he always wagged his tail, not his tongue." Corson began to notice early in his work with animals in his practice that patients spoke more often and significantly longer once the dogs were in the sessions. This observation illustrates the comfort that the animal promoted in the therapy environment, resulting in the patient feeling more at ease to communicate (1975, pp. 19–36).

In 1977, the Delta Foundation was formed in Portland with Dr. Michael McCulloch (a psychiatrist) as its first president. McCulloch once said, "In an age of research when it's tempting to reduce human emotions to biochemical reactions and to rely heavily on technology of medicine, it's refreshing to find that a person's health may be improved by prescribing contact with other living things." The organization changed its name in 1981 to Delta Society, and its mission, now known as Pet Partners, is to demonstrate and promote positive human-animal interactions and to improve the physical, emotional, and psychological lives of those they serve. At this time, the Delta Pet Partner Program has more than 11,000 Pet Partners who visit schools, hospitals, nursing homes, and convalescent homes in order to provide unique opportunities to improve the mental and physical well-being for the numerous people they serve (About Pet Partners; see References).

Over the last thirty years, several other organizations have come into being. Therapy Dogs, Inc. was incorporated in 1990 and is based in Cheyenne, Wyoming. This organization has 12,000-plus handler-dog teams in the United States. In addition, Therapy Dogs International (TDI), was established in the late 1970s in New Jersey. It certifies all breeds of dogs; in 2011, it was reported that 24,000 handler teams were registered in the country (Therapy Dogs International; see References).

THE ROLE OF AAI

According to a recent document prepared by the American Humane Association (2009), AAA and AAI are valuable forms of treatment, especially when it comes to enhancing motivation. It was indicated in their document that a growing body of evidence in the literature suggests that the opportunity to interact with therapy animals can help motivate clients to comply with the therapeutic process. This motivation carries over and assists the clients in engaging with the therapist as well as their overall interactions in general. This paper also discussed a study by Lange, et al. (2007), which found that, when dogs were included in an adolescent anger-management therapy program, they seemed to motivate participants to stay engaged in the therapeutic process. These works support the logic that animals act as catalysts for social engagement — there is much truth that happiness often comes in the form of a warm puppy.

It has been often documented over the years that the presence of a companion animal, especially a trained therapy dog, can help lessen the distress experienced by children during medical examinations or, for that matter, when they are in a hospital. In my previous book, *Afternoons with Puppy* (2008), I talked about a unique relationship between a girl named Alexann and her therapy dog, Gleason.

Gleason (who was five when this story occurred) first met Alexann in an Oregon hospital. She was six at that time and had been diagnosed with bone cancer. She was just beginning chemotherapy when the two met.

When Gleason first walked into her room, Alexann looked over and exclaimed quickly, "Oh! I love dogs! Can he come up on the bed?" Gleason looked to his owner Sue for the okay, and once a blanket was placed on the bed, he hopped up. Alexann gave him a big hug and a relationship was kindled in that first moment.

Alexann loved animals and had affectionate relationships with her pets, a cat and a dog. She thought of her pets as playmates, and they never resisted letting her do whatever she wanted, even if the playfulness was silly. Alexann and her family's lives were turned upside down once she was diagnosed with cancer. In the hospital, she had to leave her normal life, which included leaving her beloved pets. Having Gleason around allowed her to find love and security in a difficult and perhaps frightening place.

Alexann and Sue would often lead Gleason on walks through the hospital hall. They would visit the other children in the ward, and Gleason would walk slowly and gently with Alexann, often turning around to look at her as if to ask if he were going too fast. She began chemotherapy in June of that year, and Gleason was there almost every day she had a treatment.

Despite the changes in her health and appearance (she lost her hair), Gleason seemed to see Alexann as the same girl, one with a big smile and even bigger dimples. When she was released from the hospital, Alexann and Gleason continued to meet.

In one instance they met at a ceramic shop so that Alexann could make her parents' Valentine's Day gifts. On her head, Alexann wore a wig and a hat. When the three entered the shop, it was full of kids, all of whom became quiet upon seeing Alexann in her wheelchair. Alexann became quite self-conscious. Gleason sat down next to her and, with his presence, became a kind of bridge for the other children to use in approaching her. As children came over to pet Gleason, they struck up a conversation with Alexann. This was a memorable day for Alexann and highlighted how Gleason acted as a catalyst for her.

As I concluded in her story called "Carpe Diem," in the last weeks of her life, Alexann's condition continued to deteriorate. These were hard days for her. For the last six weeks or so, Alexann's parents stayed with her in the hospital day and night, and her sister was there during the last four days.

Aside from her immediate family, Sue and Gleason saw Alexann more than anyone else. In the two weeks before she died, she lost feeling from her waist down and was in a light coma. But when Gleason hopped onto her bed and her hand was placed on him, she would pet him and even give him a small smile. Sometimes

Alexann's fingers would cover his nostrils, but he wouldn't budge except to open his mouth to breathe. Sue said, "He loved that girl, and she loved him." When he left her side that day, Gleason licked her hand for the final time.

A memorial service was held one week after Alexann's death. Sue and Gleason attended along with many of the pediatric nurses from the hospital. Projected on an eight-by-ten-foot screen was a picture of Alexann and Gleason. There was even a pew reserved for them. The sign read: "For Gleason, the Wonderful Therapy Dog."

Elisa Sobo, a clinical professor of family and preventive medicine and pediatrics at the University of California–San Diego, has been very interested in how the human-animal bond can be used to ameliorate stress and pain of children in hospitalized settings. Sobo and her associates suggested in a paper (2006) that AAT serves to distract children in hospitals from pain and thus assists in maintaining their comfort level throughout treatment.

In their paper, Sobo and her colleagues identified eight situations where a therapy animal could assist a hospitalized client. In some situations, the dog provides a distraction from pain, acts as a source of companionship and fun, and helps a child to feel that he is at home. As noted with Alexann and Gleason earlier, Gleason displayed all of the elements described by Sobo in his relationship with Alexann. Specifically, a visiting dog offers a calming alternative to the child and provides much-needed company. And, just as Sobo noted, Gleason brought great pleasure and joy to Alexann and at times kept her mind off her health concerns. Having Gleason visit made the hospital a more normal living environment.

Therapy animals also can be used to support children in other ways. The Youth and Pet Survivors Program (YAPS©), based at Children's Hospital Colorado Center for Cancer and Blood Disorders, is a pen-pal program that matches pediatric oncology patients with dogs and cats who have survived cancer or other serious medical conditions. It is the first such program of its kind. Children and pets (via their owners) establish relationships and communicate through letter writing. This process allows children the unique opportunity to share feelings about having cancer with a safe, unconditionally loving animal. In the case of the YAPS program, children and dogs that have cancer correspond with one another (see Youth and Pet Survivors Program in References). This is a novel and terrific idea, especially for young, elementary-age children who have great imaginations.

From a practical perspective, over the past twenty-five years I have written hundreds of letters impersonating (on behalf of) one of my therapy dogs to many of my patients. I wrote these letters to help support these patients, many of whom were dealing with issues of death, bullying, loneliness, and failure. Rather than receiving a warm-hearted note from me, my words were disguised and written in the voice of one of my faithful therapy dogs. In my book *Afternoons with Puppy*

(2008), I dedicated an entire chapter to highlighting some of these letters. I was amazed with how well-received these notes became. Comparatively, the YAPS Program has provided a forum for many children to express their feelings via their unique relationship with their canine pen pals. Let's meet one pair.

Pepper, a Pomeranian, has two kinds of cancer (a brain cancer and a cancer of the lymph system), and Toby, a fourteen-year-old boy, has both autism and neurofibromatosis type one cancer, which includes an optic-glioma tumor (brain tumors that occur in or around the optic nerve). They have been writing each other a couple of times a month since starting their pen-pal relationship. Toby tries to respond within a couple of days after receiving each note. According to his mother, writing to Pepper has helped Toby a great deal. She explains:

> In some of his letters he expresses his frustration and excitement as to what is going on. This is so important, because often he will not verbally share how he is feeling, and to be able to put it down on paper helps him to overcome his fears and unhappiness. I think it does help, because Pepper has the same type of tumor and Toby feels he can relate, even to a dog. He has mentioned that Pepper can understand because they have the same type of tumor.

They even share a human hero, Temple Grandin. Over the years, Toby relishes getting letters from Pepper, and they are becoming not only pen pals but also real friends. Every letter is signed with, "Your Chemo Buddy, Toby."

In his many entries, Toby confides in Pepper about his daily life, his family, and his struggle with cancer and chemotherapy (which he calls his "torture"). In his letters, he also talks about the goodness in his life. In one letter, Toby wrote to Pepper about the effects of being partially blind (because of his cancer) and how he now uses a cane, which he named Yoda II. Pepper responded by writing, "I'm glad to hear you do well with your cane. I had a hard time getting used to having just one eye. Sometimes I still get stuck in a corner since I cannot always see my way out. Makes you real happy for all the good things we still have." One thing is for certain — cancer hasn't been able to deprive either of them of their unique and special friendship.

ANIMALS AS A SOCIAL CATALYST

Perhaps the most common use of any AAI is to facilitate or ease social interactions, or to be a social catalyst. It is amazing how an introduction to a therapy dog can bring a smile to a face and act as a simple icebreaker. I am told often by therapists and volunteers about how a therapy dog's presence helps people feel at ease. For example, at Victory Health and Rehab, one patient refused to leave her room for more than a week. The facility was reaching the point where they would have to remove her by force, but first they called for a therapy-animal visit. Chance and his handler came to visit this particular patient. The handler explained to the patient that she and Chance were a little warm from visiting so many patients and wanted to visit with her in the hallway. She quickly and wholeheartedly agreed to go anywhere in order to pet Chance. She spent twenty minutes outside of her room, which allowed the staff time to thoroughly clean it.

I mentioned earlier how the comfort level of my patient Matthew was always improved from having all of the dogs surround him. In many ways, the therapy dogs eased the stress he experienced while attending therapy. It also really helped to establish and support my rapport with him. My connection to my clients has always been stronger because of the animals. Because my dogs are so gentle and loving, perhaps they see me in a more gentle manner. Having a calm animal in a therapy session also projects a safe environment.

Over the years, many have commented in books and scholarly journals that animals can act as a link in conversation between a therapist and the client. In fact, this is why many therapists incorporate therapy dogs into their practice. The dogs' presence creates a sense of comfort, which then promotes the relationship between the patient and therapist. It also makes it easier for a patient to express difficult feelings.

In my thirty years of working in AAT, I have seen innumerable situations where children and adults who had initially been resistant to attending sessions seemed to just relax and become more comfortable because animals were in the room. This allows the therapist to more properly engage with the client and make him feel comfortable. I have treated children with a vast array of conditions over the years. Some have displayed selective mutism, where they are anatomically able to talk but are unwilling to speak in a public setting. Other children display severe anxiety. I have also treated children with developmental and learning disorders as well as teenagers who are chronically depressed. The anxieties of these patients were greatly reduced throughout therapy with the help of the various therapy dogs. In fact, the animals seemed to invite the young people into therapy, encouraging them to want to be there. Having a therapy dog around a professional allows that person to be viewed in a more humane and kind manner. Many families have voiced that when they see me around my therapy animals, I seem more gentle than when the animals aren't around.

A key element of an effective partnership between a clinician and a therapy animal is fluidity in their interactions. I have always used the analogy of dancing like Fred Astaire and Ginger Rogers to explain this phenomenon. When they danced, they did it with such grace; the same must occur in therapy. Both the therapist and the therapy dog need to be in harmony in order to work efficiently and effectively together. To cement this unique relationship, therapy dogs must demonstrate " affiliative behaviors" (such as friendly and positive gestures) to people. Dogs that demonstrate affiliative behaviors when they see a person walking down the street are apparently thrilled to meet a human being. As a rule, these dogs appear innately more interested in interacting with humans than they are with toys or other objects.

Animals can be incorporated into a therapeutic setting in other ways, too. For instance, I sometimes pair people with specific animals. If a person has certain difficulties, I match that individual with a therapy dog that has experienced similar struggles. This has proven to be a catalyst for a specific therapeutic discussion. I've had some birds and dogs (and even a bearded dragon) that were abused early in their lives. When a client who has been abused realizes that these animals experienced a similar history, it allows him to talk more freely about his own history. An animal also can help the therapist explain things that may be more awkward if the animal was not part of the discussion. In one case, I worked with a child who had encopresis (a soiling disorder), which was a very difficult thing to talk about. When he met a bearded dragon named Spikey that also had chronic constipation and suffered from similar challenges, the patient was able to talk about his own challenges more easily, particularly when he saw Spiky dealing with the same issue.

When some individuals come to therapy, their defense mechanisms go up and they become more tense and apprehensive. I therefore try to walk casually with a client to encourage a sense of calmness. While we walk, we begin to talk about relevant issues. While I would often walk with a client under normal circumstances, with a dog it is very, very natural to do this. Animals can become an integral part of the therapeutic process in so many unique ways. One strategy is the use of "reading dogs."

Reading Dogs

As children, many of us found our dogs' comforting while we snuggled up and read a book. Over the years, my dogs have lain next to many children, listening to them read. I wish they could tell me which story was their favorite. The unique aspect of this process is the dogs' eagerness to snuggle and share a story with any child who wants to read. We even built reading to dogs into a large research project that examined how therapy dogs can help facilitate therapies for children with ADHD. Of note, we have observed that when children read to the dogs, they genuinely relax. I've heard numerous other tributes about this process. Sometimes reading is just the beginning of a warmhearted relationship.

There is also scientific support for the notion that this program can be beneficial. Friesen (2009) suggests that canine-assisted reading programs are successful because dogs enhance the situational interest of children and motivate them to want to read out loud. Smith (2009) found statistically significant differences in improvement in reading fluency over time between early elementary-age students who read to dogs and those who did not. It appears that being surrounded by the dogs relaxes the readers and makes them more comfortable.

I had the opportunity to talk with Kathy Klotz, executive director of Intermountain Therapy Animals (ITA), the organization that founded the Reading Education Assistance Dogs (READ) program. Kathy explained that ITA was founded in 1993 in Utah and has more than 350 volunteer teams (a team consisting of a person and his own pet). In 1999, one of ITA's board members, Sandi Martin, posed a question to Kathy about applying human-animal interactions in a reading environment. As a result, ITA launched pilot programs in libraries in November 1999 and in elementary schools in January 2000 that eventually became Project READ, the first literacy-support model that utilizes therapy animals to help young children improve their reading skills and feel more comfortable with reading. Project READ targets children in their crucial formative years (grades K-3).

Kathy emphasized that "the READ model is much more than just a dog in the room or a bunch of children all taking turns reading to one visiting dog. What ITA did, rather, was to develop a full literacy-support model around this irresistible idea based on the partnership with therapy animals and their handlers." According to Kathy, the key to success is: (1) removing all peer pressure on the child and (2) employing a handler and dog who engage with each child individually, forming a relationship that can be trusted and relied upon, and within which the child feels safe, secure, comfortable, and accepted.

Kathy also shared testimonies she has heard over the years from numerous children who have spent time with a reading-support dog. A few of the typical and quintessential responses from the children in the programs sound like this.

"It seems like they listen more. Mostly when you read to people, they're looking around, not listening to you."

"Bailey never interrupts me or tells me what to do."

"My mom is always telling me to hurry, and the dog never does that."

"If I tell Buster my secrets, I know he'll never tell anyone else."

"Sometimes I stutter, and the dog never laughs at me."

"I know if I make a mistake, he will never go tell my friends that I'm stupid."

Sometimes the program supports children in ways other than learning to read. One Project READ volunteer states:

When one boy, eight years old, had his turn, Ernie stayed especially close, kissing the boy, nuzzling him, offering his big paw. When Ernie was lying down beside the boy, the boy kept one hand on Ernie, petting (him) constantly. The timer went off but the boy didn't move. He softly said, "My dog died." It turns out that his dog was the same age as Ernie. A car had hit him three weeks earlier. Just getting the boy to talk about his loss seemed to help.

Another loving example comes from Mary Domes, who explains the unique relationship that grew from the reading experience between her therapy dog, Journey, and a boy named Joshua.

Joshua came to read at the library when he was seven years old. At that time, Mary and her dog, Journey, volunteered at the local library in Wisconsin. Mary is a dog trainer who started volunteering with her dogs in 1997. She heard about a therapy-dog group in Chicago and thought her dog Brody (her first Golden Retriever) would be a great fit. She went to Chicago to get Brody tested and he passed. They then started volunteering at a nursing home, and Brody showed her how valuable he could be as a source of support for others. Journey, one of her registered therapy dogs, began working at the age of six. Mary brought Journey to a READ program at the library once a month, and this is where they met Joshua.

When they first met, Mary had no idea that Joshua had autism. She thought he was full of energy and had a short attention span. It was only after they read together for seven to eight months that Mary was told about Joshua's diagnosis. Joshua loved Journey and only wanted to read to him. Mary made sure that Journey was available when Joshua came to read once a month. They actually spent two years reading together before Journey passed away.

Looking back, there wasn't an immediate connection between Joshua and Journey. Initially, Joshua would read a page and then would say that he wanted to leave. Over time, Joshua improved, and he would bring books that he wanted to read. When he and Journey first met, Joshua sat far away from Journey. In time, they sat progressively closer as they grew more familiar with one another. Joshua started to spend more time with Journey and began to touch and pet him more. It took about six months before Joshua could read an entire book to Journey. By then he would be petting Journey the entire time he was reading. Journey made the experience more meaningful by focusing on Joshua. He'd look at Joshua when the boy read and would follow Joshua's finger as he pointed out pictures in the book. Sometimes Journey would lay his head on Joshua's lap. Watching them interact was quite touching. Mary even taught Journey to put his paws on the pages of the book, and Joshua loved this. Joshua loved to hug Journey, and Journey was very accepting of the hugs. Observing Journey's patience with Joshua taught Mary how to be patient as well. Journey helped them both to relax. When Joshua calmed down in the presence of Journey, it gave Mary more quality time with Joshua.

Journey fell ill the Thanksgiving of 2010 and died in early 2011. Mary found out that surgery, chemotherapy, and radiation were not going to help. She decided to bring Journey home to make him as comfortable as possible for the rest of his life. In December 2010, Mary phoned Joshua's mom and let her know what was going on. Journey made his last trip to the library in December. Mary asked Joshua's mom if her son wanted to go to Mary's home to read to Journey in January 2011. Joshua's mom asked her son and they decided to go for a visit. Journey was not doing well but perked up when he saw Joshua. Mary explained to Joshua that Journey didn't have many days left, and Joshua, despite his young age, understood. Mary had selected some books for Joshua to read, but he didn't want to read any of them. Instead, Joshua walked to her bookshelf and selected a book called *The Dog Chapel* (2002). Joshua had never read the book but somehow knew that was the right book to read. The story is about a chapel built to say goodbye to dogs. It talks about a Labrador Retriever who earned his angel wings. Joshua told Journey that he, too, had earned his angel wings. Joshua's mom and Mary were in tears at this scene. Journey understood the emotions of Joshua's mother, and he went to put his head in her lap.

At the end of this last visit, Journey walked Joshua to the front door (this was unexpected). As Joshua left, he touched Journey's head and said, "I'll see you in heaven." Journey had left his paw print on this boy's soul.

ANIMALS AND CHANGING THE MILIEU

I am clear that having animals in an environment changes the way we view that living world. It makes us feel extremely comfortable. When an animal enters my office, the space is transformed into a very comforting environment. Fish swimming in tanks, dogs walking up and down the hallway, and even birds greeting us are all part of that "ecosystem." In fact, in 1975, Mugford and M'Comisky wrote a paper about how having a variety of birds in a convalescent home can provide an impetus for social interaction. The animals themselves were a social catalyst in conversation and brought a calming effect to the space. At this time, people began to look seriously at social environments in rehabilitation and healing centers. One well-respected therapeutic community is Green Chimneys in Upstate New York.

I recently caught up with Sam Ross, who was the founder of Green Chimneys. In my opinion, Green Chimneys is the best example of a living environment that incorporates animals to help support the lives of children. The philosophy of Green Chimneys is based on the belief that healing and rehabilitation can occur when the environment in which the treatment is facilitated is enriched and natural. Green Chimneys has gone beyond what is commonly done in treatment facilities. The setting integrates pets, farm animals, horses, and wildlife directly into the programming with resident children. It has received both national and international recognition due to its pioneering work in this area.

While I was talking with Sam, he shared a useful metaphoric anecdote to explain the underlying goal of his sanctuary: "There is a child who is gently holding a caterpillar and is stopped by a woman asking him what he is doing. The boy quickly responds that he needs to help the caterpillar find a rock so that he can be safe and eventually become a butterfly." Perhaps that is what Green Chimneys has become for many children over the past several decades — a safe haven.

In 1948, when Green Chimneys first opened its doors, it did so with eleven children. From the beginning, the population included children from families in crisis due to illness, divorce, separation, or the death of a parent. Today, the farm is filled with animals, including two Bactrian camels. It also has fifty-one injured birds of prey in flight cages, a few deer, and various breeds of waterfowl residing in a protected display cage with a pond.

Sam explains, "Since our founding in 1947, children and animals have lived together. The program provides care for a large collection of injured wildlife. The children we serve learn to care and take responsibility for these animals under the careful watch of staff. They soon learn that having animals around full-time means twenty-four hours per day of vigilance and care. The children learn that if they love the animals and treat them kindly, the animals will provide unconditional love. They learn responsibility, sharing, caring, and empathy from their experiences." Sam believes that many children and their families are drawn to Green Chimneys because of the animals. He explains that when the youngsters first arrive as a resident or day student, it is a scary event in their lives. He believes that, at this point, the animals and the farm environment prove their value. "We must let the children have as much time as possible with the farm and garden activities. It will help them feel comfortable. It will help them find a friend who is equally interested in the same things.

"Thanks to the interaction with animals, children are able to actualize two basic needs that impact feelings of calm, security, and control: the need to love and the need to be loved."

Before we ended our conversation, Sam reminisced about the many children whose lives have been influenced by his sanctuary. He quoted from a letter sent by one of his former students: "I came to Green Chimneys when I was five years old.

All the values that I have in my life today really came from this place. This place was a family. It was my family."

INCORPORATING ANIMALS FOR TEACHING

Using animals in assisted interventions teaches children and adults specific life lessons. Taking care of an animal, and learning the aspects of animal husbandry, can be very valuable for individuals. Over the years, I've observed children with autism and other forms of developmental disabilities who have gained tremendous benefits from being engaged in animal husbandry.

A wonderful illustration of working with animals for teaching is the Positive, Assertive, Cooperative Kids (PACK) Project at the University of California–Irvine (UCI). This program was established in 2010 at UCI and led by Dr. Sabrina Schuck. It integrates canine-assisted therapy into a social-skills-based intervention.

Several components of the PACK project involve therapy dogs. One is free play, where children get a chance to interact with the dogs. This includes activities like playing with a Frisbee, ball throwing, agility training, basic grooming, and husbandry. Children have the opportunity to bond with the therapy animal with no contingencies.

Another goal is to teach children values through humane education, the core of which is learning how to treat living beings with kindness and respect through our relationships with other species. Two other unique components of the program include times during which children have the opportunity to read to the dogs, learn to be "good teachers," and have a chance to train puppies in obedience. Of key importance for the children is that, through this interaction, they can learn what it means to be a good teacher and how knowledge can effectively be shared with others. This novel project might prime children for learning new information and keep them more engaged when working on their skills. (See the Project PACK Recruitment Brochure in the References section.)

The PACK Project demonstrates how such activities could help children with ADHD self-regulate and build self-esteem. The animals might heighten the children's attention and focus and positively reinforce them. Furthermore, this kind of intervention helps children become more socially assertive.

Children learn that a good teacher is fair and respectful, and that he cares about those with whom he works. The PACK Project also teaches children about how to act as instructors while using a calm voice, speaking clearly, using good eye contact, and making sure, of course, that the dog pays attention. Although the children think that THEY are teaching the THERAPY DOGS, in many ways THEY are learning self-regulatory skills that empower them to be more in control of their own behavior. They must learn self-control for the dogs to favorably respond to them. In an interview with Lindsay Hayley, a staff member of the project, she explores her impressions of one child. Let's meet Jacob.

From the moment I met Jacob, he stood out among the other students. An eight-year-old boy with a raspy voice like "The Godfather" is bound to make an impression. Despite his tough demeanor, he proved to be one of the most sensitive and genuine kids in the group. Prior to the beginning of the PACK interventions, Jacob's parents shared concerns of how their son may treat the therapy dogs because of his behavior toward their family dog. They mentioned how he squeezes their dog too tightly, and they were concerned he lacks empathy. During the first session, Jacob voluntarily spoke about his dog during the "end-of-session challenge." He didn't enjoy walking his dog because of his dog's slow pace and the responsibility of picking up after him. Yet each week, Jacob spoke about his dog through an increasingly positive lens. About halfway through the intervention sessions, his mother noticed a significant change in her son's demeanor toward their dog at home. She said he's much more gentle and affectionate toward their dog and is even protective of how others behave around him.

Another common challenge for PACK members is speaking at an appropriate volume. Their conversational voices range from a quiet whisper to a forceful shout. Jacob was a unique case—he mumbled in a low, raspy voice and was one of the most challenging kids to hear or understand. But around the dogs, he quickly learned to use a strong, assertive tone, and he became one of the most effective teachers in the group.

In the program, the therapy dogs reinforce many of the key pro-social behaviors. During the first couple of weeks, children struggle with giving directions to the dogs. Rather than saying the command once, they tend to repeat it several times within a few seconds. It's fascinating to watch the children's transformation with their interactions with the dogs. They learn from observing how the dogs respond to the different ways the commands are given, illustrating the importance of patience, acceptance, and persistence.

It's easy to lose sight of how tough life can be as a child, especially the lives of some of the PACK children. Many children with ADHD are viewed as a nuisance and often carry the most heartbreaking stories. Abandonment, expulsion, rejection, and academic failure are just a few of their common challenges. But at PACK, it is very apparent that the dogs possess the ability to provide a sense of relief and comfort for the kids. These qualities are beneficial to any person, and dogs are an often overlooked yet incredible resource of companionship free of judgment and full of unconditional love.

ANIMALS ACTING AS CATALYSTS FOR EMOTION: COURTROOM AND COMFORT DOGS

Therapists also spend much time incorporating animals in their practice to help support the emotional capacity of clients while they are expressing feelings. Therapy animals can soothe patients in ways that a therapist cannot. Dogs also offer therapeutic touch, which is extremely important. Phil Tedeschi, a clinical professor at the University of Denver, has been involved in the field of AAT for many years. He talks about the importance of therapy dogs in courtrooms, particularly when children are involved. In many ways, the animals' presence may lend comfort and stability to an environment of challenge and dispute. Simply having animals there can make a child feel more relaxed and comfortable.

Although therapy dogs are not yet used in many courtrooms, those who have experienced the presence of the dogs describe witnesses being able to complete a difficult testimony or work through overwhelming emotions with the help of the courtroom dog. The presence of a dog makes a stark environment like a courtroom less intimidating and more familiar feeling, especially for children. Phil explains: In Colorado, the Paws Assisting the Legal System (PALS) Program was started, using the Courthouse Dogs Program as a model. Pella is the first dog in the PALS Program, and she works together with Detective Amber Urbans at the Aurora Police Department.

"This program is used as a means to introduce the calming and comforting effect of a dog to traumatized children and adults with developmental disabilities during the ordeal of a criminal investigation. The safe and stable environment allows the recitation of the events by the victim or witness to be more thorough and less traumatizing" (Aurora Citizens' Police Academy Alumni Association Newsletter, Fall 2012).

Child advocates are working to add court-facility dogs to the lists of acceptable support systems. If a trained dog or established program is not present in a courtroom, it is possible for an advocate or lawyer to make a motion to seek a dog out if they feel a client could benefit from the support. The question, though, is whether the presence of a safe dog is able to help us get more accurate information from a victim or witness during a criminal investigation. It is understood that sitting and petting a safe dog helps to release oxytocin in the brain, which helps in trauma recovery. The petting of the dogs can increase feelings of safety and boost optimism and our overall sense of well-being.

Many child victims suffer from accommodation syndrome, which makes them unbelievable and bad witnesses. The fear they experience often triggers a flight-or-fight response, making them unpredictable, disorganized, and unable to keep their story straight. If a safe dog can intervene soon after a crime, oxytocin floods the child's brain, signaling to the child that a defensive mechanism is not necessary. The child feels less anxious, more at ease, and more comfortable describing unpleasant or painful events. The idea is to change the neurological and psychosocial experience of a victim earlier in the process to help the child heal and to aid in the investigation process.

When child victims or witnesses interact with a safe dog that is not going to blame or shame them, they can be honest. What is whispered to the dog in safety can then be said out loud to the police. Children who have been assaulted may feel weak, that there is something wrong with them, or that they deserve to have been assaulted. When a dog chooses to interact with them, the experience challenges this belief of inadequacy and weakness, and it changes the children's neurological and psychosocial experience. It helps childen feel that what has happened to them is not their fault. And the calming presence of a dog makes it easier for a child to be in the courtroom. One seventeen-year-old who was testifying against her biological father found it very difficult and had to take many breaks. With a courthouse dog present, the same teen felt more comfortable testifying in court and did not require as many breaks.

It is important that the dog be able to behave appropriately in the courtroom. Court-facility dogs must be well trained to sit silently and motionless so as not to distract the jury or the witness. In fact, the dogs sit under the stand in a way that the jury cannot even see them. Pella is trained to be non-reactive and non-obtrusive in court and should not distract the jury or the child in court. This is all to prevent any biases from developing among the jury.

Pella, a Labrador Retriever/Golden Retriever mix, is the first therapy dog of her kind in Colorado and only the second dog owned by a detective involved in forensic interview work (most dogs that are utilized in forensic interview work are owned by a victim advocate or a forensic interviewer). Pella has been in the PALS Program since May 2012. She currently assists in forensic interview work, mostly with children and some adults who have developmental disabilities. Most cases relate to sexual abuse, physical abuse, or neglect. In some cases, the child is a witness to a traumatic death (e.g., dad killed mom). Detective Urbans explains in an interview on December 3, 2012 that "dogs are not judgmental or accusatory; nothing a person can say would shock a dog. Pella's presence in the forensic interview process provides emotional support to the child. The forensic interviewer is able to get better information from children when they feel calmer and safer. They are able to speak more clearly and are less nervous talking to a dog than a police officer. Although the investigator needs to remain neutral during the interview process, the dog is able to show support for the child."

Pella is currently preparing to attend her first hearing in court with a five-year-old girl. To prepare for the hearing, Detective Urbans takes Pella to visit the courtroom and gets her accustomed to the environment. In court, Pella will be asked to lie down underneath the chair of the witness stand; this will provide the witness with support as she testifies.

Eight to twelve minutes before and ten to twenty minutes after the forensic interview, the child gets to interact with Pella. Detective Urbans will facilitate the interaction between the child and Pella to enable rapport. The child can pet Pella, and Detective Urbans will teach the child some commands and get Pella to show off for the child. Detective Urbans typically gets Pella to shake, to close doors, and to jump on and off the couch.

During the interview, only the child, the forensic interviewer, and Pella are in the room. Detective Urbans watches them on a video screen next door. Pella has to be well behaved in a room without her handler present. The forensic interviewer is given basic training on how to handle Pella and ensure Pella's safety during the interview. Pella was selected for her job because of her great demeanor and calm personality. She is generally non-reactive and tolerates children pulling on her or lying on her. Detective Urbans has great faith that Pella would never hurt a child. On one occasion, Pella did not react when a little boy started pulling on Pella's mouth during the interview. Pella is also not disruptive during the interview and stays silently on the couch next to the child. Sometimes, Pella even falls asleep on the couch. The children generally pet Pella as they answer the interviewer's questions. If the child is distracted by Pella in the interview room, Detective Urbans will intervene and take Pella out of the room by saying that Pella needs to go potty and will meet the child when the interview is over. This is so the child will not think it's his fault that Pella had to leave the room. Fortunately, this hardly happens.

Pella is sensitive to the sentiments of the people around her. Pella met a family with two boys who came from a culture that did not like dogs. The family was from Africa and did not see dogs as pets that are loved by their families. The father avoided the dog completely, while the children were hesitant about interacting with Pella. The boys wanted to pet her at the back and not her head. They would shrink away if Pella turned her head to look at them. Detective Urbans asked if they wanted Pella to go with them for the interview and they said yes. Detective Urbans always gives children the choice to take Pella into the interview. Pella, who normally lies sprawled out on the couch next to the child or has her head on the child's lap, decided to curl up in a ball at the end of the couch furthest away from the child. It was as if Pella could sense that the children wanted her there but were not comfortable getting too close.

In another case, a three-year-old boy had sustained significant injuries and did not want to stay in the interview room with the forensic interviewer. The boy kept trying to leave the room. When Pella was present, the boy was able to stay in the room for twenty minutes and was able to talk to the interviewer. His parents later mentioned that Pella's presence helped the boy to open up and talk.

Many children (especially the younger ones) who have been physically or sexually abused often do not understand that what has happened to them is wrong, especially when the perpetrator is a family member. Much self-blame occurs. Pella's presence helps them to change their perception and to associate the experience of talking about the abuse with someone as a positive process. This makes talking much easier for the child. This is especially true for older children and teenagers who dislike talking to a forensic interviewer.

In one case, a teenage girl who was physically and sexually abused found it very difficult to tell her story. She would not look at the interviewer and made no eye contact. She appeared to be crying, but the interviewer could not tell, because the teen's face was turned away. Pella was then introduced to the girl, and the teen appeared to be a different person. As she petted Pella, she was now able to make eye contact with the interviewer and could share her story easily. It was as if two different girls were talking.

Pella also hangs out in the lobby with children who are waiting for their interviews. Her presence helps them to relax and calm down. The child is able to talk about something other than the case. The presence of Pella, as a safe dog, aids the release of oxytocin in the child. Seeing how calm and comfortable Pella is helps the child to associate the place as safe and worry-free. Children often take on the stress of their families, and watching their families worry about the case causes the child to feel stressed as well. Pella calms down the children and puts them at ease. She also helps the children transition into the interview room. Many young children are hesitant to leave their parents for the interview; knowing they can take Pella into the interview helps them to attend the interview without their parents.

Pella is currently not involved in investigations with offenders, although Detective Urbans sees the potential in this. She would consider evaluating it case by case. Her main concern is for Pella's safety, especially in the case of violent crimes. Safety measures would include not having the offender hold onto Pella's leash and having two detectives on hand during the investigation, one of whom is focused on the suspect and the other on the dog.

Outside of work, Pella is a totally different dog. She is playful and energetic and enjoys playing with her tennis ball. She gets along well with the other dog and cat at home and enjoys playing with them.

For the dog to work well with the forensic interviewer or in court, a relationship must develop between the child and the dog. The stronger this relationship is, the more likely it is for the dog to be able to help the child feel less anxious and able to share accurate information.

As we see over and over again, dogs seem to have an intuitive sense of what a person needs. Dogs often sense when people want their space or when individuals need the dog to be near them. Therapy dogs are beginning to appear in emergency departments now, for the same reasons that they are present in courtrooms. They calm the environment, sense when people need affection, and add an element of normalcy to a scary and unfamiliar environment, particularly for children. Emergency departments where dogs visit regularly have noticed a great difference in the overall energy of the waiting area — nearly all patients and staff report positive changes. Patients even report a shorter or more tolerable waiting time.

DOGS IN DISASTER RESPONSE

Because dogs have a calming impact on people in various stages of pain, sickness, injury, or mourning, it is no surprise that they may be helpful right at the scene of a tragedy. The presence of comfort dogs is growing at natural disasters, shootings, and other major traumatic events. Their intuition pays off greatly for frightened and shocked people who struggle to find words for their feelings during such horrible events. Dogs do not require words and are willing to sit silently without expecting any conversation. Mark Condon, co-founder of Canine Therapy Link, says of his experiences with his dog, "I always tell people who go through our training program: trust your dogs to know what to do. If you let them, they know how to act once they know what their job is. The person has the potential to just get in the way more than anything." In these situations, too, we see how dogs can create connections and provide comfort that other people simply cannot offer.

Animal-assisted, crisis-response dog-handler teams that are qualified to help in situations like Hurricane Katrina, the Sandy Hook School shooting in Connecticut, and 9/11, go through specialized training to offer comfort and emotional support to victims, emergency responders, and anyone affected by the critical incident or disaster. Dr. Lois Abrams and Deborah Hatherley are both involved as mental-health consultants with HOPE Animal-Assisted Crisis Response (HOPE ACCR) (see References). HOPE AACR is one of a few organizations in the country that works in disaster situations, including hurricanes, school shootings, fires, bombings, tornadoes, floods, and memorials for fallen warriors.

In large-scale disaster situations, certain groups fill the same role for every event. Governmental agencies, such as local, state, and sometimes federal emergency management and the health department, are supported by many non-governmental volunteer agencies, such as the American Red Cross and other non-profit relief agencies, including faith-based relief organizations. Some are in charge of food, some first aid, others shelter, and others debris cleanup as well as other functions. Now that comfort dogs have joined the ranks in the aftermath of traumatic events, dog-handler teams are able to bring some much-needed normalcy and familiarity to people experiencing trauma and shock. HOPE AACR trains dogs for exactly these sorts of events. The work is difficult and carefully orchestrated in collaboration with the other organizations. "In the aftermath of the VA Tech shooting," Hatherley explains, "the HOPE AACR dog-handler teams were invited by the American Red Cross to support their mental-health volunteers. As the professional mental-health volunteers walked around providing comfort, many students said, 'I'm okay,' and wouldn't open up to talk about what had happened. However, the students, sometimes in groups, readily approached the comfort dogs. They started talking about their own dogs and their family. Then the conversation changed, and eventually they started talking to the handler about their perceptions of what had happened and how it was affecting them personally. The dogs helped this connection to happen. That, in turn, opened the doors for the handlers to offer further 'emotional first-aid support' and refer them to the Red Cross mental-health volunteers for follow-up if needed. So we are triaging in a way — we can connect people in greatest need to professionals, who at first may find it difficult to engage them in conversation."

Professionals in AACR are working to identify best practices in this new and growing field. They plan to strengthen their public identity as a necessary component to the recovery efforts of such events. Dr. Abrams explains that there are many misunderstandings about their work and that the public needs to be educated about the value of their work and how it is done. The HOPE AACR group responds to disasters by invitation from those directly involved. They operate differently than other therapy dogs — AACR dogs must know how to respond to potentially chaotic situations, unpredictable emotional reactions, and even to various modes of transportation.

Dr. Abrams says of their training, "Dogs have to be at complex animal-assisted therapy level for a year, for at least twelve visits, and then they go through screening that is much more intense than the evaluation used for therapy dogs. They use role-plays and simulated situations. They test everything out, and some dogs don't make it; they're often too young or not the right temperament for crisis-response work. Dogs must feel confident with the handler and know that the handler is going to take care of them. Not everyone can do it, and not everyone who wants to can."

Handlers do not need to be therapists or to be in a helping profession at all. Volunteers are welcome to do this work; they go through rigorous training alongside their dog. They learn active listening skills, which both Dr. Abrams and Hatherley identify as the most important skill to have when working with people in crisis. Everybody goes through crisis-response training and is prepared for what they might encounter. A number of teams go to each crisis together. After each crisis, everybody debriefs the experience and observes their dog for signs of stress or fatigue. A team leader is present at all events — someone who is in charge of ensuring the dogs' safety and well-being. Hatherley says that the most important aspects of the training are for the dogs to trust their handler and for the dog and handler getting ongoing education and training. The role is particularly stressful and difficult, and everyone must be aware of the challenges and risks. However, the potential is great, and these dogs make a huge difference in how people cope with disasters.

Mark Condon has been working with his therapy dog Dutchess for years. When he brought her to the memorial site after the Sandy Hook Elementary shooting, he did not know what to expect. He noticed how quiet, even silent, the town was as people waited in line at the gas station or walked up the sidewalk. It is difficult to know just what to do in such a situation. He quickly realized the value of Dutchess's presence for this mourning community. In the midst of heartbreak sat Dutchess, a silent pillar of warmth and support and a refuge from having to know what to say or how to act. Dozens of people approached Dutchess that day. Some, relieved for a moment of reprieve from the tragedy, made small talk about what Dutchess and Mark do. Some wanted to understand how Dutchess, blind with her eyes surgically removed, lives so happily after losing her sight to disease. Perhaps they felt some inspiration in relating to the suffering of someone else. Most people, though, just sat with her, embraced her, pet her head, and cried. One young girl, clearly shaken by the event and likely in shock, embraced Dutchess and sobbed into her soft fur. Dutchess embraced her back, leaning into her and absorbing her sadness.

Dutchess has always known what to do. When kids are happy and excited, Dutchess gladly reciprocates the joy. In times like the Newtown tragedy, Dutchess knows her role. She doesn't need sight to tell her the mood of the people around her. People who see her at work seem to know she has a special knack for the job. Mark's experience at the Sandy Hook Elementary shooting is telling of the great power of this work. As he and Dutchess walked down street on their way home from the memorial, several surprising interactions took place. They were encountered by people calling out of their car windows, "Thank you for coming!" Dutchess brought comfort, support, and love to the memorial that day. She may not have known what happened, but she knew what was needed of her and was glad to give it.

SERVICE AND MEDICAL ALERT DOGS

Service dogs have been trained to help people with various needs for generations. We are familiar with the amazing skill and help provided by seeing-eye dogs, dogs that help with mobility, and dogs trained to assist for a variety of handicaps. Now there is a new area of health care being greatly served by the help of dogs, and it is becoming increasingly popular around the globe. This new form of help is bringing independence and security to people who once were debilitated by a variety of medical conditions.

According to Claire Guest, the CEO and director of operations for Medical Detection Dogs in the United Kingdom, "Dogs are renowned for their sense of smell." In fact, Stanley Coren and Sarah Hodgson in their book, *Understanding Dogs for Dummies* (2007), they report that dogs can smell about 1,000 to 10,000 times better than humans. For example, Bloodhounds have 300 million sense receptors when compared to humans, who have about five million. Consequently, it seems logical that dogs could be trained and used to sniff odors omitted by various diseases. "Cancer cells release small amounts of volatile substances," and the dogs at Medical Detection Center are trained to detect them. Interest in enlisting the help of dogs for their refined sniffing was first highlighted by William Pembroke in 1989.

Numerous other papers have followed, and they demonstrate how dogs can be helpful in medically identifying disorders. In particular, Dr. Guest (a psychologist) and her colleagues published a groundbreaking study in the *British Journal of Medicine* in 2004. In this study, the trained dogs were capable of smelling the odor in the urine of a person's bladder with 56 percent accuracy. The study provided the first proof that dogs could identify a unique "odor signature" that was associated with cancer. This was the first clinically robust trial to be completed and published in the world.

In 2011, a group of scientists (Cornu, et al.) reported the results of a Belgian Malinois's ability to detect prostate cancer in human urine samples. After a robust and comprehensive training period of two years, the dog's ability to discriminate urine from cancer patients from a control urine was tested in a double-blind procedure. The dogs correctly selected the cancer samples in thirty out of thirty-three cases. Of the three incorrect cases, one was actually re-biopsied and was found to have prostate cancer.

Dogs have been trained to identify numerous other odor changes in our bodies, such as hypoglycemia (low blood sugar). When these dogs become aware of the lower blood sugar, they "warn their owners or get help before the symptoms are felt. The dogs will bring their owner any necessary medical supplies, such as glucose and blood-testing kits. They can also be trained to push alarm buttons," Guest points out.

I had the opportunity to spend an enjoyable afternoon with Dr. Guest while speaking in Lleida, Spain, at a conference on animals and people. She is a tremendous resource about the future of service animals. Not only could she attest to their benefits scientifically, she also personally benefited from a dog's skills. She shared with me:

> I wouldn't have believed that my dog Daisy would help me spot a very early-stage breast tumor. Daisy was trained as a cancer-detection dog and she had sensed bladder, renal, and prostate cancers from urine samples, but not breast cancer. This is why I did not expect the following occurrence. One afternoon after work, I put Daisy in the back of the car to take her for our usual walk. When we arrived, I opened the back of the car by the field. Instead of jumping out to run on the field, Daisy jumped at me and pushed against me hard. It was then I felt a slightly bruised feeling on my left breast. It felt like a deep bruise.
>
> The pain from the bruise didn't disappear right away, and after a few days, I wondered if I felt a lump. I decided to go to my general practitioner (GP) to check on it. The GP thought there was a lump, so I was referred to a consultant. Further tests and biopsies showed that the lump was benign, but a mammogram showed an area of concern very deep — well below the lump. Core biopsies confirmed the cancer. Without Daisy, I wonder how long I would have waited.
>
> To convey her message, Daisy had begun acting strange around me and kept jumping up and down. I couldn't feel the lump at first but was told that, by the time I would've felt it, my prognosis would have been poor."

Today Dr. Guest has seen a number of cases in which dogs are helping to sniff diseases like colon, kidney, and bladder cancer. Research carried out by her organization, the Medical Detection Dogs, is groundbreaking, and hopefully, in time, they will be able to detect breast cancer at an early stage and save hundreds of lives. While lives can be saved, others experience a great improvement with their quality of life thanks to these dogs. Having a seizure-alert dog (an SAD) enables people to be more independent and to experience safer seizures, and even the occurrence of seizures has decreased for people who own an SAD. Independence among those with any of these debilitating conditions can be increased for overall improvements in their lives.

While the dogs' sense of smell is what enables them to recognize diabetic changes, oncoming seizures, cancer, narcolepsy, and other ailments, we now know that dogs can also detect medical issues through small and subtle behavioral changes that other humans cannot detect. Rupert Sheldrake's book, *Dogs That Know When Their Owners Are Coming Home* (2011), describes several accounts of dogs having a "sense" about when people are coming home, how to get home if they're in a new place, when something has changed or is about to happen, and when somebody is sick. Perhaps, according to his anecdotes, there is even more than smell and behavior detection going on. While we may not yet have much written evidence of these promising events, we know through our lived experience that this is largely an untapped resource for our well-being.

———

Animal-assisted interventions provide useful alternative therapy for many individuals. Although the efficacy of AAIs is continuing to uncover the evidence needed for scientific acceptance, the interventions have achieved considerable notoriety and public acceptance. For example, in the past six months in the United States, it was almost an expected outcome that the "therapy dogs" would be volunteering at the tragic disasters experienced in the Northeast of the United States. These dogs' abilities to share empathy and warmth made their presence welcome and very desired. The same fact holds true when we see therapy dogs working in hospitals, schools, libraries, and retirement centers. Their roles are now more common and accepted by the general public.

When I began utilizing trained therapy animals, the process was novel and unique. Many didn't seem to understand why I was doing this, and in some cases, the interactions were received with guarded skepticism. We can only imagine what it was like for people like Boris Levinson and some of the other pioneers who were met with resistance and doubt! I am happy to report that, although there still may be some resistance, in most cases the application of animal-assisted therapy is graciously received. These animals not only make various forms of therapy more inviting and warmhearted, they also seem to motivate clients to make the difficult changes in their lives, both physical as well as psychological, that clinicians may not have been able to accomplish without them.

Matthew's involvement with his canine friends was highlighted at the onset of this chapter. Not only did these interactions bring him comfort and joy, they also therapeutically enabled him to express his feelings and learn strategies to relax when he became agitated. Although the animals were initially there as a social catalyst for Matthew, the end result has been far more powerful than could have been expected. As the narrative about Matthew revealed, his connection to my pack of canine co-therapists has promoted his engagement and cooperation. Over the last thirty-five years, I've witnessed this outcome with many of my other patients.

Another example would be the dogs' effect on my dear client Angie, who I've known since she was six years old. Angie literally loves all animals. In Angie's wallet, she carries some of the pictures that she has taken over the years with the various dogs she has befriended. She has adopted them as members of her family circle and has had the dogs over for visits. These four-legged creatures have brought more to Angie's life than words can describe. They have helped her in times of emotional difficulties, and their lives have great meaning to her. They consistently let her know that she is appreciated and that they love being around her. More than anything, Angie's relationship with them is the link that connects all of us together. This metaphorical link brings true meaning to the cliché "the healing power of puppy love." As we end this chapter, we may realize that assisted animal intervention still needs more empirical evidence to support its claims. I strongly believe, however, that we cannot underestimate the power of a cold nose and a warm heart. The animals' contribution and engagement into a therapeutic process may unlock resistance and obstacles and allow a person to move forward to his new tomorrow.

CHAPTER SIX

MAGIC:
Take Me to Pooh Corner

"If ever there is a tomorrow when we're not together…there is some-thing you must always remember. You are braver than you believe, stronger than you seem, and smarter than you think. But the most important thing is, even if we're apart…I'll always be with you." — Winnie the Pooh

For some of us, nostalgia is a wonderful comfort. We find ourselves drifting back to a childhood safe place filled with magic and joy. When writing his books on Winnie the Pooh, A.A. Milne created a special place called the Hundred Acre Woods, where a young boy and his bear friend could run, laugh, and play. In many ways, I believe we all want to have a place we can turn to where we feel safe and secure; we all want to find our own Pooh Corner.

In early May 2010, I was invited to speak at the Luminaria Ceremony for my university's Relay for Life event. These relays raise funds for cancer research, and, more importantly, they spread awareness and provide a place to celebrate the lives of those impacted by this dreadful disease. The Luminaria Ceremony is the high-light of the relay. In most cases, the ceremonies preach remembrance and hope for a tomorrow free of cancer. My talk was filled with optimism and aspirations for the woman I love, my wife, Nya, who had battled cancer. It was the story of how a cold nose and warm heart, packaged in a bundle of fur, was able to kindle hope in a chasm of despair.

My story began in April 2005, when our friend's Golden Retriever had a litter of puppies. Our friend asked if we would be interested in having one, and Nya was a bit resistant, as she always is when we consider adopting new creatures. After much begging from me, she agreed, and we welcomed our new Golden puppy, Magic, into our family.

A week before this, my wife had gone in for her yearly mammogram. The following day, she was asked to come in for a CAT scan. The news was not good; she had been diagnosed with breast cancer. She was initially apprehensive to tell anyone the results. When she went to pick up Magic a few days after receiving the unsettling news, she put the busy little puppy into a small crate in the car. Magic began to whimper, and Nya spoke gently to her, saying, "I know how you feel. I'm nervous, too." Their journey together was about to begin.

About a week after Magic joined our family, my wife had surgery. Over the next several months, Magic became my wife's best friend. They were inseparable. For a young puppy, Magic was keenly interested in Nya and would never leave her side. One daily ritual was particularly special: they would hold hand and paw together for hours, often in silence. One evening several months later, Nya said to me with tears in her eyes, "I guess we were supposed to get her. Taking care of her keeps me busy and brings me joy. She brings me happiness and things to do so that I don't have to sit around and worry about myself."

As my story unfolded at the Luminaria Ceremony, I likened Magic's relationship with Nya to the channel that pulled my wife out of despair and provided her with a measurement of hope. It's amazing what people find to hold onto their normalcy; they need to continue to have purpose in their daily lives, and it is with that purpose they seem to find the strength to persevere. While Magic may not have solely saved Nya's emotional life, she was absolutely instrumental in helping return it to her.

What I have always found inspiring was Nya's strength for always having hope. The human body is able to cope under incredible circumstances, even when being deprived of substantial quantities of essential things that sustain life. However, when hope goes away or is lost, we give up the fight and the spirit is broken. The story of Pandora and her box best describes this phenomenon. As the mythological story goes, Zeus gave Pandora a box with specific instructions not to open it. Impelled by her curiosity, Pandora went against Zeus's instructions and opened the box, releasing all the evils of mankind onto Earth. One thing remained in the box: the spirit of hope, huddled in a corner. With hope, Pandora was healed and mankind was given this intangible, incorporeal weapon to fight against the evils in the world and survive what misfortunes might befall them.

Many use the word "hope" to describe several emotions. In my opinion, hope is much more than being optimistic. Hope is an internal belief that helps kindle perseverance. Vaclav Havel, a respected author and the first president of the Czech Republic, once argued in his book, *Disturbing the Peace* (1990) that hope is definitely not the same as optimism. He noted that hope shouldn't be inferred as a "conviction that something will turn out well, but the certainty that something makes sense, regardless of how it turns out." Hopefulness can be a healthy way of thinking that allows us to move forward.

Hope is what Magic provided for Nya. Magic knew, and still knows, how to get past Nya's emotional armor. Magic is able to pick up on nonverbal cues and engage Nya even when a direct invitation isn't given. When she was a puppy, she would just wander over to Nya and nudge her way into her human friend's soul.

Nya has been cancer-free for almost eight years. Her remarkable relationship with Magic is stronger than most I have witnessed. Although my wife hesitates to admit it, they are soul mates, and it is still amazing to watch the two of them together. I often find them sitting next to each other, silently gazing into each other's eyes and holding paw and hand. It is a heartwarming sight that never grows old.

Jerome Groopman, the author of *The Anatomy of Hope* (2003), was once quoted as stating, "To hope under the most extreme circumstances is an act of defiance that permits a person to live his life on his own terms. It is part of the human spirit to endure and give a miracle a chance to happen" (p. 81). It was belief in hope that I was trying to convey to all of those people listening to me at the Luminaria Ceremony as I told my story about my wife. Some took Kleenex out of their pockets and wiped away tears. Perhaps their tears weren't just for Nya but also for the memories of those they had lost or the lives they were celebrating.

At the end of my talk, I introduced Magic to the audience. She may not have understood what was said during the twenty minutes prior to her entrance, but her maturity and warmth projected onto the field. She was now an adult dog, but her love for life and people had not changed since she was a puppy. The audience was surprised to see her and equally as astonished when Magic carried a bouquet of roses over to her best pal, Nya, who was standing nearby. They embraced, and after Nya took the flowers from her, Magic put her paw out to be held. Like any other day since she was a puppy, they were connecting. My talk had ended, but images of the two of them together continued to resonate. Their connected paw and hand represented a unique symbol of hope; the interlocking of souls signified the hope for a healthier tomorrow, a hope for life and living.

Some years after that talk, I spoke to a cancer survivor. She told me that, during her recovery period, what she despised the most from others was hearing their negativity. "I hate to be around Eeyores!" she exclaimed. Eeyore is the donkey in the

Winnie the Pooh stories who seemed to always see the negatives in life. "I don't want to be pitied. I am still living, and I want to be surrounded with people who are upbeat and positive." Her story inspired the name of this chapter. When we think of Pooh, we reflect upon the relationship between a teddy bear and the love he shared with his friend, Christopher Robin.

This chapter has two major dimensions. It briefly explains the biology of hope and how this outlook nurtures healing and quality of life. This discussion is followed by stories that illustrate how our love and commitment to our companion animals can be the impetus for finding hope in life and returning to a better place. I call this place Pooh Corner, where life continues to be normal — or, if we dare, better than normal. Pooh Corner is a calm space filled with warmth and love. Magic may not have taken Nya to a new physical place, but Nya was in a better mental place because of her relationship with Magic. This dog helped her find her Pooh Corner.

THE MAGIC IN HOPE

For some people, hope is all they have. Goethe once said, "In all things it is better to hope than to despair" (Sundberg, 1998, p. 34). Hope gives meaning and purpose to moving forward in life. Without hope, how can we optimally exist? Most of us would agree that we cannot live an optimal life without hope. It is a frame of mind, a belief that becomes the foundation of our spiritual survival. Hope provides us with the energy that often pulls us out of despair. It integrates living in the moment with a sense of optimism for a better tomorrow. Hope nurtures our soul and fills it with faith and passion for life. It is that mindset, which includes a sense of optimism, which allows people to climb back into life and persevere.

In their book, *The Human Side of Cancer*, Holland and Lewis (2000) state that only in recent years have oncologists begun to squarely confront the emotional impact of cancer and its treatment and understand the fact "that emotional states of people play a large role in the acceptance of treatment and perhaps in the outcome as well" (p. 68). According to Norman Cousins, in his book *Head First: The Biology of Hope and the Healing Power of the Human Spirit* (1989), a strong will to live, along with other positive emotions such as faith, love, purpose, determination, and humor, are biochemical realities that can affect the environment of medical care. Cousins suggests that positive emotions are no less a physiological factor on the upside than the negative emotions are a factor on the downside.

Jerome Groopman (2003) points out there is no real specific definition of hope, but he does explain that a healthy amount of hope can block pain by releasing the brain's endorphins and enkephalins. These neurotransmitters actually mimic effects that are similar to morphine and help us feel better and more at ease. Hope helps us build our resilience and armor to cope with daily challenges and fears. It is hope that inspires the courage to overcome fear.

According to Cousins (1989), brain researchers now believe that the body and mind are closely intertwined. What happens in the body can affect the brain and vice versa. He suggests that hope, purpose, and determination are not merely mental states; rather, they have electrochemical connections that play a large part in the working of the immune system and, indeed, in the entire economy of the total human organism. Cousins offers that positive emotions might provide a buffer against the immunologic effects of stress, possibly reducing the risk of disease. What this really means, according to Cousins's work, is that any progress regarding coping with a disease involves not denial of its existence, but "rather a vigorous determination to get the most and the best out of whatever is now possible" (p. 78). Even the most positive attitudes are no guarantee of a cure, but they can help create an environment conducive to receiving and responding well to medical care and can enable an individual to get the most out of whatever may be possible. From all of this comes a simple idea: having something meaningful in our lives, such as the companionship of a loving pet, helps us maintain a more hopeful and positive outlook on things.

Richard Davidson, a professor of psychology and psychiatry at the University of Wisconsin, explains in *Emotional Life of the Brain* (2012) that hope is an emotion that consists of both cognitive and emotional aspects. When we hope for something, we employ our thoughts or cognition to configure what we are thinking about. More importantly, hope provides what Davidson calls an "emotional forecast," which allows us to feel more comforted because we believe something positive is out there for us.

IMPLICATIONS FOR HOPE

Although I have been in the field of human-animal interaction for decades and have witnessed how the power of companionship and love can help people in need, it really wasn't until after I witnessed the impact Magic had on my wife that I became convinced of the power of the bond, or what I'm now calling storge (*see* Chapter 1, p. 19).

Perhaps in the future, improved scientific research will help us prove and explain how these relationships make tangible differences in people's lives. Unfortunately, today scientific skepticism in using words such as "love" in a medical context still persists. As many of us realize, however, faith and belief are positive alternatives to negative thinking, and for some of us, faith alone is what allows us to heal and move forward. Like homeopathy, perhaps faith can be an alternative in the healing arts.

Albert Einstein once stated, "Everything that can be counted does not necessarily count; everything that counts cannot necessarily be counted" (see References). Several aspects of life often leave us stumped when we're trying to decipher why certain things occur. Nevertheless, we continue to witness the healing effects of relationships. Although some may need more thorough explanations of why these outcomes occur, for many of us, just witnessing the experience is proof enough. As Ann Berger, M.D., chief of pain and palliative care at the National Institutes of Health (NIH) in Bethesda, Maryland, says (in a personal communication), "They see a patient with a pet, and watch their patient's face light up. That's just not a small thing to ignore. It's a big deal for most people who understand and appreciate the outcomes that love from an animal can give."

In *The Handbook on Animal Assisted Therapy* (2010), Dr. Berger and I co-authored a chapter wherein we discussed the differences between curing and healing. Although some may see these two terms as somewhat interchangeable, they actually are not. We suggested that practitioners always hope to cure patients from their illnesses. Beyond curing a patient, however, we hope for that individual to also be healed, meaning that he learns to enjoy a more meaningful quality of life. "When a person can't be cured, one can still die healed — having a sense of wholeness as a person. We may not always be able to add days to lives, but we can add life to days" (p. 303)."

The statement of adding "life to days," especially for those who may have limited time in their lives, is of utmost importance. The following examples tell the stories of people who have found this solace and relief in the form of a companion animal. Research has demonstrated over the past thirty years that our relationships with pets can enrich life, especially in times of medical difficulties. Pets can act as a social support and help us find meaning in daily living. In a paper by McNicholas and colleagues (2005), the researchers found that relationships with pets seemed to have a positive impact when patients were coping with the early stages of bereavement, as well as after the treatment for breast cancer. The researchers suggest that, although support from an animal should not be considered as a sole alternative to help those in need, pets have certain advantages, especially in their ability to demonstrate consistency in the relationship.

According to David Spiegel (1996), a leading psychiatrist from Stanford University, people with cancer, and perhaps with other illnesses, benefit from psychosocial support to augment medical treatment. He argues that the literature has shown these supports to improve cancer outcomes and quality of life. Social supports such as expressive therapy help people build bonds, detoxify and demystify dying, help reorder life priorities, and manage symptoms. As discussed in the previous chapters, our relationships with others, including our connections with animals, can act as a strong social support. Many people struggle daily to find a sense of happiness and normalcy in their lives. The following three episodes illuminate this position.

LESSONS LEARNED FROM ANN

Even before Nya developed cancer, I was keenly interested in the roles of pets and visiting animals with people who had chronic and terminal illnesses. During this period, I met many like-minded people, one of whom was Dr. Ann Berger (mentioned above). Ann is a true believer in complementary and alternative therapies in supporting her patients, and she sees a strong role for animals in the lives of her patients. Originally, I thought that this belief stemmed from her professional curiosity, but I quickly learned that Ann's insights on the value of pets also come from her own life experiences.

Ann has had numerous health challenges in her life and has used her positive outlook and her deep faith to help her adjust. In 1999, she was diagnosed with breast cancer, and in January 2000, she had a double mastectomy. In 2007, Ann found herself easily fatigued. After looking into the matter, she ended up requiring heart surgery at Johns Hopkins University. She had a congenital heart problem that apparently had existed since her childhood but had never been identified. Today, Ann continues to battle her ailments and now has other health-related issues. She finds it difficult to breathe at times; recently it was discovered that she has a neuromuscular disorder similar to muscular dystrophy. Now, with the support of a ventilator at home, Ann is able to breathe more easily. Despite these many challenges, what has never changed in this remarkable woman is her will to live and her desire to lead a fulfilling life!

Ann believes animals can help people become happier. In a personal communication she said, "They are a good distraction, and their interactions may decrease pain for a short period of time." She believes that relationships with animals bring normalcy into periods of life where normalcy has abandoned people. She accurately describes what many with a chronic or terminal illness may feel: normalcy is what is the most absent for them. Chronically or terminally ill people feel that they have lost control of their lives. Ann feels that interactions with companion animals are wonderful distractions that may help ease this feeling. "When you have this type of visit, you're bringing the two together. In the person's eyes this is an adorable creature. It's something that just feels great."

Ann's quest in her medical practice has always included trying to bring normalcy back into the lives of those who feel discombobulated, and she has had some amazing outcomes from incorporating animal visitations with her patients. She shared with me a tea party she organized for a patient under her care.

The patient was a thirty-eight-year-old woman who initially came in to get a thyroid removed. Upon further tests and observations, however, a malignancy was found. This young woman, who had been set to be married in a month, was placed in intensive care. Needless to say, she was devastated. Ann decided to grab a tea cart she kept in her office and went to the patient's room to break the ice and make the family feel more comfortable, even during this difficult time. In essence, she wanted to project normalcy in the midst of a difficult moment. Ann's belief is that the same rationale should be given to visiting animals.

In our chapter of *The Handbook on Animal Assisted Therapy* (2010), Ann explains that "out-of-the-box" creativity can be used as a provocative and wonderfully constructive structure within an integrative, palliative-care model of relieving chronic pain. This model should take into account a holistic view, with the patient and family always in the forefront. Therefore, serving tea creates a comfortable environment for shifting focus away from suffering, allowing the patient to share a happier, more desirable moment with family, friends, and health-care givers. This offers them a setting to converse, verbalize wishes or concerns, or simply reminisce. Ann has developed numerous other types of special opportunities that she integrates to help foster a milieu of hope. For example, she will use team "theme days" such as sun-fun and Mardi Gras, along with signature hats or boas, as diversions from the white-coat attire patients are so used to seeing. "Spontaneous celebrations of life, such as setting the TV channel to a game played by an inpatient's favorite football team, or sending an outpatient to a performance by his favorite musician, have reminded patients that their life is more than suffering" (p. 307).

In some ways, what Ann and her colleagues do, even if it is only for a few moments or hours, is to allow their patients to revert to a calmer life — what I have been referring to as our Pooh Corner.

In her early days at NIH, Ann encouraged animal visitations as part of the care for some of her patients. The initial policy permitted animals to visit patients but only allowed certified therapy animals. The guideline was eventually changed to permit families to bring in their pets if the patient was actually dying.

Ann notes that we have to find goodness in life, and she has integrated this way of thinking into her work with her patients. In her personal communication she said, "People who are battling illnesses don't want you to only focus on their maladies. They are still living, and many would like to also focus on the positives. For example, some may be asking themselves, 'How do I seal a void in my life? At the end of the day, what gives me purpose?'"

Ann has had three dogs over her adult years, but her second dog, a Bichon Frise named Shomer (meaning Guardian), played an immensely important role in her life. Similar to Magic and Nya, Shomer and Ann connected deeply during her bout with cancer. He sat with her diligently throughout her recovery period: "He laid by my side and never left me. He always paid attention to his humans and their needs." This was perhaps the most salient aspect of their relationship. Shomer always seemed to be looking after the family (especially Ann), while the other dogs in Ann's life had never entirely done that. It is apparent that the attention and pampering Shomer provided strengthened their relationship.

Liberty Hyde Bailey, who is considered the father of modern horticulture, once said, "A garden requires patient labor and attention. Plants do not grow merely to satisfy ambitions or to fulfill good intentions. They thrive because someone expended effort on them" (see References). Just as plants thrive when they are given proper care, relationships are enriched when they are sprinkled with loving care.

As was noted earlier, Ann experienced heart difficulties when she was forty-seven years old and was scheduled for surgery at Johns Hopkins. The family planned to stay in a Baltimore hotel while Ann was recovering in the hospital. Her two children requested that they bring their dogs with them on the trip. Ann's first response wasn't favorable, because she believed that taking the dogs would make it more difficult for her husband to balance the needs of all family members. Additionally, the children were nineteen and sixteen years old, and Ann didn't feel the dogs were necessary. It was her son Stephen (who was actually attending Johns Hopkins at that time) who brought this request to her attention. Stephen adamantly told his mother, "We need the dogs to comfort us; we're scared. After all, we thought we were going to lose you and you would die after your breast cancer surgery. We want them with us now." After hearing her son out, Ann agreed, and the dogs joined the family when she had the surgery. The two of them together helped to bring some normalcy and support back into the family.

Ann told me that her favorite Disney character is Winnie the Pooh. She even has a Pooh bear in her office. This symbolically emulates my perception of a Pooh Corner. Ann leads her life by recognizing the importance of all the blessings life has presented to her. She remains very positive and leads life day by day. In many ways, Ann's narrative helps us all understand how and why she views the therapeutic benefits of animals in our lives. The feeling of normalcy that comes from living alongside these beautiful creatures creates a more healthy quality of life.

DAVID, DEBBIE, AND CHEWY

"Quality of life " is the mantra that David Oliver follows. His story is one of perseverance and determination in finding his silver lining. David was diagnosed with nasopharyngeal carcinoma with metastasis in the lymph nodes and bones, stage IV. Although he is coping and staying positive even with health challenges, he has accepted his fate and knows this cancer will eventually take his life. David says in a personal communication, "I am trying to live every moment rather than die. For some strange reason, because I love life so much, I am not afraid to die." On the other hand, he is deeply sensitive to the effect that his health has had on his wife. He is convinced that the process of watching a loved one die is much harder on the caregiver than on the one whose life is going to end. His mission in his final chapter of life is trying to make provisions for his wife Debbie so that she will be able to move forward. One of his secret ingredients in this transition is a two-year-old Shih Tzu–Affenpinscher named Chewy.

David and I became better acquainted when I viewed a video he and Debbie produced called *Man's Best Friend*. In one segment David expressed his feelings about his illness through the eyes and voice of their two-year-old Chewy.

In the video, Chewy sums up how David feels and suggests what he believes is his dad's greatest concern living with cancer. "He talks to me all the time," Chewy says, "and he constantly tells me 'always take care of Mom,' so I know what my job in life is all about. I need to take care of both of them, and when Dad is gone, to give special attention to her." These powerful words give us a glimpse into David's mind and allow us to recognize his greatest fear: life for his beloved family after he is gone.

David is quick to share his joy and hope in his daily life because of his interactions with Chewy. He says, "When I would come home between chemo treatments (six of them, with twenty-one days between each with horrific side effects), it was Chewy's diligent and warmhearted attention that made my life bearable. Chewy would climb into my lap, lick my face and chin, and, believe it or not, seek out my neck and lick it long and hard." David incredulously wondered, "How in the world does he know that the cancer spread from lymph nodes in my neck to bone?" As we discovered in chapter 5, this natural response may be much easier to explain when we realize the incredible strength of a dog's sense of smell. Chewy may have been drawn to David's cancer because he sensed something different there.

The remarkable relationship David has with Chewy is very touching. In David's words, "To have him snuggle up to me takes my mind off my cancer. He accepts me just as I am, doesn't make me answer any questions, and loves me unconditionally. I don't have to call him to say, 'nap time!' He watches my every move and knows, perhaps before I do, when and where I will be when I hit the hay."

When I awaken and my eyes open, there he is, waiting for me. Who could ask for more?"

David's mantra is living life to the fullest. He seizes and relishes all the moments he has. He is a living testimony to the Renaissance ideal of *carpe diem*. Researchers like Holland and Lewis would agree with this mindset. Their research (2000) stresses that, in order to feel fulfillment in life, we must appreciate every moment, a day at a time. In so many ways, the task of dealing with cancer and other debilitating diseases seems less overwhelming when we break it up into small chunks and find purpose and joy in what we have. This way, we allow ourselves to focus on getting the most out of each day, despite our illness. In so many ways, a glimmer of hope and a personal desire for living is almost self-fulfilling. It nurtures our soul and motivates us to want to have more.

David says that dogs are marvelous companions, but in his case, Chewy's companionship may have taken the relationship to a new level: "I talk to him, share my secrets, hug and snuggle, play and sleep with him; you can't get closer than that. He never talks back, but more times than not, I wish I knew what he was thinking. Those eyes will look at me and I can easily discern happiness, joy, sadness, messages like 'let's play,' and I will swear to it, understanding. The latter comes across when he jumps in my lap, gives me a knowing glance, and curls up for a snooze. He often chooses to do this when he knows I am suffering. During chemotherapy treatments, his snuggles were ubiquitous. I loved it. And now, even in this good period, he continues to comfort me."

Social scientists have also studied the value of companionship and have developed some conclusions. For example, the research by Spiegel and Kato (1996) highlighted that patients with cancer who had the fewest contacts with people each day were 2.2 times more likely to die of cancer over a seventeen-year period than those with greater social support. Bryant (2008) proposes that most humans seek out social support to help them adapt to difficult situations. She believes that social support is an important foundation for healthy functioning and strongly believes that pet companionship should be considered as an excellent alternative for people.

In reflecting upon David's comments, it is critical that we conceptualize and recognize the importance of an animal in the life of a person coping with illness. Pets may often symbolically represent some aspect of the person's life experience or needs (McNac, personal communication). As the end of our life approaches, we may lose more and more of our autonomy as we become increasingly dependent on caregivers. When we have a strong attachment to our pets, a deep symbolic meaning is tied to these relationships. For some of us, the animals in our life are every bit as important as other family members, particularly at the end of life.

Dr. Edward Creagan (2002), a professor of medical oncology at the Mayo Clinic, agrees with this position and fiercely argues that an indisputable mind-body connection is anchored by pets. While presenting at the PAWSitive InterAction Conference, he said, "I prescribe pets to a third of my cancer patients to help them cope with the rigors of their terrible disease. I consider getting a pet to be one of the easiest and most rewarding ways of living a longer, healthier life" (Creagan, 2002). Dr. Andrew Weil, a prominent physician in the field of integrative medicine, echoes this comment in a personal communication: "Living with companion animals reduces focus on self." He believes that excessive focus on our self undermines health and suggests that interacting with companion animals helps neutralize the harmful effects of stress. Both of these points are applicable to David's testimony.

Chewy's life allows David to focus on the well-being of another creature rather than solely on his disease and resulting ailments. Instead of being the one to receive and require caretaking during his battle with cancer, David has become a caretaker himself, looking after and sharing his time with his beloved pup. For example, Chewy needs walks every day. In fact, Chewy makes David and Debbie get out for a walk at least four times a day, which translates into forty minutes of exercise. Chewy also seems to refuse to relieve himself in their own yard; instead, he insists on being walked so he can soil the neighbors' yards — and, of course, the further from the house, the better. This means that David and Debbie usually have to walk a decent distance prior to Chewy being satisfied and comfortable in relieving himself. David also humorously shares that Chewy meanders all over the neighborhood, introducing himself to the other dogs and their owners, and "they, in turn, ask me how I am doing, ruffle the back of Chewy's head, and share the latest neighborhood gossip. Chewy won't let me disengage or withdraw from anything. He is a magnet attracting others, and I have become, over time, very grateful for it."

It is a definite fact that many of us are positively impacted by the attentiveness that animals give us. Their unconditional attention, or as my friend Gail Melson calls it, "thereness," can be extremely powerful to anyone who is in need of "refuge from the strains of human society." We can see how Chewy provides this form of "thereness" for David and his family.

Dean Martin, one of the members of Sinatra's Rat Pack, used to end his television show with the song "Everybody Loves Somebody Sometime." When talking about his relationship with Chewy, David noted, "I always loved that song and the meaning it has for all of us. Dogs, and I'm sure other pets, can be that 'somebody' to someone. They have for me, and they will for Debbie. The importance of love and affection cannot be underestimated, especially at the end of life. When I hug Chewy, he looks me in the eye, gives me a lick, snuggles closer, and reminds me that I am the luckiest man alive."

David loves Chewy and recognizes how important he is in his daily life. He states, "Licking and loving me is, however, small potatoes compared to what Chewy does for Debbie. When she cries in the middle of the night, he will leave my side and snuggle up to her." One night, while David pretended to be sleeping, he saw Chewy inch up to Deborah's face and begin licking away her tears. David adamantly believes that he and his wife are beyond lucky to have Chewy in their lives, regardless of their grim circumstances: "I'm so happy she will have him when I am gone. Chewy knows she needs comfort and relief from it all."

I had the opportunity to also speak with Debbie about her perceptions of David's battle with cancer. She described herself as a realistic person. Being in the field of hospice care, she understands the condition of her husband's illness. Despite her logical understanding of things, on an emotional level the situation is very different. She admits that this journey has been challenging.

While speaking with Debbie, I noted that it was difficult for her to talk about her husband's illness and the thought of him dying. However, when we refocused our discussion to Chewy, her voice perked up. She laughed as she talked about how Chewy made her take him on walks around the neighborhood. In a sense, Chewy forced her to take care of herself — to go outside and breathe the fresh air around her. Debbie confessed that Chewy not only makes her laugh but has become a wonderful companion and a source of support during this difficult time.

For her, the hardest thing is to think about when David is gone. However, he constantly reminds her that she will not be alone. "Chewy is your dog. He's going to take care of you when I am gone." For now, they are a family living in the moment as best they can and loving each other to the fullest. Their lives are filled with hope and courage to live one day at a time. Although hope may not bring a cure, it will allow them and others who are able to hold onto it to live more fulfilled lives despite dire circumstances.

RICK AND RILEY

In Chapter 1, I introduced you to my colleague, Rick Timmins. Rick is a wonderful person who has a true love of companion animals, and he shared with me his relationship with his dogs. A few years ago, he and his wife, Marcia, had a wonderful opportunity to adopt a dog named Riley, who was about two years old. About a year after they got Riley, Rick was diagnosed with Hodgkin's disease. He was alarmed at this diagnosis of cancer, even more so because his first wife had passed away from lung cancer. Additionally, Marcia's mother had just died a day prior to the diagnosis, so Rick was by himself when he received the alarming news. After returning home from the doctor's office, all he could think about was how he was going to tell his wife and his daughter that he had cancer. Emotionally, he was in an awful place and at a total loss for what to do or say. Upon entering the house, to Rick's surprise, Riley reacted differently to him. Usually, he would greet Rick with an enthusiastic welcome, but that afternoon, he just walked over to him and lay by his side as Rick sat and contemplated his situation. Rick recalls that they seemed to sit like that forever. Riley just looked at him solemnly and calmly. Rick really believed (and continues to believe) that, in that moment, Riley sensed that something was wrong.

Over the next several months, Rick underwent chemotherapy. His body weakened, which impacted his ability to take his usual long walks with Riley, in which Riley would often run off by himself in the woods and not really keep an eye out for Rick. However, as Rick's health changed, his four-legged friend stayed closer. He seemed to recognize the need to slow down and remain nearby as Rick's abilities were now restricted. There were days when Rick didn't feel like getting up and he would stay in bed. On those days, Riley would stay very close by, becoming his nanny, so to speak.

Upon completing his chemotherapy treatment, Rick essentially "hit the wall." He became very weak all of a sudden. Unfortunately, Marcia had gone out of town, leaving Rick home alone. He fainted and landed on the floor. When he awoke, Riley was sitting attentively next to him. Luckily, his daughter had planned to come over that day, and when she arrived, she helped Rick up and took him to the hospital. On that day, Riley had a dual purpose: he nannied and watched over Rick before help arrived, and he provided solace to Rick's anxious daughter as she was helping her dad.

Rick reflected how significant that time was with Riley. His faithful companion gave him the support he needed. As Riley aged, his health declined and their roles reversed. Riley developed gastrointestinal issues when he was thirteen, and he slowed down due to arthritis. It was Rick's turn to be the nanny. The two of them would still walk together, but this time it would be Rick who walked slowly because Riley couldn't walk as fast. Rick constantly watched over Riley because he didn't want him to unduly suffer; he wanted to protect him from the pain he was experiencing, a desire that many of us have when we witness suffering.

One morning, while Rick was reading, Riley came over to him and put his paws on him. He wanted to go for a walk. Rick opened the door and off they went. Their walks were now rare, but Riley seemed to want to go. He moved more quickly that day, and it was a terrific outing. When they returned home, Riley seemed content just lying on the carpet near Rick. That was his last day of life. It is a warmhearted memory that still chokes Rick up when he talks about it.

Hearing Rick recount his life events makes me realize how important it is to capture and treasure even the smallest moments in life. Yann Martel (2001) concluded in his book, *Life of Pi*, "It's important in life to conclude things properly. Only then can you let go. Otherwise you are left with words you should have said but never did, and your heart is heavy with remorse" (p. 279). Rick and Riley were able to say their good-byes, and in so many ways they acted as spirited souls, lifting each other in times of need.

CINDY, BOB, AND MOLLY

In this last scenario, we meet Cindy and Bob. They have been together for more than twenty years, and though they never had children, they did have Molly, their beloved Toy Poodle. They knew she was special the moment they brought her into their home ten years ago. Molly came into their lives after Cindy and Bob had experienced a great deal of loss: Cindy had lost her father and Bob had lost his brother and two close friends. They decided they needed something to bring unconditional love into their lives after these events. Cindy recalls, "From the very first moment Molly came into our lives, there was a comfort level and peaceful feeling that made us feel safe, happy, and fulfilled."

Although Molly bonded quickly with both Cindy and Bob, it became quite evident early on that she was a "daddy's girl." She slept by Bob's head every night and still does. It is not uncommon to see Molly and Bob snoozing together in his recliner or to watch them playing together on the floor. Molly quickly became the apple of their eyes and was instrumental in bringing the couple closer. Molly had such a warm temperament that the couple had her certified as a therapy dog and began taking her to hospitals and convalescent centers. Little did they know how important Molly would prove to be.

Over time, Cindy began to notice that Bob was acting differently. He became very forgetful and didn't seem to be behaving like his old self. He was eventually diagnosed with Alzheimer's disease. As Bob's disease progressed, Molly went from being a therapy dog for others to being a therapy dog exclusively for Bob. At first, Molly would just alert Cindy when Bob was getting into something he was not supposed to, such as the refrigerator. As Bob's condition declined, Molly became more aware and in tune with Bob and began to alert Cindy when he would get up from a nap or in the middle of the night. Molly quickly turned into Bob's protector by making sure she alerted Cindy anytime Bob was in trouble. At one time, Bob had many interests, but now he only seemed to be interested in Molly. She was his link between the past and present and provided continuity for him. Molly also provided Cindy with constant reminders of the good amidst this frustrating disease. Today, Molly is the thread that keeps their relationship together; she is the calm memento of the love in their relationship that sometimes gets forgotten because of the stress of caring for someone with Alzheimer's on a daily basis.

Cindy describes the normalcy and happiness Molly brings to the couple during this very challenging time and shares a story that exemplifies the love Molly gives each day. Molly was sitting with Cindy and Bob in their big living room chair: "For years this was our routine; the three of us would sit and watch TV together. People with Alzheimer's are restless and anxious and can't seem to sit comfortably for long periods of time. This one afternoon in particular, Bob seemed more relaxed than usual as we sat together. For over an hour we enjoyed the program and held hands as we each petted Molly. This was heartwarming to me, and it felt like nothing was even amiss in our home. As we each lovingly stroked Molly, who was now was nestled in our laps (having her head on one of us and her rump on the other), Bob slowly looked over at me and said, 'This is our family.' We both smiled at each other, and as tears welled up in my eyes, I felt in that moment that he was truly present and alert. For that moment he was the husband I remembered — a memory I hold onto deep in my heart."

Today, both Cindy and Molly demonstrate their love for Bob with words, caresses, doggie licks, and lots of hugs. He responds periodically to their actions with an "I love you, too" or "Thank you for taking care of me." One day he surprised Cindy by looking into her eyes and telling her, "I love you without fail." The moment he uttered those words "was a gift to hear, a true gift for all the many long and sometimes frustrating hours it takes to keep his life comfortable and happy. I could never do what I do for him without my Molly by my side and his. She is my saving grace, and I say grace daily as I give thanks to her."

—

"What day is it? It's today!" squeaked Piglet. "My favorite day," said Pooh. These are simple words uttered by a childhood imaginary playmate. They are words that celebrate our existence. In a perfect world, it would be beautiful for all people to be excited about living each day to its fullest potential. This isn't a perfect world, however, and some people's lives are filled with harsh realities. The purpose of this chapter was to learn from people who have had to struggle with harsh realities and have still tried to find the silver lining in their lives. The highlighted stories in this chapter focus on people who found comfort and meaning in their lives with the support of their beloved pets. This was the common thread that helped them persevere in difficult moments. Their admiration for companion animals seemed to bring life back into their battered existence. This isn't as unusual as you may think. Most of us have outlets that help us through difficult moments. For some of us it is our pets; for others, it may be gardening, photography, music, or being around our human family. However, the end result is comparable. The individuals in this chapter have found something to make their lives meaningful. They also have found things that allow them to continue finding normalcy in their existence — something that motivates them to get out of bed every day.

These channels help most of us build resilience to overcome adversity. James Pennebaker, a social psychologist at the University of Texas in Austin, has discovered in his research that people who find meaning in the face of adversity and develop solutions to overcome their struggles are ultimately healthier in the long run when compared to those who do not. How do most of us find meaning in our lives, especially in difficult moments? Sometimes the answer may be staring us in the face, but we may choose not to see it. For the people in this chapter, the common silver lining was the companionship and relationships they had with their beloved animals.

In early April, we took several pictures of Nya and Magic for this book at local parks and a beach in Southern California. I wanted so much to capture the genuine love that they share. I must admit, it was a bit of a selfish act; they are two individuals I dearly love, and I wanted a photo that would commemorate their bond. I believe we captured some special moments, but it may be hard to completely bring to life the true spirit I have witnessed over the years, which is the essence of their relationship. Pictures only capture what can be seen in a given brief moment, but they often don't capture what has been felt. Nevertheless, as you look at the photo of them (at the start of this chapter), I do think it captures their love. You now have the ability to fill in the blanks, so you can appreciate their significance in each other's lives.

It has been slightly more than eight years since the two of them met — two frightened souls who were connected by chance. Who would have fathomed the significance they each would have in each other's lives? In Magic's case, it was moving to a new home and beginning life as a puppy; it was a new start in her journey of life. In Nya's case, it was dealing with the uncertainty of her diagnosis, her surgery, her recovery, and the rebuilding of a life after cancer. Over the years, these two have become lifelong soul mates. Each night I have the tremendous pleasure of witnessing the miracle of their love as I sit and watch them softly engage one another. Both have aged, but their commitment and devotion to each other are still as remarkable today as they were when they first met. Just like Christopher Robin, Nya often joins her four-legged friend in a place we can only enter if our mind lets us. Pooh Corner is a place where we can all go to find tranquility and peace; it is a place that we all could benefit from finding, even if we don't struggle with more serious difficulties or challenges. It is a place that helps us feel appreciated and loved. We should all take moments in our lives to find our own Pooh Corner: the corner filled with those who bring joy, human or non-human. It's worth finding. Close your eyes. Who knows, maybe your "Magic" will invite you to go there now.

CHAPTER SEVEN

OUR "FOREVER" COMPANIONS:
Remembering and Cherishing the Bond

"Say not in grief 's/he is no more' but live in thankfulness that s/he was."
Hebrew Proverb

April 30 may not be the most remarkable day in history, but some astonishing moments and events have occurred on that day. Big Ben stopped at 12:11 P.M. for fifty-four minutes in 1997. That event made international news. The ice-cream cone made its debut at the St. Louis World's Fair on that day in 1904 (a day for which I am deeply grateful). Perhaps the most significant event for Americans that occurred on that date was in 1789, when George Washington gave his first Inaugural Address.

But for two specific families, April 30 now has a completely different meaning. Although their lives were lived in parallel, these two families will always be connected because of similar life events that occurred on that date. One had some warning; the other came very quickly. Here are the two stories.

In one part of California, Steve and Pat sat in silence as they witnessed the last breaths of their beloved Louie. On the early morning of April 30, Louie could no longer stand, walk, or control his bowels. That is when the phone call was made to his lifelong veterinarian, Dr. Cooper. Louie passed on just before noon that Saturday while lying peacefully on his bed next to the family room recliner. Pat and Steve rubbed and patted Louie gently as Dr. Cooper injected the sedative and then the medication that would end his life. Life would become significantly different for Pat and Steve. The loss of Louie would leave a large hole in both of their hearts.

I have known Steve for a couple of years as a colleague at Cal Poly, the university where I teach. Steve is a widely accepted scholar in educational leadership, and although I respected his academic contributions, we became friends because we both loved dogs. Steve was proud of his Louie, and we would often spend moments talking about their adventures and the therapy work that he, Pat, and Louie did with seniors in nursing homes.

Steve and Pat adopted Louie almost on a whim one Saturday afternoon in May 2003. Although they had been talking about getting a dog for weeks and had been poking around the Internet, investigating various breeds, they weren't completely convinced that having a pet in the home was what they really wanted. Neither Pat nor Steve had owned a dog since their childhood years, so in a very real sense they felt they were entering "alien territory." They were excited but also a bit nervous when they pulled into the PETCO parking lot to check out the pet-adoption day sponsored by a local rescue group "Four Paws."

Almost immediately they spotted the most handsome Boxer either of them had ever seen. He looked like the canine version of Paul Newman. As they approached Louie, his energy and affiliation for people was immediately apparent. Small for his age (approximately ten months), very skinny, and with a stubby tail wagging hard, he came right over to them to say hi. He had a beautiful black-mask Boxer face, with arching eyebrows and a perfectly shaped head. He had a peanut-butter fawn coat, his ears were soft and floppy, and he had a white breastplate and four little white paws. Steve and Pat rubbed and petted him, and they received a number of doggy licks. They were smitten. The "deal was sealed" when Louie, exhausted from an afternoon of pets and rubs, curled up and fell asleep on Steve's feet (yes, ON both of his feet). To this day, Pat and Steve remain convinced that Louie chose them and that the foot-sleeping incident was merely his way of saying, "You will do; wake me up when we go home."

When Louie was just about two years old, Pat was convinced that he needed a job — after all, Boxers are a working breed. Since idle hands (or paws) are the devil's workshop, and since Boxers are an exceptionally energetic breed, a job seemed to be just the right thing to satisfy Louie's social proclivities AND just the right thing to provide him with a sense of purpose. A local animal-therapy organization named Paws for Healing caught Pat's eye — and it seemed like a perfect venue for Louie and for them. They signed up for training and before long were weekly visitors to two local nursing homes. Louie took to the work like a fish to water. The patients, many of whom were elderly and without much social contact, absolutely loved him. He nuzzled, nurtured, and licked each and every person who showed an interest. During one unforgettable visit, an end-stage patient with Alzheimer's named Adelle, who for months had shown no signs of awareness or lucidity, opened her eyes, smiled, reached out and petted Louie gently as he rested his head on her lap. Although Louie's impact on the patient was intensely moving, within seconds after Adelle's reaction to Louie, a staff member broke out in tears. "This is the first time since her arrival that Adelle has shown any signs of recognition or emotion," he said misty eyed.

Every week for five years, Louie visited his nursing-home friends, making new pals and touching countless hearts along the way. He loved his job and was never more "at home" than when he was in service to those in need.

Steve shared with me several of the health battles that Louie experienced in the latter part of his life. In August 2010, Louie underwent surgery for a degenerative spinal disc. A few months later, on December 27, 2010, Louie seemed a little slow during his afternoon walk. The family figured that, after several days of holiday festivities, he was understandably tired, so they thought nothing of it. But by the next morning, something had gone horribly wrong. During breakfast, Louie wobbled in circles around the family room, bumped his head into the wall, and was clearly disoriented. He didn't want to lie down, but he could barely stand up. They rushed him to the University of California–Davis veterinary hospital. At first, the doctors agreed that his symptoms were suspiciously similar to those experienced by a dog with severe back pain. They sent him home with medication. Within hours, his condition worsened and they brought him back to UCD. Later that night he stopped breathing. The doctors revived him, but something was clearly wrong. This had to be far more ominous than a spinal injury.

Later that day, a full-body MRI revealed their worst nightmare — three brain tumors, a tumor in the carotid region of the neck, and more degenerating spinal discs. In essence, this was a death sentence, or so Steve and Pat feared. Seemingly out of nowhere, their little boy went from a dog on the mend to a dog about to die. The neurosurgeons were thorough, thoughtful, professional, and simply wonderful as they diagnosed Louie's conditions and explained to them possible treatment options. "What would you do if Louie was your dog?" Pat asked. Simultaneously, both surgeons stated that they would let him go. But Steve and Pat weren't ready. This was too much, too soon. They needed time. After much deliberation and through teary eyes, they responded that if there was any chance Louie could be helped, they wanted to take it. They knew the odds were not favorable, but in no way were they prepared to let him go without a fight.

The brain cancer was clearly the most ominous and immediate threat. The MRI revealed a lesion that looked like a large water balloon in the forebrain and two smaller lesions near the cerebellum. The surgeons explained that, without a tissue sample, they couldn't determine how to treat the lesions other than performing risky and invasive surgery. Steve and Pat took a chance and went ahead with the brain surgery.

After an eight-hour operation, the surgeons emerged from the operating room with both good news and bad. The good news was that they had successfully removed the large, fluid-filled sac and had relieved the pressure on Louie's brain. The bad news was that they were unable to retrieve a tissue sample of the lesion itself. Louie was out of immediate danger, but they were no further along in knowing how to treat his other brain lesions (other than high-risk surgery).

The tumor on Louie's neck was another problem altogether. It had entwined itself throughout the carotid artery and surrounding blood vessels and could not be extracted. Moreover, without knowing the nature and mitigating effects of his brain tumors (the most serious threat to his survival), there was no effective way of treating the neck tumor. After a week of recovery, Louie came home with anti-inflammatory and anti-seizure medications. The doctors were supportive and guardedly optimistic. Steve and Pat were committed to Louie's full recovery and once again for several weeks nursed and attended to him 24/7.

After two months, Louie had once again shown incredible resilience. He seemed fully recovered from the brain surgery and was back to his old routines. "God willing," they thought, "Louie has beaten the odds." However, the positive gains lost ground. A follow-up MRI in late February revealed that the brain tumor had returned. The doctors stated that he had days, or perhaps a few weeks, to live. The end came on April 30. As Louie received the medications that would end his life, Pat softly sang his favorite bedtime song, "Nighty night, sleepy sleep, Mommy loves her good boy," while Steve whispered in his ear, "Daddy loves you forever" and "You're my best boy." They both struggled to hold back their tears because they didn't want to upset Louie, but as he drifted away, they couldn't help but think that he knew what was happening.

After a few moments, Dr. Cooper took out his stethoscope and checked Louie. "Everything is quiet," he said softly. For the first time in several months Louie looked genuinely at peace. And then for Pat and Steve, the tears came.

On that same Saturday, in a different part of the state, not knowing what was occurring at Steve and Pat's household, I, too, was about to experience a devastating outcome. It was 11:20 A.M. I was growing impatient and anxious, waiting for a call from my wife. You see, our oldest Golden Retriever PJ (ten and a half years old) had become overly lethargic over the past few days. She hadn't been in any apparent discomfort, but a clue for us was the evening before when she didn't finish her dinner. Anyone who was familiar with my beloved PJ knew that she loved food as much as I did. She was known never to refuse food. My wife called and was able to get an appointment for PJ with our veterinarian at 10 A.M.

I was waiting at work for the call. It was not unusual that visits would take that long, so I stayed positive. I even went out for a few minutes for a break, and when I returned, I received the dreaded message. It was vague but seemed very urgent.

The news was devastating. PJ had a large mass around her kidney and spleen. She was bleeding internally and had only 12 percent of her blood left in her system. The prognosis was bleak. I told my wife that I would be right over. Before leaving my office, I rummaged around, looking for a short children's story that I had read to all of my dogs before their passing. Although in my heart I was still trying to find hope, I was preparing myself for the worst-case scenario. The end was coming sooner than I ever imagined, and saying good-bye to my "forever dog" would be the hardest.

Saying good-bye to all of my beloved companions has always been hard! Over the years, I've had to do this several times, and although I loved them all dearly, PJ was different. We just had a very unusual, amazing bond. She was my "forever dog!"

PJ was my beloved pup who entered my life after the death of my first therapy dog, Puppy. Puppy was terrific at helping people feel at ease, and we were very closely connected. We had been inseparable for more than ten years; wherever I was, she was by my side. We were soul mates. When she passed away, I was heartbroken. Six months after her death, my sons presented me with an incredible gift. They knew how much I missed my old buddy. Their gift came packaged in a simple card.

> We don't have your gift in this envelope, but this is the best present we will ever give you. We will see your "golden" smile again because this is a certificate for a new "Golden Puppy" who isn't yet born.

In 2008, I wrote an article for *Dog Fancy* in which I explained the significance of this wonderful gift.

> Once I became open to a new puppy in my life, I passionately got involved. A couple of months later, I witnessed the birth of her litter. I immediately fell in love with a light blond Golden identified only with a red piece of yarn around her neck. I decided to involve some of the children I worked with in selecting a name for Ms. Red. Eventually, I opted for a touching suggestion by an eleven-year-old patient. "I have the best name in the world, Dr. Fine. Why not name her PJ? Although she will grow up and be her own dog, naming her Puppy Jr. (alias PJ) will keep Puppy's spirit alive." That day, Ms. Red became PJ. It was perfect; we had come full circle.

Perhaps all of these factors had an impact on our relationship, none more so than our connection. We were just like two peas in a pod. However, like all life events, ours was about to end, at least on the physical side . . . but back to our original story.

When I arrived at the veterinarian's office, PJ was lying on the ground. Although she appeared tired, she wagged her tail and gave me eye contact. My eyes twinkled just seeing her. I immediately lay next to her, and I even coaxed her to eat two small biscuits I had brought along. I spoke with the veterinarian about the prospects of additional treatment and quickly realized that there were few options. The only humane choice was to euthanize her. I told the veternarian that I needed time to have some closure with my good buddy. During those moments, I held her close to my heart and told her how much I always loved her. In my heart, I knew I told her this often, but I also knew time would cheat me out of doing so tomorrow. Shortly after that, we went through the process. In only a few moments, her last breath was taken in my presence. I remember the veterinarian saying that she was almost gone but that she had a strong heart. Although at that moment my own heart was breaking, I smiled and said, "You got that right." In only a few moments, my life had changed forever. I went in to hold onto my dear friend, and I left carrying only her collar, a baggie of some of her fur, and a mind full of memories of a life I would never forget. For some she may have been just a pet; for me she will always be *"My Forever Dog."*

For both the Davis and Fine families, April 30 would never be the same. Our hearts broke that day and have been mending ever since. I know (and I hope Steve and Pat do as well) that, in time, we will heal and be able to put our beloved companions' lives in a different perspective, but for now, both families find themselves pondering their life circumstances and are attempting to move forward.

DOES THE HURT GO AWAY?

Loss is never easy. Over the years, I have mourned the loss of several companion animals. Some have died of natural causes while others have been euthanized. Each death has impacted me differently, and each loss has left its imprint. Does it get any easier? Not really! Each of my beloved companions has blessed my heart. I remember each one differently.

"Remember" is such a cold word. It echoes a past that I dearly want to hold on to. It reflects a period that I want to cherish in my mind for eternity. Will all of my memories of the days spent be enshrined in my mind, or will they gradually fade? These are perhaps just a few worries that many of us have as we lose our beloved companions. We don't want to forget. We feel we owe it to our pet to not forget him — not even one detail. That becomes the challenge. Over time, it is natural to forget, perhaps not the major moments but some of the minor daily occurrences. However, the small moments are what we want to cherish the most, because, as a collection, they comprise our full relationship.

Death may be more easily accepted when we have watched our companion suffer, and we feel a sense of relief when the end comes. All of us know when our companions suffer. They don't act like the partners we have known over the years. We often respond to loss with a wide array of emotions. Nevertheless, over time, most of us do heal and work through our emotions. We find ourselves understanding and accepting loss.

Loss can be devastating. While grieving is experienced differently for all of us, the outcome is usually the same — a sense of pain and emptiness. Rachel Remen, a nationally recognized physician and prolific writer, views grieving as contributing to

my forever friend

PJ

Dogs are not our whole life,
but they make our lives whole.

-Roger Caras

our recovery. She writes in her poem "Choosing Life Again" that "Grieving is not about forgetting. Grieving allows us to heal, to remember with love rather than pain. It is a sorting process. One by one you let go of things that are gone and you mourn for them. One by one you take hold of the things that have become a part of who you are and build again".

I like this explanation but also know that the process can be very painful and complicated. We mourn because we FEEL the hole in our heart that needs to be mended! We mourn to preserve the memories of the departed so they will be transformed into our personal treasures. However, as Dr. Remen points out in her poem, we grieve so we don't allow ourselves to get caught in our past.

We mourn because we are afraid of the uncertainty of the future. I remember many years ago when I worked with a young mom whose child was experiencing a serious behavioral disorder. During a frustrating moment in her visit, she uttered, "Will there ever be sunshine after this hurricane?" Her words have resonated in my mind for more than twenty years now, as she sat next to me, hopeless about what her tomorrow would bring. We spoke for several minutes, and by the end of our conversation, she felt some hope for a better tomorrow. Her words echo what many of us feel in our time of loss. Will there ever be sunshine in my life again? How will I live my life without my loved one? In time, most of us do realize that the sun will continue to set and that the tomorrows of our future will have many new events in store for us.

The death of each of my pets has left a hole in my heart. All of the losses have been hard. Love has no boundaries in my household, and all of our companion animals have been significant members of the family. As such, each loss is painful. I have always wondered why I renew my love with other pets, logically knowing that my heart will be broken again. However, I've come to realize that, in the end, the unconditional love that I share with my four-legged and winged family members is worth the painful emotions I may experience at the end of their lives! They are a blessing to me, and I must cherish what I have while I have it.

Perhaps what makes the grieving for an animal companion more challenging is society's lack of appreciation about the strength of the bond between companion animals and their guardians. How often have we heard, "Why are you so miserable? It was only a dog," or "Just go and get a new one." As such, many of us aren't comfortable publicly mourning our loss because we're afraid of being misunderstood. Our society has still not sanctioned grieving the loss of an animal, which seems only to compound the problem. Perhaps in time we will see this become a more accepted practice.

Unlike the ceremonies performed when fellow humans pass on, ceremonies are not usually performed to allow us a sense of closure when a companion animal dies. Companies don't traditionally provide bereavement days from work for the loss of an animal. Some of us believe that others will look at us oddly if we asked for that formal time. We end up feeling embarrassed, and instead, we conceal our feelings rather than deal with them. I can't count the times I have talked with people who have lost their pet and then have hidden their emotions because they feel that others won't understand.

SAYING GOOD-BYE TO MY GRANDFATHER AND PUPPY

My first experience with the death of an immediate family member was my grandfather, who died only a few days before Yom Kippur, the Jewish Day of Atonement. My grandfather was a very important person in my life. I didn't grow up with a dad, and in many ways he was my surrogate father. I remember flying home the eve of the Holy Day with tears in my eyes. I use the story of my grandfather's death to segue into discussing another difficult day in my life — the death of Puppy, my first therapy dog and the namesake for PJ. Puppy started to show significant signs of aging by the end of 1999. She tired more easily and was often found napping in my office. She had aged gracefully, and my "girlfriend" was now a beautiful "grand dame."

On the eve of Yom Kippur, almost seventeen years after I flew home for my grandfather's funeral, Puppy had begun to decline significantly. In fact, she had been struggling the entire week, but on that day, she couldn't keep much food or water down. Many years later I would begin to understand that the dying often refuse food and water as a way for the body to prepare for the end of life. I sat with her for several hours, getting her to occasionally lick an ice cube. By early morning, the end had almost arrived. At about 8:15 A.M., with Puppy's head in my lap, her heart stopped, and in a moment she was gone. I cried like a baby.

As I explain in *Afternoons with Puppy* (2008), "It was Yom Kippur, another Day of Atonement — another year when death paid a visit as it had seventeen years before to my grandfather, and, as I did so many years earlier, I went to the synagogue that morning with a feeling of emptiness and a bruised heart."

I bring up this story because, in most cases when I told people what had just occurred, they remained silent. They didn't know how to respond. However, one friend who also was a true dog lover sat with me and listened. He understood, and for the moments we sat in silence that morning, the bond between us was enhanced.

A few months prior to Puppy's passing, I had agreed to present a lecture at the National Conference in San Francisco on "Pets Are Wonderful Support." I had almost finished the entire PowerPoint presentation prior to Puppy's death, and many of the slides had pictures of her. As I explain in *Afternoons with Puppy*:

> I almost cancelled speaking at the conference because I thought it was
> too soon to share my personal impressions of the value of animal-assisted

interventions. However, I decided that if I kept the talk more informational, I could avoid becoming emotional. As I stood before the audience, I was surprised that I didn't feel any emotion when discussing Puppy's contribution to my therapy work. As the lecture progressed, I became more confident that I could share more intimate details. I couldn't have been more wrong.

At the end of the lecture, I decided to tell a story about one young boy named Alex who had been very moved by Puppy's death. I told the audience how I could still see him looking at me and innocently asking, "Will I ever see her again? Is she in heaven, Dr. Fine?" And then he said, "I really hope she is okay. I miss her." I told the audience that at first I was speechless. How to respond? Somehow I managed to pull it together and have a good discussion on death and loss. Alex told me, "She made me feel at home, Dr. Fine, and that is what I will miss the most." I went on and explained to the crowd, as I had to Alex, that Puppy was a blessing.

Although he and I would never see her again physically, she would be in our hearts forever. As his eyes filled with tears that afternoon, he looked at me and said, "I am happy that I met her. I will miss her a lot. Things will be different around here without her. I will say a prayer for her tonight. I know she is making a new home in heaven." I spoke to my audience of how I knew Puppy's influence on Alex would continue to bless him forever.

It was the word "forever" that did it. For the first time in my professional life, I began to weep in front of my audience. I was so embarrassed about becoming emotional, especially in front of such a large audience, that I looked down at the floor. I had thought I could avoid those emotions. I was hesitant to look back up. What would I see — laughter, pity, and people flying up the aisles in a hasty retreat? But I had to finish; I had to make an exit. I took a deep breath and looked up. No one had left. All of them were sitting quietly, and many were crying right along with me. Death has the power to bond us all together.

On October 19, 2000, I went to San Francisco to give a lecture and was joined by my peers, by other professionals, in holding a memorial service for Puppy. I realize now that I had never truly grieved, that I had put it off in telling only of her death and my effort to comfort my patients during their loss.

It now has been more than eleven years since Puppy died, and I continue to think about her and that lecture of October 2000. However, I now see her loss much differently, not because I miss her any less, but because the immediacy of my loss has changed and I have had time to put her life in a different perspective.

EMOTIONS OF LOSS

We all will feel various emotions when our companion animals die. There really isn't a formula to explain our individual responses, because we all respond differently to death. The intensity of our grief often depends on how attached we were to our pet and where our companion animals fit into our lives at that time. Research suggests that attachment and the intensity of our relationship have a direct association to our grieving. The closer we are to our pet, the more significant our response may be (Podrazik et al., 2000; Sharkin and Knox, 2003).

Our reaction to our pet's death is also related to whether or not he was older and died of natural causes. While this sort of passing can still be devastating and painful, it is more expected (Melson and Fine, 2010). Death of an older companion animal is an unfortunate facet to the circle of life. However, when death occurs because of euthanasia, some of us may feel guilty, especially if we are left with doubt. We may begin to second-guess our decision and wonder if we could have done something differently to prevent that final outcome. Veterinarians traditionally try very hard to discuss health-care options with guardians. Some do explain when the animal's health is so frail that the kindest thing we can do for a pet is to induce its death humanely through euthanasia. On the other hand, when a pet dies from an accident, our sense of guilt may rise exponentially, especially if we believe that the death was due to our negligence.

When I talk with individuals about their loss, they often share their preoccupation or obsession with thinking about the deceased. That fixation may continue for quite a long time and may cause numerous side effects, including sleep challenges, absentmindedness, and withdrawal. Anger, a sense of numbness, hopelessness, and even helplessness are other emotions that we may experience.

STAGES OF MOURNING

A few months after PJ passed, I decided to attend a workshop on death and grieving with David Kessler. David was a student and close friend of Elizabeth Kübler-Ross, the individual who is best known for putting a face to how we understand death today. Her theory explaining the stages that we may experience when we lose someone close to us gives structure to our concept of what is normal grieving and mourning (Kübler-Ross, 1969, 2005). These stages identify the feelings that we go through and provide a recipe for understanding what we can expect when we lose someone dear to us. In most cases, many experts agree that the process of grieving includes accepting the reality of our loss, realizing that the loss may cause painful feelings, and eventually adjusting to a new life without our animal companion.

Kübler-Ross identifies the first stage as denial, a defense mechanism that we use to avoid reality. For example, when a pet becomes gravely ill, we may question the diagnosis. How many of us have gotten a second opinion when our pets have had a devastating diagnosis? We are hoping for an alternative finding and don't want to believe what we are told.

After the denial stage, Kübler-Ross identifies four other possible stages. The anger stage highlights the frustration we may encounter because of the helpless feelings we experience. We begin to question why and lash out as a consequence. The strongest emotions are released in the anger phase, but our anger may be expressed at any point during the illness or at the final outcome.

Bargaining is highlighted during the third stage, when some of us may try and ask for a second chance. I recall feeling that emotion while I was sitting in the veterinarian's office with PJ. Although we had a short time, I discussed every possible option before we selected the final alternative. I remember when my first dog Goldie battled cancer; it was very hard for me to make a decision. Goldie was my first dog, and the end of his life was my first experience with death — an outcome that tore my heart apart. Although I knew he was very ill, the responsibility for the decision was so hard to put into action. Once my wife and I made the decision — because we realized how much pain he was in — we arranged for a veterinarian to come to our house to perform the procedure the following week. I had not met this veterinarian before, but we had been told that he was very empathic.

That week I spoiled Goldie. We spent most waking hours with each other. His last night in our home, I slept by his side. There were moments when he gazed into my eyes, wondering why I wouldn't leave his side. When the veternarian came over the next day at the lunch hour, Goldie and I were in his favorite spot of the house, under the table. The veterinarian noted that he could examine Goldie one more time before he would perform the act. It was as if I went through all of Kübler-Ross's stages in five minutes or less. I wanted to bargain and hope that everyone would be wrong, but the bargaining wasn't going to help that day. Once the veterinarian also agreed with everyone else's diagnoses, we talked about what was going to occur next. Goldie rested peacefully on my lap and didn't seem to mind the moisture that was coming from my eyes. His passing would be my first experience with euthanasia, and I will remember that day for the rest of my life. I actually read him a story about always loving him and inscribed a note in the book to memorialize Goldie. The book now has four other inscriptions on that page.

According to Kübler–Ross, the final two stages involve depression and acceptance. When we are depressed, tears flow more easily, and daily activities may be harder to perform. Depression is a normal outcome, but if it is pronounced, pervasive, and more long-term, additional support may be necessary.

When we reach the stage of acceptance, we try to move forward, which eventually may include sharing our heart once again! We accept our loss as we integrate the memories into our life without our pet. By talking about the departed, their souls are never entirely lost. Their memories are intertwined into ours forever. In this way, we find a lasting connection with our loved ones while we embark on our new life without them.

Psychologist J. William Worden (2009) explains mourning somewhat differently from Kübler-Ross. He doesn't view mourning as a series of stages but rather as four tasks that we attempt to work through as we grieve. In his research, he found that mourning wasn't really a state of mind but instead a process that we all need to go through to reach a point of closure. The process begins with an attempt to confront the reality that our loved one is gone. The task can be cumbersome and painful for some and may take a long time to work through. The second challenge or task is confronting the pain of grief. During this task, we need to feel the honest pain and navigate through it. Later in this chapter, I'll highlight strategies that can help us during this portion of grieving. Many believe that it is counterproductive to suppress the pain and not deal with it. When we suppress feelings, grieving does not sink in and delays the healing process.

The latter two tasks deal with our ability to move on and make healthy adjustments to our lives. Worden explains that the third task is adjusting to a life where the departed is no longer there. In Task 3, we are confronted with rebuilding our lives, and the last task is moving on and investing our emotional energy into a new life. Although it may be hard to imagine that this can actually occur, many of us have found love once again in a new relationship while holding on to positive memories of a time gone by.

The process of mourning allows us to confront grief. It provides the time we need to adjust to a new journey in life. The mourning period allows us to deal with loss and put it into a new perspective.

COURAGE TO MOVE FORWARD: LIFE AFTER LOSS

Is there such a thing as "closure" after the loss of a loved one? There is nothing simple about death, and moving forward is equally as complicated. When we feel love in our heart, and when that is taken away, it is only natural that we feel pain. And the pain is different for each of us. Reaching a sense of closure may be easier for us than it is for others. But with time, most of us will learn to accept loss while preserving and honoring the memory of our departed loved one.

We all cope differently when we move forward toward developing closure. Some of us may find it helpful to talk with others, while others may want to be left alone for awhile. I still remember talking with a friend of mine who had a wonderful yellow Lab. Whenever I wrote her notes, I'd close by writing, "Dogs leave their paw prints on your heart forever." When her Lab passed on a few years ago, she wrote me that, although she loved and missed him so much, she couldn't feel the paw print on her heart. In fact, she felt a hole that needed to be mended. Writing her emotions and expressing her thoughts were helpful in her journey of recovery. She wanted to let me know how she was feeling, and by listening I allowed her to express these pent-up emotions.

Not every approach will be embraced by everyone. Individuals will select options that best suit their needs. As such, there are so many other options to consider. Some may find visualization helpful in capturing moments in their mind and revisiting them, while others might prefer to reminisce about events in their pet's life. By reflecting on those pleasurable times, they contemplate how important their companion animal was to them. Some talk freely and openly about their feelings of grief, while others creatively write or draw as an expression of their emotions. Some may find solace in joining support groups to talk with others who experienced similar losses. The end result is that everyone finds unique ways to help in the process of healing. The loss of a loved one hurts at first, but healing does occur. Let's take a glimpse at how some people worked through their emotions.

Let's recall Steve and Pat and their beloved Louie from the beginning of the chapter. They shared with me that, no matter what the "grief experts" say, they believe there is no easy way to cope with the loss of a deeply loved companion. They stated in our interview that "there's no way to close the door, to transcend time and space, or to rectify your feelings of love and loss. For a time, grief simply becomes you." Nevertheless, Steve and Pat found a few options that supported them. A few weeks before his passing, they wrote a letter to Louie's closest friends in the neighborhood to explain the gravity of his condition and to invite them to come by the house to say good-bye. With each visit, Louie "held court" and greeted each friend with a wagging tail and a kiss. These "good-bye sessions" allowed Pat and Steve to share feelings and memories with others who also loved Louie.

Because Louie was a working therapy dog who had established numerous relationships with people in nursing homes, Steve and Pat knew that his passing would cause these individuals great grief. A week after his passing, they identified many of his favorite floppy toys and brought them to his very best friends at the nursing home — and that included patients *and* staff members. With each toy, Pat attached a little note of appreciation. This gesture was emblematic of Louie's kindness and was gratefully (and in many cases tearfully) received by each of Louie's friends. Through this simple action, Louie's work lived on.

Louie was not only a therapy dog but in a very real sense a teacher. For all who knew him, Louie gave new meaning to living in the present, demonstrating boundless joy, and appreciating the little things in life. Pat and Steve donated Louie's body to the veterinary school at the University of California–Davis so that students and doctors could learn about his devastating conditions and through this knowledge help other dogs.

As we can see, Louie continued to "heal" others even after his death. Even today, Pat and Steve still visit Louie's nursing home friends.

Louie's cremated remains are home with the Davis family. They plan to eventually take them to the top of the 500-foot hill behind their home and neighborhood and set them free — just as Louie would want. Above all else, Louie loved to run free, to gaze at the hill behind the house, and to explore the great outdoors and all of its creatures. Moreover, since Louie was "the neighborhood dog," it is most fitting that he spends eternity reigning over his "domain."

I've had the privilege of meeting many guardians of animals. One of my cherished friendships has been with Diana. In fact, if I were to be reincarnated as another species, I would love to come back being Diana's dog. She is such a caring, warmhearted person! My relationship with Diana was kindled over a decade ago when I first met her beautiful Golden Retriever named Savannah. Savannah mentored PJ at the dog park and taught her some of the appropriate puppy manners. She and I quickly became close buddies. Whenever she would see me, she would run over for pets and of course treats. Although we didn't see each other often, whenever we would re-encounter one another, I'd be greeted with a wagging tail, a cold nose, and what I call "the doggy samba dance."

On April 12, 2008, Diana came home and noticed that Savannah had a pronounced limp. She thought Savannah may have injured herself and took her to the veterinarian the following Monday. To Diana's dismay, X-rays revealed Savannah had bone cancer. Savannah went through amputation surgery to remove her painful leg and this was followed by chemotherapy. Throughout the process, Savannah was a real trooper, and her quality of life didn't seem to waver. Her health impairments made us closer. When I heard about the surgery, I began visiting her weekly. It was like an uncle visiting his niece. She was always was excited when I arrived and was especially curious about what treats I had brought for her. She would even get annoyed with me if I gave her canine siblings too much attention. I was her friend, and I was there for her. These are moments I will cherish forever. Our visits went on for about eight months. Savannah lost her battle on New Year's Day 2009.

Diana was lost without her Savannah. She told me that the day Savannah passed on was one of the hardest days of her life. She fell into a deep state of grief that seemed never ending. During that period, Diana decided that she would do several things to help herself heal and to preserve Savannah's memories close to her heart. These are all strategies that we can put into place to treasure our bond.

Diana put together a rather sophisticated digital slide show about Savannah's life. She told me that, from the day Savannah came into her life, she started taking photos of the times they shared together. Diana felt that a slide-show tribute would be an effective way to relive and capture her memories. She spent four months going over hundreds of photos. Some brought her to tears, especially in those early weeks of working on the slide show. However, Diana felt the tears were therapeutic. It allowed her to express her pain and work through it (very much like we discussed with Worden's tasks). As she became more involved in the project, she found she was smiling more than crying and remembering the happier times they had shared. By the time the slide show was completed, she could only smile, realizing what a treasured life they had experienced together. She also began to appreciate that Savannah's passing would never erase all those memories.

Diana found solace in other venues, including the support she gained from others who were in various Golden Retriever support groups. Many of her friends counseled her and lent her support in her time of grief.

Diana also created a special place to preserve Savannah's life. She had heard about a woman who designed custom urns that incorporated etched photos. The artist captured these memories and crafted an urn that expressed the importance of Savannah's life to Diana. Today that urn is hosted in a special place in Diana's home. Inside the urn are some of Savannah's special mementos, such as her Therapy Dog vest, locks of her fur, her favorite toy, and an angel.

In conjunction with the creation of the urn, Diana reserved some of Savannah's ashes to spread at her favorite beach. Several months after Savannah passed, the family took a trip to Cambria, California, where Diana spread Savannah's ashes in the ocean where she took her first swim and where numerous annual photos were taken. Diana even purchased a lovely locket in which to place some of Savannah's fur. Just wearing the locket and having it close to her heart has brought Diana much comfort.

Maria Milito, a disc jockey in her native New York, found comfort in letters that she received from her listeners and authored a book highlighting several of them. In October 2006, Maria lost her Pug, Clarice. She was devastated. In our talk, Maria revealed the outpouring of support from her listeners when they heard of Clarice's passing. Many sent her e-mails and cards to acknowledge her loss and to provide her with kind words of wisdom. She decided to write *Clarice and Friends … How They Helped Mend the Hole in My Heart* (2011) to share these words of encouragement and to help others deal with their loss and realize that they are not alone. The book incorporates a collection of e-mails sent to her when her Clarice passed away.

Over the sixteen years that Clarice was alive, Maria often spoke of her antics and their bond while on the air. In fact, whenever she made public appearances, she was often greeted with questions about how Clarice was doing. I can relate to that. I sometimes feel like chopped liver when I get reacquainted with older patients. Their first comment usually is not about me. Most often they ask, "How are the girls?" They sincerely want to be updated on their new antics.

Writing has always been a strong therapeutic alternative for people to express themselves and their feelings. When Clarice died in September 2006, Maria posted a blog about her loss that informed many of Clarice's friends. She wrote:

> Clarice the Wonder Pug died peacefully in her sleep this past Monday, about six weeks shy of her sixteenth birthday. Of course she was a very special dog to me, as all of our animals are special to us as they should be — from howling like a mad dog when I played Bob Marley's "Jammin'" to waking up from a coma-like sleep when she heard the sounds of a pretzel bag opening. In almost sixteen years together, we've been through divorce, moving a few times, job hirings, job firings, deaths, and life. The one wonderful constant has been Clarice. And even until the end, she was the Wonder Pug, dying exactly as I had always hoped she would — in her sleep in her bed in our home. . . . after an hour and a half as they predicted, Clarice came home with us . . . this time in a small wooden urn with a place for her photo in the front. Of course she'll always be in my heart as well as yours. That will be one of the most difficult parts, I think. I'll be back with you tomorrow. I just need another day to chill and process the past forty-eight hours.

Maria was surprised at the outpouring of support she received from her listeners. She found comfort and solace from the e-mails. Each note seemed to help her realize that she was not alone. Writing the book was therapeutic. It allowed her to work through her feelings and organize the e-mails in a manner that could help others who have loved their pets and lost them. The book is divided into various themed chapters. Here are two of Maria's favorites, and she explains why they are important to her.

The first e-mail Maria discussed with me was from a person in Nashville, North Carolina, who listens to the radio station online. This e-mail actually was the catalyst for the subtitle of the book. Ellen wrote Maria to express her condolences and to tell her how she felt when her dog Tully had passed on. Ellen noted that she still had difficulty talking about Tully without crying. She let Maria know that it was okay to cry and that over the months the tears would become easier. However, she did emphasize that the pain would leave a hole in your heart. The words "hole in your heart" hit Maria like a baseball bat. They accurately captured the feelings she was experiencing without her Clarice. Maria could speak, walk, breathe, and sleep, yet all of her daily functions were more difficult because of this artificial hole in her heart. Maria found herself using that quote when any of her listeners wrote her about their loss. It seemed to capture what most were feeling!

The second e-mail was from a listener in New York City. Vinny talked about how his girlfriend's cat, Ella, would always walk across the pillows at night above their heads. The night she died, they both felt her walk across the pillows, and then weeks later they heard her bell ringing throughout the house. As Vinny wrote, "The cats have always been there to comfort us before they left, and there's no reason they should stop now." The e-mail struck Maria with its similarity to an outcome she had felt a week after Clarice passed away. That specific weekend, Maria had some family over for dinner. Her sister heard a noise and asked if she had squeaked her sneakers on the floor. Ironically, Maria and her mom had just heard the same sound. The noise was similar to the high-pitched whimpering Clarice would make as she walked around the apartment. Although there was no logical explanation for these sounds, their close connection to Clarice and her everyday presence for the last sixteen years could have created them.

I have also instituted similar remedies to help me cope with my losses over the years. Walking and hiking have always been cathartic for me to work through my feelings. I often walk in the company of my dogs. In these private moments, I find the solitude in the outdoors that helps me express my emotions.

The day after PJ died, I went to a ceramics shop and made a memorial plate in her honor. The store was filled with many young families as I sat with my wife, making the plate (and bugging the salesperson with several questions). The process of making the plate and designing an urn (the same as Diana made for Savannah) was very therapeutic.

Both of these activities helped me express some of my emotions that I may have tried to bury. They allowed me to put my relationship with PJ into perspective and to develop something permanent that would help me store my memories for eternity. Even more important, these actions helped me realize that if I did things to remember PJ's life, she would never be forgotten — a concern that worried me the most.

I also found it helpful to write. A couple of years after my black Lab, Hart, passed on, these efforts culminated in the publication of a children's book, *Give a Dog Your Heart and Love Will Come Your Way* (2010). The book is a beautiful story about my son Corey and his best childhood friend named Hart. The story is a tribute to their bond, and it explores how I helped Corey understand and cope with her death. *Give a Dog Your Heart* allows children to hear Corey's story and learn how he dealt with his loss. In fact, when PJ passed on, many of the ideas that were suggested in the story, including completing the workbook at the end of the book, were extremely helpful to me in expressing my loss. Although the book was written for children, the content is valuable for any pet partner.

As noted earlier, it is also helpful to join a support group. Throughout the nation, several veterinary schools and humane societies provide crisis outreach assistance. For example, Iowa State University College of Veterinary Science has a free hotline that anyone can call at any time. The service is funded by IAMS and is run by veterinary students (1-888-478-7574). Additionally, Cummings School of Veterinary Medicine at Tufts University also has a similar hotline: (508-839-7966). In addition, the website http://vetmedicine.about.com/od/petlosssupporthot-lines/Pet_Loss_Grief_Support_Hotlines.htm is an excellent resource that lists a number of referrals for support groups and pet-loss hotlines.

—

Life does not end with death, especially if we keep alive our memories. Victor Hugo stated, "The tomb is not a blind alley, it is a thoroughfare. It closes on the twilight, it opens on the dawn." Although our companion's physical presence has been taken from us, if we integrate this animal's significance into our lives, his importance to us will never end.

No doubt, the hardest aspect of pet loss is that we fall in love with a species whose lifespan is traditionally shorter than ours. This stance is elegantly shared in Irving Townsend's *Separate Lifetimes* (1986), when he writes "We choose to surround ourselves with lives even more temporary than our own life within a fragile circle, easily and often breached...We still would live no other way. We cherish memory as the only certain immortality, never fully understanding the necessary plan" (p. 172). In essence, we make these loving choices regardless of the fact that, in time, our hearts may break. In fact, when we talk with others about having companion animals in our lives, most respond by saying that the affection and devotion received overshadow loss. I guess heartbreak is the sacrifice we make when we fall in love!

Death is unavoidable, but the sense of despair is optional. All people respond to loss differently and have the right to grieve. The ultimate challenge is how to overcome loss and allow that love to continue to live through you. In time, most of us will heal and realize that between birth and death is something we call living. It is that life — the time between those life markers that we must hold on to so that we can cherish the memories of our departed loved one — human or other.

Isla Paschal Richardson once stated, "Grieve not, nor speak of me with tears, but laugh and talk to me as if I were beside you...I loved you so...'twas heaven here with you." These are the words that we can only hope to follow. We cannot cheat death even if we try, but the realization that we can celebrate and cherish the bond that we have is what makes loss livable. Richardson's message helps ease our consciousness. These are the words that I selected to be etched on PJ's urn. Although it would be wonderful to have her nuzzle at my side, this is the reality I will live with for eternity.

It is now more than two years since my buddy passed on. Never has a day gone by that I haven't spoken her name or thought of her. In each instance (even now as I write), a smile comes to my face and a sparkle in my eye lingers on. My memories of my beloved PJ are still freshly etched in my mind. I would be lying if I said that I don't miss her, but over time, I know I will heal, and the loss will be less painful. PJ's soul and the souls of all our departed companions will bless our lives forever, especially if we allow them into our hearts.

We now have a new family addition named Ketzy. She is an adorable butterball — a fluffy Golden Retriever who bursts with love every moment she is up. Her energy captures what I have loved the most about all of my companions. Her spirit, curiosity, and unconditional love make life more worthwhile. She is Ketzy, a new being, not a replacement. I know I am ready to share love again.

For some, the waiting period is shorter, and for others it will be longer. But when the time comes, we know we are ready! That doesn't mean there won't be some bittersweetness. As the new chapter begins, it doesn't mean that the older chapter closes. My belief is that my life with PJ (and all of my companions over the years) is a part of me. Her soul will radiate in my heart forever. She has made me a better human, and in that vein, a better mate for a companion animal. She has taught me so many things about relationships. For now, I must allow my heart to fall in love again and to respect the position that "all lives have beginnings and endings and it is the middle that we will cherish forever." We cannot be afraid of enjoying and savoring that life. We must celebrate what we have while we have it.

To honor these two special souls, I will conclude by toasting, "Here is to my middle with PJ and my new beginning with Ketzy. May my life become richer because I allow both of you to capture my soul."

As Roger Caras, a past president of the ASPCA, once said, "Dogs are not our whole life, but they make our lives whole." Our animal companions do enrich our lives and bring us great joy! With love, pain does come. Our comfort is knowing the time that we did have, and cherishing those golden memories.

CHAPTER EIGHT

NEVER BE AFRAID OF SHARING YOUR HEART—LOVE WILL FOLLOW

*I*t seems like yesterday that I begged my wife Nya to let me have my first dog. It was 1984 and we had been married six and a half years. I acted like a small, eager child pleading for his first pet, trying to convince her that we were ready for this new furry addition to our family. We talked about getting a dog for almost two years and finally the moment was right. We were ready to add one more jewel to our family! It was probably one of the best decisions we ever made. Goldie introduced us to the countless joys of sharing life with a companion animal, especially if we're willing to share our heart fully. That was more than thirty years ago, and we have no regrets — only gratitude for having our eyes opened to the immense love of a canine companion. Our lives have been changed forever.

Since then, we have had a blessed life living among our family of critters with many glorious days along with, unfortunately, some days filled with great loss and sorrow. Despite this, we wouldn't trade any of these days for all of the tinsel and tin in the world. Collectively, these days have become our life. We now appreciate, more than ever, how our lives become richer when we share it with others. Let's remember that, when we give love, love usually finds its way back to us.

Oscar Wilde once declared, "The only reward for love is the experience of loving. The elation only occurs when we open our hearts to a special someone" (*see* References). It is "this loving" that fills our souls and becomes the fuel that enriches our lives. For those of us who have allowed our hearts to become entwined, we reap the ultimate benefits of the bond — being loved and sharing our love with another being. I have learned over the years to believe that love is blind and doesn't discriminate what can be shared between humans and nonhumans. What *is* critical in our love is our willingness to open our hearts and become connected.

As discussed in Chapter 1, familial love, or "storge," is perhaps the most dynamic aspect of our relationship with companion animals. Our commitment and devotion are fueled by this familial love, which results in a give-and-take between us and our companion animals. This is what makes the bond so meaningful for both parties. When my dogs greet me at the door, I don't wonder if their reaction is because they admire me; I know it is a genuine sign of affection that we both feel toward one another. The familial love that we experience promotes our connectivity. It allows our bond to become an affair of the heart.

I learned many years ago never to be afraid of sharing my heart. Perhaps I experienced this the most when I became a father to two boys. And my love has grown exponentially as I have shared it with my family — both human and animal. When we are willing to open our heart, love will always follow. This is a life lesson I have learned with so many, including my beloved companion animal friends.

LET'S TAKE A TRIP: TRAVELING THE COAST TO FIND THE TRUE MEANING OF THE BOND

"Move over, Charley!" Ketzy and Magic are my co-pilots to Northern California. In the spirit of John Steinbeck and his Standard Poodle Charley, it is befitting to begin this last chapter by following the footsteps of this prolific writer. Steinbeck chronicled his travels with his beloved Poodle to find out the meaning of life in America. Like Steinbeck and his Charley, Ketzy and Magic joined me on a short sojourn up the coast of California to meet a plethora of pet lovers and to help me understand the meaning of companion animals in people's lives.

That was the major intention of our adventure, but on the way, I made an even greater discovery. Just like Dorothy and her whirlwind adventure to the Land of Oz, the yellow brick road that I followed brought me even closer to those I love the most. I saw my girls, Magic and Ketzy, differently with their eyes wide open with excitement — anxious to encounter new places and people. I witnessed the love to be found in the relationships of others; I also was aware of the extreme devotion that I have for my tight-knit pack.

We simply had a blast! Although I spend considerable time with my dogs at work, we rarely take road trips, especially like the one we just took. The joy they both expressed when they jumped into the SUV we rented was priceless. They knew something exciting was going on, but they weren't sure where we were going. Both lay comfortably in the back seat as we rode the coastal highway to Northern California.

On our trip to Carmel, we took a few detours. We stopped for some walking and potty breaks in both Santa Barbara and San Luis Obispo. In San Luis Obispo, after walking the girls in a park near a small creek, we stopped at a small pet boutique where they went in to do their own shopping. Magic immediately headed to the snack bar, where various bones and treats were on display. She was in doggie heaven and let us know which treats she wanted. Ketzy, on the other hand, as the toy connoisseur, ran to the closest rack of balls and toys and grabbed everything she could hold as she vocalized her pleasure. The associates in the shop just giggled as the girls wandered around the store, doing their version of "power shopping." It was like taking a couple of kids into a toy store, but I must confess, the girls acted much better. We left the store with a few yummy treats, a couple of stuffed toys, and Fourth of July bandannas for both of them.

I noticed a large sign in the store advertising a festival in late July called "Golden in the Park Days." In previous years the event was a smashing success. Apparently hundreds of Golden Retrievers and their human caretakers attend and hang out for the day; this year would be no exception. It would have been a fun adventure, but it wasn't in our plans. Today we were heading to the pinnacle of our Land of Oz Tour, which was to visit the Cypress Inn in Carmel, California. Carmel is one of the most dog-friendly cities in the United States, and the Cypress Inn is partially owned by Doris Day — the actress and animal-welfare advocate.

As we drew closer to Carmel and the hotel, Magic seemed more curious than Ketzy to see where we were going. She edged herself closer to the front and lay comfortably between the two front seats. She knew something was up. Magic has always been much more intuitive than little Ketzy, so we wanted to make sure there were not too many surprises in store for her. When we entered the Cypress Inn, it was an eye-opening experience. Just imagine a foyer filled with a carpet of dogs all lying comfortably on the ceramic tile while their human counterparts were talking or oohing and ahing. The girls were delighted to see the jar of biscuits on the reception counter ready for the eager puppies arriving. The treats were similar to cookies that are presented to adults and children at all Doubletree Hotels. In any case, the dogs were excited to have a treat right when they walked in.

This was Ketzy's first time staying at a hotel, so she seemed a little apprehensive when she walked in. There were so many new smells, different surroundings, and a sea of new faces all around. For me, it was amazing to watch my dogs and the other dogs soak in this opportunity. So many questions were racing through my head, including why people would choose to travel to this dog-friendly destination.

Doris Day became a co-owner of the Cyprus Inn many years ago. Today it is a wonderful resort for dog lovers to vacation with their dogs. As such, many veteran customers were sitting in the lounge, sipping wine and eating appetizers with their dogs by their side. In most cases, the dogs were well behaved and comfortable in this environment.

Carmel is a true haven for animal lovers. Everywhere you turn, dogs are walking and people are shopping and dining with their furry companions by their side. We went to several venues and were welcomed with open arms. The highlight of Carmel, at least for the dogs, was the leash-free beach. I wasn't certain what to expect; I knew Magic would be pretty laid back, but I didn't know how Ketzy would react. I knew she'd have a blast fetching the balls, but would she come back when recalled? I'll fill you in on our glorious days at the beach a little later.

The trip to Carmel was personally magnificent! Dogs were everywhere, and there was a tremendous respect for the human-animal bond. I found myself smiling as I witnessed so many living testimonies of people connecting with their companions. Many of the guardians sat by quietly soaking up the pride they felt. Some even posed for pictures. But mostly, it seemed like a regular day as people and dogs just hung around.

For me, this was a great opportunity to travel with two dogs for whom I had deep affection. The older dog has seen much in her life and was obviously excited about being on a road trip, but it was a much different experience for the young one, Ketzy. I will relish the experience for a lifetime. It was like observing a young child on her first trip to Disneyland. So much was new for Ketzy, and everywhere she turned gave her a different adventure. Her eyes were wide open as she experienced an abundance of new scents and sights. Perhaps one of her greatest challenges was the lack of grassy areas in downtown Carmel. Ketzy had to get used to relieving herself city style, which meant finding patches of grass or dirt (and not large lawns). I never realized how challenging this would be to dogs that are used to lots of green space in which to romp and take care of their business. More importantly, I wasn't as sensitive as I should have been to the challenges of urban living, particularly when it comes to caring for companion animals.

LESSONS LEARNED ON THE ROAD

What I learned on our road trip was how much these animals were a part of my life and how much they meant to me. Watching both Ketzy and Magic — one a fast stepper, the other one a bit slower — play, love, and spend time with each other.

I laugh when I think about entering the hotel room. It was somewhat small compared to the space we have at home. When Ketzy wandered in, she panted and appeared anxious. Both my wife and I got her to relax by gently rubbing her back and talking softly to her. We were committed to making this a positive experience for her. When she was about ready to fall asleep, we flipped off the lights and quickly rolled into bed. Early the next morning we woke up and never stopped doing something. We visited the beach several times. Ketzy was a real trooper. She galloped through the sand and had so much fun. What kept her coming back (thankfully) was the ball throwing, an activity she loves.

Ultimately, the trip was filled with encounters of many like-minded people who loved their dogs. These interactions, as well as the sheer joy of watching our dogs love hanging out, made this "Steinbeck adventure" a trip to remember. We met countless people who also felt endeared to their dogs. There was Harry, a Golden Retriever who was almost thirteen, with Jerry and Pam. I met Pam early in the morning as I was quietly leaving the hotel to take Magic and Ketzy on their first walk. Ketzy sat patiently as Pam and I spoke for a few minutes. Ketzy was eager to romp and sniff on the beach, but she remained patient. Pam noted that this was their first trip with Harry to the Cypress, although they had traveled with him to other hotels in the United States. She told me that it was a very special weekend because she and her husband were celebrating their thirtieth anniversary. The vacation wouldn't have been complete if they had left Harry at home. He was aging, and Pam wasn't sure how many more anniversaries he would be with them. So Harry joined the couple as they celebrated their years of marriage together.

Throughout the morning, as both our families wandered around the sites in Carmel, we bumped into each other a few other times. Smiles could be seen from the celebrating couple as they shared their walk with their beloved Harry. He was not an imposition but rather a jewel in their family crest.

What I recall the most about our encounters, however, was turning around as they were about to leave the hotel to go home. Pam gently led Harry back to the car, and as he was about to enter the vehicle, Pam bent over and embraced him. In silence, she seemed to acknowledge how important he was to her and how critical his presence was during their celebration.

Then there was Bella, the Standard Poodle who had breakfast with us. Bella's owner has a neuromuscular disease and was traveling with her dog just because she didn't want to leave her at home with a babysitter. The family travels often, and whenever possible, they like having their dog with them. In essence, taking Bella along wasn't about being responsible; it was about spending time as a family, both human and non-human.

So what did I discover? What information could I share in the spirit of Steinbeck's commentaries on America? A hard act to follow! Perhaps the greatest discovery is that it is more commonplace today to see people taking road trips with their entire family, including companion animals. Vacations today are very different from what they were fifty years ago. At that time, many began bringing their dogs in from their backyards and allowing them into their bedrooms and homes. Does that mean we are more connected to them now? I'm not sure. I do know that it is more acceptable today to openly share our love and devotion to our non-human companions.

Our companion animals provide a social lubricant that reaches across the trivial barriers that keep people from getting to know others. The dogs become an immediate conversation point for many people. They begin chatting, "Hey — nice dog. I had a Golden when I was a kid. How old is she? Where did you get her?" Several people have even stopped their cars in the middle of a busy intersection (perhaps not the safest choice) to comment how beautiful my dogs were. By taking our dogs with us on daily walks, simple errands around town, and lengthy car trips, my wife and I know and enjoy the company of many people who we ordinarily wouldn't have met; when we have a dog with us, who needs Facebook?

When I think of Doris Day, I contemplate my own childhood and the many movies I watched in which she had the starring role. In *The Man Who Knew Too Much*, she performs a song that is apropos to this discussion. "Que Sera, Sera" has simple lyrics, but it does have something to say about our inability to read the future: "The future's not ours to see, que sera, sera." She was right. We never really know where the future will take us, but we can help shape our future with the actions we take today. The words we speak and the actions we take today are creating tomorrow's memories. We just need to make plans and adjustments. The love between animal and human will become as natural as sunshine.

Our road trip perhaps wasn't as monumental as Steinbeck's, nor was it as glorious and as publicized. Nevertheless, for a humble family, we were in awe with what we discovered during our California Coastal sojourn. Love and commitment were in the air, and smiles of joy were abundant. Families seemed more complete when their pets were along for the drive. I cannot tell you how often passersby stopped us, wanting to pet Ketzy or Magic. Then they would reminisce about their pets at home (or those who had passed away), and for a few moments, I received some joy by holding onto my girls.

The most serendipitous and yet eerie discovery on our trip was the unplanned meeting with the spirit of John Steinbeck. Well, not exactly his spirit, but wait until you hear what happened. After spending the morning driving the seventeen-mile scenic route of Carmel, we headed for a short drive to nearby Monterey. Guess what happened? While walking along Cannery Row, we walked smack dab into Steinbeck's statue. I must confess, it was an eerie feeling to see him right in front of me. This was very unexpected. Although he was not physically present, if he could speak, what would Steinbeck tell me about Charley? What words of wisdom would he share about their bond?

The experience felt very much like the recent Woody Allen film, *Midnight in Paris*. In it, Owen Wilson plays Gil Pender, who has the chance to meet many of the remarkable writers from the past. One night he gets lost in the side streets of Paris. At midnight, he gets transported back to the 1920s and meets his literary heroes, including Ernest Hemingway and F. Scott Fitzgerald. He hears firsthand their perspectives on life and literature. In one scene, Hemingway tells Gil, "No subject is terrible if the story is true, if the prose is clean and honest, and if it affirms courage and grace under pressure." Gil listens in awe as his hero shares his wisdom.

Unfortunately, I don't have this same luxury with Steinbeck. It would have been terrific to hear his insights, but I am left only with impressions of what I hope he'd share. Hopefully he'd be pleased about the transformations we are witnessing today in the acceptance of human-animal interactions. But what he would actually say remains a mystery. Any ideas?

HE IS THE GIFT

Years ago, I met David Frei at a fundraiser in New York City. He believed that the critical components to a strong bond with our companion animals related to our connectivity with and respect, commitment, and love for our pets. Many of us know David as the co-host of the annual Westminster Kennel Club's dog show in New York City; however, David is a trailblazer for companion animals, and he is a strong advocate of the therapeutic benefit of animals in our lives. David is the president and chair of Angel on the Leash, a popular visiting therapy-dog program throughout the country.

While we chatted on an assortment of subjects, including the Westminster, he noted that the day after the show, many of the winners visit several of the morning talk shows. Over the years, some of the dogs also have visited a few other venues, including hospitals and the Ronald McDonald House.

David shared with me some stories about various dogs, but one of them stood out. It was about James, the Springer Spaniel who was the winner of the 2007 show. David offered accolades for James in the ring, but most of his commentary focused on James's presence with others. "James was probably the most interactive therapy dog I have ever witnessed," he commented to me. His testimony about James's warmth peaked my interest. I decided to contact Terri Patton (James's owner) and learn more about this remarkable dog.

Terri and I had several wonderful conversations over a month's time as I tried to decipher why David had such high praise for this young dog who died in 2011. Terri was quite open about her admiration for James. You could hear in her voice the genuine love and respect she had for him. She spoke in a loving tone as she reminisced about her little brown dog. The essence of our talk led her to disclose what was the most important to her and to their lives together. It was a simple comment. "Just being with him! James was my gift," she said. His presence was why she fell in love with him, not the trophies. Their souls connected. Many believe that our souls are the highways that connect us to another dimension. Our connection allows us to celebrate and to link in a very special way. This is a process that only those who have been there can truly understand.

Terri often talked about James as her little brown dog. "He was always special to us," she shared. "Even as a puppy, he had an incredible presence of tenderness. It was his inner beauty that captivated all of us. He just drew you in and made you feel complete. Little did we know what the future held for him and us."

The first three and a half years of his life were spent cultivating life experiences that would ground James and teach him to be a gentleman (as Terri remarked) in the real world. Obedience and Rally classes, as well as visits to various senior graduated-care facilities (for persons with dementia and Alzheimer's) and pediatric oncology centers, filled his time. During these visits, his quiet gentleness allowed individuals to connect with him on a deep level. James always seemed to know instinctively who needed him the most, and he really could "work a room" — like a movie star — never leaving anyone out.

At three and a half, and looking the part of a mature show dog, Terri and his handler, Kellie Fitzgerald, thought he was ready for competition. Kellie took him to competitions in Louisville, Kentucky, but his first attempt lasted only three days.

When he returned home, he went back to doing what he loved best — visiting his fans at the elder-care facilities and the children at the hospitals. Even when patients weren't supposed to have dog visitations, they would see him passing by and beg to visit with him. He remained home for another year until Kellie felt he was ready to go back into the ring.

At the age of five and a half, he and Kellie, his co-pilot, started out on a new journey. Little did they know what life had in store for them! The first year of James's career resulted in a rocket-like shot to the top. With so much more potential, he continued his career for another year and made it to the top yet again. He achieved the number-one Sporting Dog and number-two dog in the All Breeds status awards.

Many dogs retire at Westminster, and this was going to be Terri's decision. He already had won Best in Show at the AKC Eukanuba Invitational in Long Beach, California, and an English Springer Spaniel Field Trial Association (ESSFTA) Specialty Best in Show.

The second day of judging at the Westminster in February 2007 meant James would be shown at the Breed level first, then Group and Best in Show levels, all on the same day. He won the Breed and the Sporting Group. After the judging was complete, Dr. Robert Indeglia, a cardiac surgeon, walked to the middle of the ring and told the crowd that he wished he could give all of the seven dogs a Best in Show rosette, but tonight the award had to go to the English Springer Spaniel!

The next day at a reception for James, Dr. Indeglia said that while all of the dogs were stunning, one truly stood out. He commented that, just before James went around the ring for the final time, he looked at him as if to say, "This is MY night and don't you dare screw this up." The entire room shook with laughter. We all know that look that our canine friends can give us. Dr. Indeglia said that it was definitely James's night and that he exemplified breed perfection. But to Terri, James exemplified much more than breed perfection. He was her beautiful little brown dog who had stolen her heart.

James's biggest fans were at a nursing home called The Virginian. They loved "their champ" before he was a celebrity, and they didn't waste any time before they let everyone know how proud they were of him. Terri explains, "We were still at our hotel in New York the day after James's big day at The Garden; they were snowed in! The phone didn't stop ringing!" One phone call stood out. It was from one of the seniors at The Virginian, and she informed Terri that many of them had stayed up the night before, cheering on their pal. She called to ask that Terri bring James to visit them when they returned home. The group wanted to fix him his favorite things and see their "hero." So a plan was made that afternoon.

The first visit James made when he returned home was to his beloved seniors at The Virginian — and what a spectacle it was! You had to be there to believe it. Terri explains, "We barely had the car in park before the residents, many in walkers and wheelchairs and being assisted by aides, lined the sidewalk to see their little brown dog." Terri was awestruck at how deeply James had moved all of these people and how happy he had made them on so many levels.

Then the real treat followed — the residents prepared a lunch fit for a king. The menu included James's favorites like chicken, green beans, and doggy ice cream for dessert. He donned his "snood" to keep his ears out of his food, and he was hand fed his lunch by his doting admirers.

The depth of James's personality allowed him to form close and very special relationships with many people. And James didn't discriminate — everyone was his best friend if they gave him love and attention. He knew how to draw people in. More importantly, he knew how to hold onto them and keep them wanting more. Over the last years of James's life, he brought such tremendous happiness to everyone he met. He taught Terri and others to celebrate every day as if it could be their last. Stories abound of how he touched people in his life. Here we'll focus on three.

Terri and James visited the Detroit Kennel Club show at Cobo Hall in Detroit after his Best in Show win at Westminster. He was there to greet the crowd of thousands who were in attendance. Two one-hour sessions were arranged so that people could meet him. Nearly thirty minutes prior to each set meeting time, the crowd started to form — ten lines deep at one point. Terri was astounded. She shared that a lady in a wheelchair waited patiently near the end of the line, eager with anticipation. She was very chatty and let the people around her know how excited she was about meeting her canine hero. As time passed, Terri asked those ahead of her if it would be okay if they made space for James to get off of his bench and come to her with a greeting. They agreed, and James came to her as if SHE were the celebrity. Terri asked if she would like a closer encounter with James and she said, "I would like to hold him if that would be okay." Terri lifted him onto her lap and he kissed her on her cheek. Her smile lit up the entire hall. "I can die happy now," she said.

Two other stories were the culmination of James's many visits to the Ronald McDonald House in New York City. One friend they met there was a twenty-year-old man with cancer. The young man teased James by making "hand" gestures behind James's head and dressing him in hats while taking photographs with him. James didn't seem to mind. Terri told the young man that it was obvious James adored him. Unfortunately, the young man's battle with cancer ended his life too quickly, and in January 2008 he passed on.

A few days after his death, David Frei sent Terri an e-mail that included the funeral service program of James's beloved friend. On the cover was a photo of him with a huge smile sitting next to James at the Ronald McDonald House. At that moment, Terri understood the profound impact of their visits. James's undivided attention was a gift he shared with everyone.

On another visit to the Ronald McDonald House in New York, Terri and James met a four-year-old boy who had been diagnosed with osteosarcoma of the face, maxilla, and eye socket. Osteosarcoma is the most common type of bone cancer in childhood, but it is more commonly found in the arms and legs. James and Terri were at the Ronald McDonald House at 5 P.M. when the children were returning from their treatments at Sloane-Kettering. Although they interacted with several youngsters, one child stood out — a young boy who seemed very reserved and hesitant. James didn't waste any time in starting their interaction. He looked at the young boy, walked over, and sat right next to him. Terri walked over to where they were seated, looked into the boy's gentle eyes, and reassuringly said, "James likes you. He would love a hug and perhaps a kiss if you would like to."

At first the young lad just pet James. James reciprocated the affection and scooted closer. Eventually, they were just inches apart. To Terri's surprise, the child reached over, hugged, and kissed her little brown dog right on his head. Terri was so pleased with his response but was startled to hear several gasps in the room. She looked up and reassured the surrounding adults that James was very gentle. Almost in unison, the small group of adults responded in chorus, "No, that's not it. We have been trying for weeks in his physical therapy to get him to make a pucker like a kiss to strengthen the muscles in his face. He has resisted because of the pain he has to endure. It is amazing that James just got him to do this in only a few seconds." Terri smiled and was happy for the boy. She was very aware of how James made people feel so at ease. That was another gift of his to others. Consequently, people would go out of their way to reciprocate his kindness. In this case, it was a kiss that really came from the heart!

When James passed, Terri received several calls from people who had never met James but had seen him when he won at Westminster. They were sobbing upon learning of James's passing and wanted to pay their respects. What Terri learned from these phone calls is that James had made a difference. "You see, they watched on 2/13/07 when James put on the show of a lifetime. The truth be known, he did it because it made him happy just to be in the moment with everyone watching."

James will never be forgotten, especially in Terri's heart. Her comment that he was a gift resonates in my mind and sends chills down my spine. Although we never met, her thoughts about companion animals are very similar to mine. In so many ways, I feel connected to Terri. Our discussions helped clarify once again the true meaning of our companion animals in our lives; however, Terri's recognition that James's life was a gift to her is perhaps the most meaningful. Gifts are traditionally shared and given to others. When they are not appreciated, we set them aside. When they are appreciated, we hold them closer to our heart. James's life was his gift to Terri. He opened her eyes to the wonders of familial love (storge) and helped her see the richness that she had right in front of her. In a world where we are so concerned in finding tinsel and tin, the gift that James gave her was the most valuable — the gift of endearing, unconditional love. It was the gift of helping her find what's meaningful in life and never letting go of it.

One of the greatest qualities of any gift is when we have the opportunity to share that gift with others. James's presence allowed this to occur. He permitted Terri, on a daily basis, to share his love with others. He also allowed her to promote the belief that having companion animals in our lives is truly a blessing that can be shared and felt by many.

We all have our own stories. Each one is a tapestry of moments woven together to shed meaning on our life. During my world travels, I have spoken to thousands of people about their life moments with their companion animals. Some have made me smile and laugh, while others left tears on my cheek. One thing was always constant. Each story held significance to someone, and that person was thrilled to share the memory with me. For that one time, I entered their lives as they were sharing their gift with me. I have learned that, although there are similarities in what I hear, each story is unique and special to someone. I treat each account as such and respectfully thank all who take the time to share their stories with me. As author Gloria Gaither said, "Memories are perhaps the best gifts of all" (see References). For people like Terri, memories allow them to capture moments of yesteryear and continue to keep them alive. What we do and say today is creating memories for tomorrow.

Gifts therefore are life blessings that appear to us in all shapes and sizes. Blessings shouldn't be viewed only as prayers but as special life experiences that have been given to us. They are valued blessings only if we acknowledge their meaning to our lives. Ralph Marston writes, "What if you gave someone a gift, and that person neglected to thank you for it — would you be likely to give another? Life is the same way. In order to attract more of the blessings that life has to offer, you must truly appreciate what you already have" (*see* References). Those of us who appreciate our blessings are predisposed to apply or remember them. So let's spend more time commemorating those blessings. Let's hear a few more tales and appreciate the gifts that such life experiences were to each of the following people.

YOU HELPED ME EARN MY WINGS

My youngest son, whom I mentioned in the first chapter, had a personally heartwarming relationship with a Peach-Faced Lovebird named Coshi. Corey adopted Coshi in 1990, and the bond between them was remarkable. Corey was only in preschool at the time and they became inseparable. It is one of the most remarkable relationships I've ever witnessed between a young boy and a bird. As I wrote a few years back in *Afternoons with Puppy* (2007), "Wherever Corey went, the bird tagged along. She would hang on his shirt as they went out to play. I used to get a kick out of watching Corey come to the kitchen in the morning. There he would be marching into breakfast with Coshi dangling on his shirt top. It was a sight to see. We even called some of his shirts 'Coshi's shirts,' because they were slightly chewed around the neck. It was inspiring to see how gentle this rambunctious young preschooler could be with a tiny bird, and how they could play together — something we don't normally associate with a child and a bird."

I have many fond memories of the two of them. One was how Corey would drive Coshi around in his small Batmobile. They were a real pair. You had to be there to appreciate Corey pushing this tiny bird in a little toy car. He would gently place her on the seat of the vehicle and slowly push her around the floor. She was so attentive. "Froom! Froom! Here we go Coshi!" She would gaze out the window as her Batmobile rolled through the house. Sometimes the car would make its way out onto the driveway, but Coshi would stay put! They were pals, and that was what friends do. Interestingly, Coshi took the role of the Caped Crusader, and Corey was Robin. What a very different Dynamic Duo — but one that worked well.

Coshi passed on many years ago, but it is uncanny to realize that she has never been forgotten. Since then we have never had a small bird like her. She was an engaging spirit who made her mark on a little boy's heart. Corey earned his wings during Coshi's lifetime. He grew up in front of her eyes and learned the true meaning of friendship, responsibility, and love. Coshi's death was Corey's first experience with loss, and although he mourned greatly, he learned never to be afraid of sharing his heart. The love that is generated is the magic ingredient for sustaining relationships for an eternity. In return, Coshi left her imprint on Corey. She helped in his formative years and gave him his first pair of life wings. Over the years, Corey and I still reminisce about Coshi's lifetime and all the joyful times he had with her. He even talks about perhaps getting another Peach-Faced Lovebird. He now is an adult, but there is definitely room for a small creature to share, and even though I'm sure there won't be a Batmobile driving around, I'm certain there will be love. The bond between human and nonhuman is intangible, but once you see two who are inexorably bound to one another, it is beautiful to behold.

I AM THE LUCKIEST PERSON IN THE WORLD

"I can still remember the very first time I saw Caramel, or Mel, as we call her. She was in a caged area in front of a pet store along with five or six other dogs that were waiting to be adopted. Mel, a beautiful Chihuahua mix, caught my eye, and I was immediately drawn to her. Something inexplicable happened in those next few moments. I was filled with so much emotion when I looked at her that tears began to stream down my cheeks. A bond was developing between us as we had barely begun to connect. I couldn't take my eyes off her. I knew, right then and there, that she was the dog for me and that we were meant to be together." This was the simple introduction that Pam shared with me on how she met Mel. Today, the two of them are still inseparable.

Pam doesn't know if Mel was abused as a puppy, but while she in foster care, Mel had her infected uterus removed after giving birth to two puppies. The day before she was adopted by Pam (and her husband Gary), her left eye was surgically removed and stapled shut. The veterinarian shared that the eye had no vision or circulation and believed it was best to remove it. Clearly, Mel went through quite an ordeal. Pam hovered over her for the first week, fearing that, with only one eye, she would have problems and bump into things. Fortunately, that never evolved. In fact, Pam quickly realized that Mel could see better with one eye than she could with two. That was more than six years ago when Mel first came into her life. Today the bond they share grows stronger every day.

"Mel has brought me such joy. She senses when I'm sad and reaches out to me by staying extra close or by asking for a tummy rub. Not a day goes by when I don't appreciate how much better my life is because of Mel. In turn, I do everything within my power to give her the best possible life. She is my wonderful friend." Toward the end of our conversation, Pam described how Mel completes her life. "People who see us together often comment that she's lucky to have me, but I know, in my heart, that I'm the lucky one, because I have her." I'm not sure if it was luck or fate that brought them together. One thing is for certain — they are both lucky to have found each other.

LIFE MOVES ON

Many of us turn elsewhere for support when we experience loss. Sometimes we turn to friends or family for comfort, and some of us turn to companion animals. Being surrounded by pets who need us gives us a sense of purpose.

When my sister (Roslyn) called me to tell me that she had gotten a dog, I was initially taken aback because we grew up in a household that didn't like animals. Our mother was afraid of dogs and didn't have any connection to them. She didn't understand the fuss that people made about their pets and discouraged us from interacting with them. My sister and I therefore became afraid of dogs. We'd even hide when we saw them on the street. Looking back at our childhood, it's hard to understand how we both overcame our fears. I explained my transformation earlier, but my sister's change happened many years later. In fact, I think she became more comfortable with dogs after she started to visit us in California and saw the gentleness of Goldie, our first Golden Retriever.

Following my initial surprise at her news, I understood why she was getting a dog. Bereavement takes a toll on everyone. Perhaps having a puppy in her home could help lift her spirits. My mother's death was quite unexpected. Although she had been suffering with diabetes for decades, she still had an active life. About five months after my mother died, my sister got a mixed-breed Lhasa Apso/Shih Tzu. She named her Bascha, which was my mother's middle name. Names are cleverly selected; some commemorate a life, while many of us are attracted to a certain name. My sister chose "Bascha" because it allowed her to connect to my mother's spirit. It is ironic that she named the dog in the spirit of my mother, who only very late in life began to have an appreciation toward other living beings.

Bascha has given my sister a new sense of purpose. The two spend much time with each other, and my sister enjoys taking care of Bascha as much as Bascha enjoys being around her. Their relationship is built on a common need: companionship. Roslyn (I actually call her Resei) often tells me that she couldn't imagine a life now without her dog. Bascha makes her laugh and smile and at times aggravates her and makes her sad or even angry — situations that are typical in a thriving relationship. Life does have unexpected twists and turns, so we often never know what to expect. However, one thing is certain — Bascha has become an extension of Roslyn's life.

Their interactions are helping my sister turn the pages of life into a new chapter. The book is far from finished. My hope is when Roslyn looks into Bascha's eyes, she sees a more positive future. As one of my heroes Einstein says, "Life is like riding a bicycle. To keep your balance you must keep moving" (*see* References).

YOU SAVED MY LIFE

Mathijs is an adult with autism from Belgium who loves horses. Today he has two Shetland ponies named Daphne and Patricia. However, the horse that changed and actually saved his life was named Sarah. Horses bring the best out of Mathijs; his acquaintances noticed that he become more social in the presence of horses.

Almost twenty years ago, Mathijs was riding Sarah near a frozen canal on a sidewalk covered with snow. The roads were very slippery, and it was even more challenging for Mathijs, who traditionally didn't use a saddle when he rode. That evening, a dog ran toward Sarah and startled her. Mathijs fell off her back and into the canal. His arms were flailing and he was trapped in the cold water. Mathijs shouted to Sarah to come and help him. She did not hesitate a moment and bent over so he was able to lift himself out. The incident had a significant impact on him. Mathijs became deeply connected to Sarah, who brought normalcy into his life. He attributes his relationship with her as one reason why he functions better in society. She may have saved his life that cold, wet evening, but their relationship enriched it. Mathijs had so much praise filled with admiration and love for his beloved Sarah.

When we talk about the soul, we often have different definitions. To me, our souls act as a window to an alternative dimension in life. When souls connect, they open a tunnel that allows beings to unite in a heartfelt manner. This is what Mathijs and so many of us experience when we live that bond. Our souls connect and we are able to enter a realm of love, commitment, and respect that doesn't differentiate between species.

YOU DON'T NEED EYES TO SEE THE WORLD

I recently met Donna Latella at a conference I was keynoting in New York. Donna is a professor of occupational therapy at Quinnipiac University. She shared with me her love of dogs and how they have fulfilled her life over the years. We quickly became kindred spirits when she told me that she named her most recent Golden Retriever after me. Can you believe that? I have a kindred spirit who is a four-legger. I was flattered and speechless. Donna explains, "All through the conference, I texted my husband, asking if I should tell Dr. Fine that our therapy dog was named after him. Dr. Fine is the person who inspired me to follow my dream and passion in animal-assisted therapy. His name seemed to be the best choice for this new therapy puppy. My husband encouraged me to share this with him and finally said, 'If you don't, you will regret it.' So I finally got up the nerve when sitting across the table from him. I made eye contact and proudly told Dr. Fine about my Aubrey and his work in AAT."

Since then I have tried to keep my eye on Donna and this Golden bundle of love. What I have heard is encouraging! He appears to be a true natural. Donna told me that, when we spoke in early August, it had a tremendous impact on her life. Four years ago, on this day, her beloved therapy dog and best friend Griffin, a six-year-old Golden Retriever, died suddenly in her arms. His memory and amazing work as a therapy dog will never leave her thoughts or feelings.

Griffin's loss left a large hole in Donna's heart. Fortunately, Donna still had one other dog in her life. Griffin had a twin brother, Logan. He was always shy and less confident than his brother. Although Donna loved him, she was looking for a new dog that would continue in Griffin's therapy feet. A year after Griffin passed on, Donna brought Aubrey into their lives. Logan took all of this in stride and was content to have the whippersnapper join them. Of course, Donna had big plans for Aubrey, and hoped he would continue in Griffin's footsteps and become a therapy dog. "To this day, he has exceeded my wildest expectations. He now works in hospitals, nursing homes, adult day centers, reading programs, and research projects." Aubrey also accompanies Donna to classes on a regular basis (as did many of my therapy dogs; I think Puppy would have gotten better student evaluations than I did). Donna reveals, "When he is not there, my OT students ask, 'Where is Aubrey? We need him here to decrease our stress today.'"

Most important, my namesake is a dedicated companion not only to Donna and her family but also to his dear friend Logan. One year after Griffin died, Logan suffered from severe glaucoma and needed his eyes removed. This was heartbreaking to the family. They genuinely believed that his life would be very poor after this because he also was so shy. In fact, the couple struggled with whether or not he should be euthanized, but the specialist assured them he would bounce back without a problem. Sure enough, he did and, in fact, exceeded their hopes. Logan is happier and more confident than he was with sight. He is outgoing and does everything he did before he had sight — and more. Logan has taught the couple how eyes are not needed to happily see and experience the world. In fact, it seems that eyes sometimes get in the way.

I learned a similar lesson many years ago, growing up with a grandfather who was blind all of my childhood. Although he was a simple man, he was a giant in my life. His insight and love of life were great inspirations to me. He once told me, "Aubi (that is what he called me), make a life, not a living." Today I continually try to live up to those simple yet profound words.

Aubrey, too, was a gift to the Latellas. He helped them see that love from each of our companions can be different but equally as meaningful. Aubrey has also shown the family how we all can be humble and share kindness. Donna explains, "In figuring out how to keep a blind dog safe, we noticed another gift from our wonderful Aubrey. He somehow knew of Logan's plight and, whenever he was needed, he would guide Logan by gently pushing himself against him up and down stairs, walking in the yard, and helping him avoid bumping into things."

As Donna says, "Gifts are found in many packages! My prayers were answered tenfold as we were given the gift of an awesome companion, therapy dog, and good friend to Logan, in our Aubrey. Griffin, Logan, and Aubrey have been amazing blessings. However, along the way, without expecting it, we also learned and very much appreciate how seeing the world involves so much more than through our eyes. The greatest gift they have given us is seeing life through our hearts."

A MATCH MADE IN HEAVEN

It's difficult to define what it means to bond with a dog. The process sneaks up on us without warning. It's not a rational decision but a strong emotional attachment. My good friend, Ron Kotkin, experienced this bond with his four-legged Golden Retriever named Teddy. Wherever you found Ron, Teddy was at his side, and that's how I got to know them. Ron and I became acquainted when we co-authored a book. Our friendship was the best thing that came from our writing together, and the strongest ingredient that cemented our friendship was our common love of dogs. Ron is an example of a dog's best friend. He is passionate about the animals in his life.

Ron recalls that his brother contacted him one day to tell him that his neighbor had puppies for adoption. He and his wife Loretta decided to see the puppies with the possibility of taking one home. Ron stood in the yard at the outer circle watching ten puppies when one of them headed right for him. She walked up to him and rolled on her back, coaxing him to rub her belly. In that instance, a bond was formed. Little did Ron know how strong that bond would be. On the way home, she fell asleep on his hand on the console of the car. That sealed the deal — they were inseparable.

Ron and Loretta took Teddy everywhere with them. In fact, many of their vacations centered on her. They took her for long walks no matter how tired they were.

They made up games for her and delighted in her excitement when she figured them out. Teddy loved the beach and jumped for joy when she hit the sand. It was amazing, and people would stop on the beach to watch her. They seemed to appreciate her genuine happiness, running up and down the beach and playing in the surf. In so many ways, like many of us, Ron's and Loretta's lives revolved around making her happy and basking in her affection for them. Teddy was their faithful companion.

Although Teddy is no longer with them, her spirit lives in their hearts. To this day (three years since her passing), at every meal, they always start with a toast to her. In essence, "To know a dog and open your heart fully is to learn what it is to have unconditional love." Ron, Loretta, and Teddy shared this in full measure.

It has been said that dogs are the eternal Peter Pan. They never age emotionally; they are like eternal children. The greatest gift that can be found in their relationships with us is their zest of life.

Jean Paul Richter, a German writer of the late eighteenth century, stated, "There are souls in this world which have the gift of finding joy everywhere and of leaving it behind them when they go." For many of us, the gift we receive from our faithful companions is the unconditional love that we share with them together.

LOVE HAS ITS COST

Having companion animals in our lives requires more than love. We need a sense of commitment to take care of another being, which includes our awareness of the financial and emotional demands. Chapters 3 and 4 bring to light some of these responsibilities, but here we'll focus on the importance of green space and of following a "code" for the human-animal bond.

My friend, Jose Peralta, an associate professor of veterinary ethics at the College of Veterinary Medicine at Western University of Health Sciences, agreed that, in order for a relationship to flourish, we need to put in a lot of effort. "A critical aspect to a healthy relationship with our pet companions is taking our responsibility to preserve their quality of life to heart," he told me. "Once we invite a companion animal into our homes, they become our responsibility. It is much like we act as good hosts when we have visitors. We have to ensure that the animal's needs are met at all times. For this, we need to know their needs and requirements and be prepared to meet them." Both of us (as well as other professionals in the field) understand that we must do our homework before we bring an animal home. We also must follow the suggestions in Chapters 3 and 4 about how to best integrate a companion animal into our lifestyle. In this way, we'll be prepared to provide an adequate quality of life for the animal: nothing more, nothing less.

Some students at the Western University of Health Sciences prepared a document that summarizes common questions and problems of new adopters. Their ultimate goal is to help prevent the return of the pets because adopters lack critical information that will help them be successful with their companion animal. The document is now available at: https://sites.google.com/site/projectadoptwesternu/. Dr. Peralta and I strongly recommend that all prospective adopters review this handout for its excellent insights.

The Importance Of Green Space

We all know that exercise is important for our companion animals, just as it is for us. Ironically, a couple of weeks after returning from the road trip, I got a real education on the importance of green space for our pets. While I was in Chicago for the annual American Veterinary Medical Association Meeting, I had the pleasure of meeting Stephen Jenkinson. For the last twelve years, Jenkinson, who is from the United Kingdom, has specialized in advising local governments and public bodies on how to better plan for and manage dog walking in their communities. Jenkinson passionately believes that good management and planning for dog ownership is good for everybody, including people who do not have dogs as well as wildlife and the wider environment.

He told me that "planning for dog ownership in new housing makes complete sense, when we know that across the Western world, between a quarter and a third of all homes will contain a dog. Most dog owners seek to be responsible. They will do the right thing and avoid conflict if we make it easy for them to do so, by providing ample opportunities for the amenities they most desire." According to Jenkinson, the City of Calgary's off-leash management plan is the best he has ever seen. The plan provides clear, good planning for the needs of people and their dogs and makes the city a desirable place in which to live. Jenkins continued by stating, "Making it easy to do the right thing is now recognized as the way to get good compliance with responsible dog ownership."

It is easy to recognize the way dogs and other companion animals build stronger communities, because people talk to each other and feel safer in the outdoors; the sense of community is immense. This is known as social capital. In many ways, having dogs and their humans walking in our communities provides some of the glue that keeps communities working together.

The Promise: The Code for the Bond

Magic has played an important part of my life. I perform periodically for children's shows, and I use magic in my therapy practice and lectures. I also utilize story-telling to shape the impact of the trick and make the experience more meaningful for the audience.

One of my favorite tricks is called the Beads of Prussia, in which I incorporate the lovely theme song from the film *On Golden Pond* as gentle background music while I spin my tale about the human-animal bond. In my left hand, I show the audience an empty acrylic tube, and then I hold up one of thirteen one-inch, wood-colored beads (red, green, and yellow). As the music plays, I drop one bead at a time into the tube while I explain how each bead represents a critical element in fostering our bond. Together the collection of beads represents the formula that I believe is needed to establish an optimal bond with our faithful companions.

So, for a few moments, let's imagine this is the closing of a lecture and we are listening to the opening title music of the film *On Golden Pond* arranged by David Grusin. The music captivates us as we listen and watch the bond being built in front of our eyes. We hear that the bond is special to many of us but that it will materialize only if we put into it what we expect to get out of it. The recipe is a balance of making sure we add all the ingredients fully. In no specific order, the beads are dropped into the tube, one after the other.

The first bead dropped in represents respect. We need to respect that all animals are sentient beings who are deserving of our respect. We must see them as distinct beings and not consider them humans. We need to be respectful of who they are and their needs.

The second bead represents the importance of attention. Attention is the source of sustenance that cultivates our relationships. Our companion animals deserve our attention and constantly seek it from us as well. Attention shouldn't be given only on our own accord. It is a cord that binds us. They, too, have their needs and may be in need of attention that perhaps at times we aren't as willing to share.

The third variable continues with the same theme. It is the bead of giving time. The greatest gift we can give any being, human or non-human, is time and attention. Healthy time feeds our relationships and helps them blossom. In a world where we struggle to find tinsel and tin, time is probably one of the greatest gifts. The time we spend with our companion animals is what teaches us to become engaged partners. The more optimal time we share, the more connected we will become. We need to remember the first moment when we first held that puppy close and it snuggled closer and kissed us. That was the beginning, and every time we repeated that gesture, we both became more and more engaged.

The fourth bead is now dropped into the tube. It represents the care that is needed and required to safeguard the needs of our companion animals. The bond requires this sense of responsibility because our companion animals depend on us for their needs — not only for today, but for their tomorrows as well. Our safekeeping is a lifelong commitment that covers when they are young, cute puppies or kittens *and* as they mature.

The fifth bead represents the one that most of us adore. It is engaging with our companions: playing with them and providing them with healthy exercise. Most of us, humans and non-humans, love to play and interact. The exercise that comes with this provides healthy outlets. We both benefit from this interaction.

The next three beads are typically dropped into the tube simultaneously. The sixth, seventh, and eighth are probably less luxurious than many of the others, but they are critical for optimal quality of life. They represent the importance of taking care of our companion's basic sustenance with food, water, and shelter — the critical elements of daily living. Our companions need fresh food, their water changed, and a safe place to live. Some animals lodge in our living rooms and bedrooms, while others have a safe place in our backyard. Grooming and cleaning up after them (the ninth and tenth beads) are equally as relevant.

Discipline and training is the eleventh bead and are crucial for an effective relationship. It is perhaps one of the most important elements in our formula of building our special bond. Many people misunderstand the term "discipline" as being cruel or harsh. In essence, the real meaning of discipline is training through the eyes of a disciple. We must learn to co-exist. We need to teach our animal companions to understand our needs. Dogs speak canine, and cats speak feline. These beings don't speak human, but we need to communicate our intentions for us to co-exist successfully. Perhaps we need to see ourselves as "dog whisperers," so that through the process of discipline and training we teach each other to live with one another.

The twelfth bead signifies the need to allow our companion animals a sense of dignity and integrity. They're not humans with fur but are sentient beings with their own emotions and thoughts. They are deserving of being treated in a dignified manner.

This leads us to the last bead. It is the most potent ingredient that ties the bond together, and it's the simplest of all. It's love and devotion. It's our willingness to engage and share our hearts with another special being that makes this bond complete. It is also the element that ties us together.

At this point, the theme song is about to end, and the beads are tossed into the air. Astonishingly, and to the surprise of the audience, they are magically strung together to form a necklace. The strand of beads helps the audience crystallize how all these ingredients blend together. The visual effect usually gets them to see the message clearly. It promotes the idea that a healthy combination of these elements makes the bond unbreakable.

So how do we put these ideas into practice in real life? Are we willing to make a promise to our companions that can be viewed as a symbolic commitment to them? This promise should be viewed in a similar fashion to the vow parents make to their newborn child. If so, what should this promise entail? Each of us can develop our own individually tailored vow that is personally meaningful. The critical point is that we value making a commitment that will create robust, meaningful relationships. The following is my own personal vow that I have tried to live with ever since Goldie and my crew of four-leggers and wingers came in my life.

The Promise: The Code for the Bond

I promise to love you.
I promise to be respectful.
I promise to keep you free of hunger and thirst.
I promise to keep you safe.
I promise to provide you with opportunities for socialization and affection.
I promise to provide care for you and to keep you free of discomfort and pain.
I promise to provide you with appropriate mental stimulation.
I promise to provide you with appropriate physical stimulation.
I promise that I will be your devoted mutual companion.

———

Summer has come and it is almost gone. It's hard to believe I began this project about two years ago. I also prepared several brief commentaries that I call "Bark Insights," which actually are anecdotes about life through the eyes of my various therapy dogs. In one of these insights, I discussed how we must appreciate what we have while we have it. We must learn to be happy with our loved ones and cherish them. This is the strongest message that I hope to convey. It is wonderful to understand that our human-animal interactions have both profound health and psychological benefits. But to me, these interactions are only the icing on a beautiful cake! For most of us, such benefits are not as important as having our beloved companion at our side. In the relationship itself, our true essence flourishes. In our connections — our touch and our glances between one another — these remarkable outcomes are generated.

This past weekend I visited Sean and my daughter-in-law Nelli (I prefer to call her my daughter). These were my family members who got two kittens a few months ago. This weekend was the first time I got to meet them. I haven't lived with cats for more than twenty years, but during the last few days, I had many wonderful memories. Hunter, Colby (the two kitties), and I bonded. Our initial connections were through my children, who love them dearly. It was only natural that I wanted to blend into their small nuclear family, so I spent a lot of time with the two boys. It was an amazing four days. We played, we snuggled, and we laid around in solace together. They granted me entry into their small clan, and, in their own simple way, with their playful, friendly actions, they welcomed my presence. In fact, this morning I awoke with Hunter at the head of my pillow, pawing my head gently and purring. It almost made me want to stay motionless for a bit longer. It didn't last too long, but the moment we had was priceless.

These tiny moments are filled with meaning. The two kitties have allowed me to become closer and more connected with my family. Hunter, Colby, and I couldn't actually converse, but we were able to communicate with our hearts. This connection of souls deepens our relationships with animals. As Benjamin Hart alluded to in *The Tao of Pooh* (1982), "Lots of people talk to the animals…Not many listen, though… That's the problem." In our case, in the last few days of August, not only were we able to converse and to bond — we listened to each other with our souls.

During his commencement remarks in 2005 at Stanford University, Steve Jobs, one of the founders of Apple Computers, remarked, "You can't connect the dots looking forward; you can only connect them looking backwards." We need to view these dots as various important life milestones that bring us significance. The dots are highlights of a tapestry of our lives that illustrates our history. Recognizing the significance of our dots will lead to a clearer appreciation of what is important in life. Perhaps an awareness of these dots will help us cultivate a better understanding of where our companion animals fit into our own being. The dots may not help us recall the daily details in our lives, but they will capture the most vital aspects. They will help us remember how all of our significant others, human and nonhuman, made us feel. Those warmhearted memories are the feelings that we will hold closely in our hearts. As Maya Angelou, the famous American poet and educator, said, "People will forget what you said; people will forget what you did; but people will never forget how you made them feel" (*see* References). These are the feelings that we remember for a lifetime! They become the life experiences that we will take to our graves.

The testimonies shared throughout these pages will help us to appreciate what is right in front of us before we lose that window of opportunity. We need to enjoy and be grateful for the wonders of each passing moment and capture these moments while we have them. If we can do that with the humans and non-humans in our life, we will experience fulfillment and abundance. Let's celebrate and cherish our bonds with our beloved companions. When we share our hearts fully with them, they will become our faithful companions, and the love they return to us will be our greatest reward — "a pearl of great price."

REFERENCES

Chapter 1

American Humane Association. 2012. *Keeping Pets (Dogs and Cats) in Homes: A Three-Phase Retention Study. Phase I: Reasons for Not Owning a Dog or a Cat.* Washington, D.C.: American Humane Association.

American Pet Products Association. 2012. Industry Statistics and Trends. www.americanpet-products.org/pressindustrytrends.asp.

American Veterinary Medical Association. The Human-Animal Bond. www.avma.org/KB/Resources/Reference/human-animal-bond/Pages/Human-Animal-Bond-AVMA.aspx.

Babe. 1995. Universal Pictures. Directed by Chris Nooan.

Beck, A. Personal Communication, February 16, 2013.

Berns, G. 2012. "What Is Your Dog Thinking?" www.sciencedaily.com/releases/2012/05/120504110504.htm.

Berns, G. Personal Communication, 2012.

Bonas, S., McNicholas, J., and Collis, G. 2000. "Pets in the Network of Family Relationships: An Empirical Study." *In* Podberseck, A., Paul, E., and Serpell, J. (eds.), *Companion Animals and Us.* United Kingdom: Cambridge University Press, pp. 209–236.

Brown, M.W. 1942. *The Runaway Bunny.* New York: Harper and Row.

Burnford, S. 1960. *The Incredible Journey.* New York: Bantam Doubleday Dell Books for Young Readers.

Coren, S. 2002. *The Pawprints of History: Dogs and the Course of Human Events.* New York: Free Press.

Dolphin Tale. 2011. Alcon Entertainment. Directed by Charles Martin Smith.

Farley, W. 1941. *The Black Stallion.* New York: Random House.

Fine, A.H., and Eisen, C.J. 2007. *Afternoons With Puppy: Inspirations from a Therapist and His Animals.* West Lafayette, Ind.: Purdue University Press.

Gipson, F. 1956. *Old Yeller.* New York: Harper and Row.

Grandin, T., and Johnson, C. 2005. *Animals in Translation: Using the Mysteres of Autism to Decode Animal Behavior.* New York: Scribner.

Grandin, T., Fine, A.H., and Bowers, C.M. 2010. "The Use of Therapy Animals With Individuals With Autism Spectrum Disorders." *In* A.H. Fine (ed.), *Handbook on Animal-Assisted Therapy: Theoretical Foundations and Guidelines for Practice.* San Diego, Calif.: Academic Press.

Hare, B., and Woods, V. 2013. *The Genius of Dogs: How Dogs Are Smarter Than You Think.* New York: Dutton.

Herriot, J. 1972. *All Creatures Great and Small.* New York: St. Martin's Press.

Horowitz, A. 2009. *Inside of a Dog: What Dogs See, Smell, and Know.* New York: Scribner.

Jenkins, M. Personal Communication, 2012.

Johnson, R. Personal Communication, October 12, 2012.

"Kinship." 1989. *Oxford English Dictionary Online* (2nd ed.). www.oup.com.

Knight, E. 1940. *Lassie Come-Home*. Philadelphia: John C. Winston Company.

Lee, J.A. 1973. *Colours of Love: An Exploration of the Ways of Loving*. Toronto: New Press.

Lewis, C.S. 1960. *The Four Loves*. New York: Harcourt.

Lewis, C.S. 2002. *The Chronicles of Narnia Series. Boxed Set*. New York: HarperCollins.

London, J. 1906. *White Fang*. New York: Macmillan Company.

Marley and Me. 2008. Fox 2000 Pictures. Directed by David Frankel.

McCullough, B., Personal Communication, 2013.

Melson, G. 2001. *Why the Wild Things Are: Animals in the Lives of Children*. Cambridge; Harvard University Press.

Milligan, T. 2009. "Dependent Companions." *Journal of Applied Philosophy* 26(4): 402–413.

My Dog Skip. 2000. Alcon Entertainment. Directed by Jay Russell.

O'Brien, R.C. 1971. *Mrs. Frisby and the Rats of NIMH*. New York: Aladdin Paperbacks.

Potter, B. 1902. *The Tale of Peter Rabbit*. London: Frederick Warne.

Quinn, S. 2009–2013. The Chet and Bernie Mystery Series. New York: Simon & Schuster.

Schneider, D.M. 1984. *A Critique of the Study of Kinship*. Ann Arbor, Mich.: University of Michigan Press.

Seabiscuit. 2003. Universal Pictures. Directed by Gary Ross.

Serpell, J. 1986. *In the Company of Animals: A Study of Human-Animal Relationships*. New York: Basil Blackwell Ltd.

Smith, Tami. Personal Communication, 2013.

Stein, G. 2008. *The Art of Racing in the Rain: A Novel*. New York: HarperCollins.

Steinbeck, J. 1962. *Travels With Charley: In Search of America*. New York: Viking Press.

Timmins, R., Personal Communication, 2013.

Townley, C. 2010. "Animals as Friends." *Between the Species* 10: 45–59.

War Horse. 2011. DreamWorks SKG. Directed by Steven Spielberg.

White, E.B. 1952. *Charlotte's Web*. New York: Harper Trophy.

Young, J. 2003. "Creature Comforts, Fresh Finds." *Richmond Times-Dispatch*, July 12, F3.

Chapter 2

Ainsworth, M.S. 1979. "Infant-Mother Attachment." *American Psychologist* 34(10): 932–937.

Allen, K. 2001. "Dog Ownership and Control of Borderline Hypertension: A Controlled Randomized Trial." Paper presented at the 22nd Annual Scientific Sessions of the Society of Behavioral Medicine. Seattle, Wash.: March 24, 2001.

Allen, K. 2001. "Pet Ownership, but Not ACE Inhibitor Therapy, Blunts Home Blood Pressure Response." *Hypertension* 38: 815.

Allen, K., Blascovich, J., and Mendes, W.B. 2002. "Cardiovascular Reactivity and the Presence of Pets, Friends, and Spouses: The Truth About Cats and Dogs." *Psychosomatic Medicine: Journal of Biobehavioral Medicine* 64(5): 727–739.

Anderson, W.P., Reid, C.M., and Jennings, G.L. 1992. "Pet Ownership and Risk Factors for Cardiovascular Disease." *The Medical Journal of Australia* 157(5): 298–301.

Beck, A., and Katcher, A. 1981. "Age of Aquarium." *Psychology Today* 15: 14.

Beck, A.M., and Glickaman, L.T. September 1987. "The Health Benefits of Pets." National Institutes of Health: OMAR Workshop, September 10–11, 1987. Online at consensus.nih.gov/1987/1987healthbenefitspetsta003html.htm.

Beckoff, M. 2013. "My Dog Always Eats First: Homeless People and Their Animals. Dogs Often Are the Oxygen and Reason for Living for Homeless People." www.psychologyto-day.com/blog/animal-emotions/201301/my-dog-always-eats-first-homeless-people-and-their-animals. Accessed March 26, 2013.

Cobb, S. 1976. "Social Support as a Moderator of Life Stress." Presidential address. *Psychosomatic Medicine: Journal of Biobehavioral Medicine* 38(5): 300–314.

Coleman, K.J., Rosenberg, D.E., Conway, T.L., Sallis, J.F, Saelens, B.E., Frank. L.D., and Cain, K. 2008. "Physical Activity, Weight Status, and Neighborhood Characteristics of Dog Walkers." *Journal of Preventative Medicine* 47(3): 309–312.

Dembicki, D., and Anderson, J. 1996. "Pet Ownership May Be a Factor in Improved Health of the Elderly." *Journal of Nutrition for the Elderly* 15(3): 15–31.

Eddy, T.J. 1996. "RM and Beaux: Reduction in Cardiac Response in Response to a Pet Snake. *Journal of Nervous and Mental Disease* 184(9): 573–575.

Fine, A.H., and Eisen, C.J. 2008. *Afternoons With Puppy: Inspirations from a Therapist and His Animals.* West Lafayette, Ind.: Purdue University Press.

France, A. Retrieved from www.brainyquote.com; accessed August 2013.

Friedmann, A.H., Beck, A.M., and Lynch, J. 1983. "Looking, Talking, and Blood Pressure: The Physiologic Consequences of Interaction With the Living Environment." *In New Perspectives on Our Lives With Companion Animals*, A.H. Katcher and A.M. Beck (eds.). San Francisco: Pets are Wonderful Support.

Friedmann, E., Katcher, A.H., Lynch, J.J., and Thomas, S.A. 1980. "Animal Companions and One-Year Survival of Patients After Discharge from a Coronary Care Unit." *Public Health Reports* 95(4): 307–312.

Hart, L.A. 1995. "The Role of Pets in Enhancing Human Well-Being: Effects for Older People." *In The Waltham Book of Human-Animal Interaction: Benefits and Responsibilities of Pet Ownership*, Ian Robinson (ed.). (Waltham Centre for Pet Nutrition). Waltham in the Wolds: UK Waltham.

Headey, B. 1998. "Health Benefits and Health Cost Savings Due to Pets: Preliminary Estimates from an Australian National Survey." *Social Indicators Research* 47: 233–243.

Headey, B., and Grabka, M. 2007. "Pets and Human Health in Germany and Australia: National Longitudinal Results." *Social Indicators Research* 80(2): 297–311.

Herzog, H., 2011. "The Impact of Pets on Human Health and Psychological Well-Being: Fact, Fiction, or Hypothesis?" *Current Directions in Psychological Science* 20: 236.

Irvine, L. 2013. *My Dog Always Eats First: Homeless People and Their Animals.* Boulder, Colo.: Lynne Rienner Publishers.

Jennings, G.L. 1995. "Animals and Cardiovascular Health." Paper presented at the 7th International Conference on Human–Animal Interactions, Animals, Health, and Quality of Life. Geneva, Switzerland: September 6–9.

Johnson, R., and Zeltzman, P. 1978. *Walk a Hound Lose a Pound: How You and Your Dog Can Lose Weight, Stay Fit, and Have Fun Together.* West Lafayette, Ind.: Purdue University Press.

Julius, H., Beetz, A., Kotrschal, K., Turner, D., and Uvnäs-Moberg, K. 2013. *Attachment to Pets: An Integrative View of Human-Animal Relationships With Implications for Therapeutic Practice.* Boston: Hogrefe.

Kellert, S. 1997. *From Kinship to Mastery: Biophilia in Human Evolution and Development.* Washington, D.C.: Island Press.

Lawrence, P.R., and Nohria, N. 2002. *Driven: How Human Nature Shapes Our Choices.* New York: John Wiley and Sons.

Lin, N., Dean, A., and Ensel, W., eds. 1986. *Social Support, Life Events, and Depression.* New York: Academic Press.

McConnell, A.R. 2011. "Friends With Benefits: On the Positive Consequences of Pet Ownership. *Journal of Personality and Social Psychology* 101(6): 1239–1252.

McGreevy, P.D., Righetti, J., and Thomson, P. 2005. "The Reinforcing Value of Physical Contact on the Effect on Canine Heart Rate of Grooming in Different Anatomical Areas." *Anthrozoos* 2: 33–37.

McNicholas, J., and Collis, G.M. 2000. "Dogs as Catalysts for Social Interactions: Robustness of the Effect." *British Journal of Psychology* 91: 61–70.

McNicholas, J., Collis, G.M., Kent, C., and Rogers, M. 2001. "The Role of Pets in the Support Networks of People Recovering from Breast Cancer." Paper presented at the 9th International Conference on Human-Animal Interactions, People and Animals, A Global Perspective for the 21st Century. Brazil.

Melson, G.F. 2001. "Child Development and the Human-Companion Animal Bond." *American Behavioral Scientist* 47: 31–39.

Mikulincer, M., and Shaver, P.R. 2007. "Boosting Attachment Security to Promote Mental Health, Pro-Social Values, and Inter-Group Tolerance." *Psychological Inquiry: An International Journal for the Advancement of Psychological Theory* 18(3): 139–156.

Mugford, R.A., and M'Comiskey, J. 1975. "Some Work on the Psychotherapeutic Value of Caged Birds With Old People." *In* Pet Animals and Society: a British Small Animal Veterinary Association (BSAVA) Symposium, R.S. Anderson (ed.). London.

Nagasawa, M., Mogi, K., and Kikusui, T. 2009. "Attachment Between Humans and Dogs." *Japanese Psychological Research*, 51(3): 209–221.

Nagasawa, M., Kikusui, T., Onaka, T., and Ohta M. "Dog's Gaze at Its Owner Increases Owner's Urinary Oxytocin During Social Interaction." *Hormonal Behavior* 55(3): 434–441. doi: 10.1016/j.yhbeh.2008.12.002. Epub 2008 Dec. 14.

National Institutes of Health. 1987. "The Health Benefits of Pets." Workshop Summary, September 10–11, Bethesda, Maryland. Office of Medical Applications of Research.

Odendall, J.S., and Meintjes, R.A. (2003). "Neurophysiological Correlates of Affiliative Behavior Between Humans and Dogs." *The Veterinary Journal* 165(3): 296–301.

Olmert, M.D. 2009. *Made for Each Other: The Biology of the Human-Animal Bond.* Cambridge, Mass.: De Capo Press.

Raina, P., Waltner-Toews, D., Bonnett, B., Woodward, C., and Abernathy, T. 1999. "Influence of Companion Animals on the Physical and Psychological Health of Older People: An Analysis of a One-Year Longitudinal Study." *Journal of American Geriatric Society* 47(3): 323–329.

Roberts, C.A., McBride, E.A., Rosenvinge, H.P., Stevenage, S.V., and Bradshaw, J.W.S. 1996. "The Pleasure of a Pet: The Effect of Pet Ownership and Social Support on Loneliness and Depression in a Population of Elderly People Living in Their Own Homes." *In* Nicholson, J., and Podberscek, A. (eds.), *Proceedings of Further Issues in Research in Companion Animal Studies.* University of Cambridge: Callender.

Schalock, R. 1996. "Reconsidering the Conceptualization and Measurement of Quality of Life." In R. Shalock (ed.), *Quality of Life: Conceptualization and Measurement,* Volume 1, pp. 123–139. Washington, D.C.: American Association on Mental Retardation.

Serpell, J.A. 1991. "Beneficial Effects of Pet Ownership on Some Aspects of Human Health and Behaviour." *Journal of the Royal Society of Medicine* 84: 717–720.

Shiloh, S., Sorek, G., and Terkel, J. 2003. "Reduction of State-Anxiety by Petting Animals in a Controlled Laboratory Experiment." *Anxiety, Stress, and Coping* 16(4): 387–395.

Shorb, T.L., and Schnoeker-Shorb, Y.A. 2013. *Kellert-Short Biophilic Values Indicator,* Personal Communication.

Siegel, J.M. 1990. "Stressful Life Events and Use of Physician Services Among the Elderly: The Moderating Role of Pet Ownership." *Journal of Personality and Social Psychology* 58: 1081–1086.

Siegel, J.M. 1993. "Companion Animals: In Sickness and in Health." *Journal of Social Issues* 49(1): 157–167.

Solomon, J., and George, C. 1996. "Defining the Caregiving System: Toward a Theory of Caregiving." *Infant Mental Health Journal* 17(3): 183–197.

Solomon, J., and George, C. 1999. "The Development of Attachment in Separated and Divorced Families." *Attachment and Human Development* 1(1): 2–33.

Solomon, J., and George, C. 2008. "The Measurement of Attachment Security and Related Constructs in Infancy and Early Childhood." In Cassidy, J., and Shaver, P.R. (eds.), *Handbook of Attachment: Theory, Research, and Clinical Applications,* 2nd ed. New York: Guilford Press.

Strand, E.B. 2004. "Interparental Conflict and Youth Maladjustment: The Buffering Effect of Pets." *Stress, Trauma, and Crisis: An International Journal* 7(3): 151–168.

Straub, R.O. 2007. *Health Psychology: A Biopsychosocial Approach.* New York: Worth Publishers.

Vormbrock, J.K., and Grossberg, J.M. 1988. "Cardiovascular Effects of Human-Pet Dog Interactions." *Journal of Behavioral Medicine* 11(5): 509–517

Wells, D.L. 2009. "The Effects of Animals on Human Health and Well-Being." *Journal of Social Issues* 65(3): 523–543.

Wilson, E.O. 1984. *Biophilia.* Cambridge, Mass.: Harvard University Press.

Zasloff, R., and Kidd, A.H. 1994. "Loneliness and Pet Ownership Among Single Women." *Psychological Reports* 75: 747–752.

Zilcha-Mano, S., Mikulincer, M., and Shaver, P.R. 2011a. "Pets in the Therapy Room: An Attachment Perspective on Animal-Assisted Therapy." *Attachment and Human Development* 13(6): 541–561.

Zilcha-Mano, S., Mikulincer, M., and Shaver, P.R. 2011b. "An Attachment Perspective on Human-Pet Relationships: Conceptualization and Assessment of Pet Attachment Orientations." *Journal of Research in Personality* 45(4): 345–357. doi:10.1016/j.jrp.2011.04.001.

Zilcha-Mano, S. Mikulincer, M. and Shaver, P.R. 2012. "Pets as Safe Havens and Secure Bases: The Moderating Pet Attachment Orientations." *Journal of Research in Personality* 46(5): 571–580.

Chapter 3

Abbott, K. "The Average Cost to Adopt a Dog from a Shelter." www.ehow.com/about_5445461_average-cost-adopt-dog-shelter.html. Accessed August 2013.

Almqvist, C. 2003. "Direct and Indirect Exposure to Pets—Risk of Sensitization and Asthma at 4 Years in a Birth Cohort." *Clinical and Experimental Allergy* 33(9): 1190.

American Pet Products Association. 2011. "National Pet Owners Survey, 2011." Greenwich, Conn.: APPA.

American Society for the Prevention of Cruelty to Animals (ASPCA). 2013. www.aspca.org/adopt/pet-care-costs.

Bennett, J.R.B. 2000. "Relational Experiences Between Children and Pets During Parental Divorce" (Order No. 9983989, John F. Kennedy University). *ProQuest Dissertations and Theses*, 124 pp. http://ezproxy.prescott.edu/login?url=http://search.proquest.com/docview/304653131?accountid=24826 (prod.academic_MSTAR_304653131).

Daly, B., and Morton, L.L. 2006. "An Investigation of Human-Animal Interactions and Empathy as Related to Pet Preferences, Ownership, Attachment, and Attitudes in Children." *Anthrozoos* 19(2): 113–127.

De Saily, M. 1876. "Teaching Kindness to Children." The Pennsylvania School Journal 24(April): 335.

Eddy, S. 2004. *Friends and Helpers.* Whitefish, Mont.: Kessinger Publishing (e-book).

Eliot, G., 1857 (reprinted 1998). *Mr. Gilfil's Love Story, Scenes of Clerical Life.* London: Penguin Books.

Fine, A. 2012. *Animals Make Life Richer: Exploring the Roles That Animals May Have in Promoting Warmer and Kinder Households.* Claremont, Calif.: Healing Paws Press.

Gandhi. M. www.brainyquotes.com. Accessed August 20, 2013.

Gardner, N. 2008. *A Friend Like Henry.* Naperville, Ill.: Sourcebooks, Inc.

Grandin, T., Fine, A., and Bowers, C. 2010. "The Use of Therapy Animals With Individuals With Autism." *In* Fine, A. (ed.), *The Handbook on Animal-Assisted Therapy* (third edition). New York: Elsevier Science Press.

Grogan, J. 2005. *Marley & Me and Love with the World's Worst Dog.* Sydney, Australia: Hachette. Quote from: www.goodreads.com/work/quotes/14960-marley-me-life-and-love-with-the-worlds-worst-dog. Retrieved March 14, 2013.

Herzog, H. "The Impact of Pets on Human Health and Psychological Well-Being: Fact, Fiction, or Hypothesis?" *Current Directions in Psychological Science* 20(4): 236–239.

Humane Society. 2012. "Allergies to Pets." www.humanesociety.org/animals/resources/tips/allergies_pets.html. Retrieved August 2013.

John, A. 2012. "How Much Is That Doggie in the Window? The Surprising Economics of Purchasing a Purebred Puppy." *Forbes Magazine.* www.forbes.com/sites/allenstjohn/2012/02/17/how-much-is-that-doggie-in-the-window-the-surprising-economics-of-purchasing-a-purebred-puppy/.

Jones, K. 2012. *Fetching the Perfect Dog Trainer.* Wenatchee,Wash.: Dogwise Publishing.

Katz, J. 2003. *The New Work of Dogs: Tending to Life, Love, and Family.* New York: Random House.

Leigh, D. 2011. "Lack of Allergies More Than a Pet Theory." *The Australian.* www.theaustralian.com.au/news/nation/lack-of-allergies-more-than-a-pet-theory/story-e6frg6nf-1226074509423.

Lombardi, E. 2010. "Effects of Pet Exposure in the First Year of Life on Respiratory and Allergic Symptoms in 7-Yr-Old Children." *Pediatric Allergy Immunology* 21: 268–276.

Lynn, C. 2013. "2012 Dog Bite Fatalities." www.dogsbite.org/dog-bite-statistics-fatalities-2012.php.

Martin, F. Telephone interviews, April 5, April 12, 2013.

McCullough, W.T. 1986. "The Effects of Pet Ownership on the Psychological Well-Being of

Physically Disabled Children (Animal-Facilitated, Pet Therapy, Recreation, Leisure, Lifestyle)" (Order No. 8609284, Boston University). ProQuest Dissertations ahd Theses, 148 pp. http://ezproxy.prescott.edu/login?url=http://search.proquest.com/docview /303392287?accountid=28426 (prod.academic_MSTAR_303392287).

McNicholas, J., and Collis, G.M. 2001. "Children's Representations of Pets in Their Social Networks." *Child Care Health Development* 27(3): 279–294.

Meadan, H., and Jegatheesan, B. 2010. "Classroom Pets and Young Children." *YC: Young Children* 65(3): 70–77.

Melson, G. 2000. "Companion Animals and the Development of Children: Implications of the Biophilia Hypothesis." *In* Fine, A. (ed.), *The Handbook on AAT* (first edition). San Diego: Academic Press.

Mueller, M.K. 2013. "The Role of Human-Animal Interaction in Promoting Positive Youth Development: Toward Theory-Based Measurement and Application." Ph.D. Dissertation, Tufts University.

Mueller, M.K., Geldhoff, G.J., and Lerner, R.M. 2013. "The Role of Human-Animal Interaction in Organizing Adolescents' Self-Regulatory Abilities: An Exploratory Study." Poster presented at the biennial meeting of the Society for Research in Child Development, Seattle, Wash.

Nagasawa, M., and Ohta, M. 2010. "The Influence of Dog Ownership in Childhood on the Sociality of Elderly Japanese Men." *Animal Science Journal*: 81.

Paul, E.S., and Serpell, J.A. 1996. "Obtaining a New Pet Dog: Effects on Middle Childhood Children and Their Families." *Applied Animal Behavior Science* 47(1,2): 17–29. Also available at: http://dx.doi.org/10.1016/0168-1591(95)01007-6.

Reimer, K. 2012. "U.S. Pet Ownership on the Decline" (cover story). *DVM: The Newsmagazine of Veterinary Medicine* 43(10): 1–37. Also available at: www.humanesociety.org/issues/ pet_overpopulation/facts/pet_ownership_statistics.html.

Steele, W., and Sheppard, C. 2003. "Moving Can Become Traumatic." *Trauma and Loss: Research and Interventions* 3(1). Also available at: www.tlcinstitute.org/Moving.html.

Strand, E.B. 2004."Interparental Conflict and Youth Maladjustment: The Buffering Effects of Pets." *The Journal of Evidence-Based Social Work* 7(3): 151–168.

Triebenbacher, S.L. 2000. "The Companion Animal Within the Family System: The Manner in Which Animals Enhance Life Within the Home," p. 365. *In* Fine, A. (ed.), *The Handbook on Animal-Assisted Therapy* (first edition). San Diego: Academic Press.

Walsha, F. 2009. "Human-Animal Bonds II: The Role of Pets in Family Systems and Family Therapy." *Family Process* 48: 481–485.

Wells, Deborah. 2009. "The Effects of Animals on Human Health and Well-Being." *Journal of Social Issues* 65(3): 523–543.

Chapter 4

American Veterinary Medical Association. 2012. "Selecting an Amphibian, Bird, Cat, Dog, Ferret, Fish, Horse, Rabbit, Reptile." Brochure Series.

Coren, S. 1998. *Why We Love the Dogs We Do: How to Find the Dog That Matches Your Personality*. New York: Fireside.

Deming, J. Personal Communication, February 12, 2013.

Forrest Gump. 1994. Paramount Pictures. Directed by Robert Zemeckis.

Hare, B., and Woods, V. 2013. *The Genius of Dogs: How Dogs Are Smarter Than You Think*. New York: Penguin Group.

Hart, B.L., and Hart, L.A. 1998. *The Perfect Puppy: How to Choose Your Dog By Its Behavior*. New York: Barnes and Noble Books.

Jones, K., Personal Communication, January 8, 2013.

Kingsley, E.P. 1987. "Welcome to Holland." Available at http://vialogue.wordpress.com/ 2008/06/19/welcome-to-holland-raising-a-child-with-a-disability/. Retrieved January 22, 2013.

Martin, F., Personal Communication, April 5, 2013.

McConnell, P. 2002. *The Other End of the Leash: Why We Do What We Do Around Dogs*. New York: Ballantine Books.

McConnell, P., Personal Communication, November 2012.

Moore, A., Personal Communication, April 12, 2013.

Patton, T., Personal Communication, May 27, 2013.

Sherwood, P. 2000. *The Dog Fanatic: Tail-Wagging Quotes on Man's Best Friend*. Guilford, Conn.: Lyons Press, p. 16.

Sternberg, S. "Assess-a-Pet." Sponsored by American Society for the Prevention of Cruelty to Animals (ASPCA). www.animalsforadoption.org/rvaa/assess_pet.

Volhard, J. and Volhard, W. 2007–2013. "Choosing Your Puppy." wwww.volhard.com/pages/pat.php (printable pdf).

Weiss, E. "Safer/Meet Your Match Program." Sponsored by American Society for the Prevention of Cruelty to Animals (ASPCA). www.warl.org/adopt/meet-your-match/.

Chapter 5

American Humane Association and PetSmart Charities. 2012. *Keeping Pets (Dogs and Cats) in Homes: A Three-Phase Retention Study*. Washington, D.C.: AHA.

Aurora Citizens' Police Academy Alumni Association Newsletter. Fall 2012. http://aurorac-paaa.org/.

Coren, S. 2010. "Foreword." *In* Fine, A. (ed.), *Handbook on Animal-Assisted Therapy* (third edition). San Diego, Calif.: Academic Press.

Coren, S., and Hodgson, S. 2007. *Understanding Dogs for Dummies*. Hoboken, N.J.: Wiley Publishing, Inc.

Cornu, J.N., Cancel-Tassin, G., Ondet, V., et al. 2011. "Olfactory Detection of Prostate Cancer by Dogs Sniffing Urine: A Step Forward in Early Diagnosis." EurUrol 59: 197–201.

Corson, S.A., Corson, E.O.L., and Gwynne, P.H. 1975. "Pet-Facilitated Psychotherapy." In Anderson, R.S. (ed.), *Pet Animals and Society*, pp. 19–36. Baltimore, Md.: Williams and Wilkins.

Delta Society (n.d.). "About Animal-Assisted Activities and Animal Therapy." [Note: Delta Society is now Pet Partners; www.PetPartners.org.]

Fine, A., and Eisen, C.J. 2007. *Afternoon With Puppy: Inspirations from a Therapist and His Animals*. West Lafayette, Ind.: Purdue University Press.

Friesen, L. 2009. "How a Therapy dog May Inspire Student Literacy Engagement in the Elementary Language Arts Classroom." *Learning Landscapes* 3(1): 105–122.

HOPE Animal-Assisted Crisis Response (HOPE AACR). www.hopeaacr.org.

Huneck, Stephen. 2002. *The Dog Chapel: Welcome All Creeds, All Breeds. No Dogmas Allowed.* New York, N.Y.: Harry N. Abrams.

Lange, A.M., Cox, J.A., Bernert, D.J., and Jenkins, C.D. 2007. "Is Counseling Going to the Dogs? An Exploratory Study Related to the Inclusion of an Animal in Group Counseling With Adolescents." *Journal of Creativity in Mental Health* 2(2): 17–31. DOI: 10.1300/J456v02n02_03.

Levinson, B.M. 1962. "The Dog as Co-Therapist." *Mental Hygiene* 46: 59–65 (quote on p. 59).

Levinson, B.M. 1969. *Pet-Oriented Child Psychology.* Springfield, Ill.: Charles C. Thomas.

Mugford, R.A., and M'Comisky, J.G. 1975. "Therapeutic Value of Cage Birds With Old People." In Anderson, R.S., ed., *Pet Animals and Society.* London: Bailliere Tindall.

Nightingale, F. 1859. *Notes on Nursing: What It Is and What It Is Not.* London: Harrison and Sons, p. 58.

Pet Partners. (n.d.) "About Pet Partners" (online). www.petpartners.org/history.htm.

Sheldrake, R. 2011. *Dogs That Know When Their Owners Are Coming Home.* New York: Three Rivers Press.

Smith, C.S. 2009. "An Analysis and Evaluation of Sit Stay Read: Is the Program Effective in Improving Student Engagement and Reading Outcomes?" EDD Dissertation, National-Louis University.

Sobo, E., Eng, B., and Kassity-Krich, N. 2006. "Canine Visitation (Pet) Therapy." *Journal of Holistic Nursing* 24: 51–57.

Therapy Dogs International. (n.d.). "About TDI." www.tdi-dog.org/about.aspx.

University of California–Irvine, Child Development Center. December 2012 (unpublished). Project Pack Recruitment Brochure.

Williams, H., and Pembroke, A. 1989 "Sniffer Dogs in the Melanoma Clinic?" *Lancet*, vol. 1: 734.

Willis, C.M., Church, S.M., Cook, W.A., McCarthy, N., Bransburn, A., Church, M.R.T., and Church, J.C.T. 2004. "Olfactory Detection of Human Bladder Cander by Dogs: Proof of Principle Study." *British Journal of Medicine* 329:712.

Youth and Pet Survivors Program (YAPS). Flint Animal Cancer Center, Colorado State University, Fort Collins, Colorado.

Chapter 6

Bailey, L.H. Quote from www.searchquotes.com/quotation/A_garden_requires_patient_labor_and_attention._Plants_do_not_grow_merely_to_satisfy_ambitions_or_to_/43580/. Accessed March 16, 2013.

Berger, Ann, Personal Communication, August 2013.

Bryant, B.K. 2008. "Social Support in Relation to Human-Animal Interaction." Paper presented at the NICHD/Mars meeting on Directions in Human-Animal Interaction Research: Child Development, Health, and Therapeutic Interventions. Bethesda, Md.: September 30–October 2.

Cousins, N. 1989. *Head First: The Biology of Hope and the Healing Power of the Human Spirit.* New York: Penguin Books.

Creagan, E. 2002. "Pets, Not Pills: The Healing Power of Fur, Fins, and Feathers." *Proceedings,*

Pawsitive Interactions Conference, Atlanta, Georgia, 2002, A Scientific Look at the Human-Animal Bond, pp. 7–9.

Davidson, R. 2012. *Emotional Life of the Brain*. New York: Hudson Press.

Einstein, A. Quote retrieved from http://famous-quotes.findthedata.org/1/50376/Everything-that-can-be-counted-does-not-necessarily-count. Accessed April 2, 2013.

Goethe, von, J.W. Quoted in Sundberg, J. 1988. *Hope in Times of Grief*, p. 34. Colorado Springs, Colo.: Waterbrook Press.

Groopman, J. 2003. *The Anatomy of Hope: How People Prevail in the Face of Illness*. New York: Random House.

Havel, V. 1990. *Disturbing the Peace*. New York: Alfred A. Knopf, Inc. Quote from www.brainyquote.com/quotes/authors/v/vaclav_havel.html. Accessed March 19, 2013.

Holland, J.C., and Lewis, S. 2000. *The Human Side of Cancer: Living With Hope, Coping With Uncertainty*. New York: HarperCollins.

Martel, Y. 2001. *Life of Pi*, p. 279. Orlando, Fla: Harcourt Books.

McNac, D. Personal Communication, August 16, 2009.

McNicholas, J., Gilbey, A., Rennie, A., Ahmedzai, S., Dono, J., and Omerod, E. 2005. "Pet Ownership and Human Health: A Brief Review of Evidence and Issues," *British Medical Journal* 331(7527): 1252–1254.

Milne, A.A. *Winnie the Pooh*. Quote from Goodreads, www.goodreads.com/author/quotes/81466.AAMilne. Accessed March 26, 2013.

Oliver, D., Personal Communication, August 2013.

Oliver, D. "Man's Best Friend Talks About Cancer." Videoblog #14. http://dbocancerjourney.blogspot.com/. Accessed November 11, 2012.

Skeath, P., Fine, A.H., and Berger, A. 2010. "Increasing the Effectiveness of Palliative Care Through Integrative Modalities: Conceptualizing the Roles of Animal Companions and Animal-Assisted Interventions." In Fine, A.H. (ed.), *Handbook on Animal-Assisted Therapy: Theoretical Foundations and Guidelines for Practice* (third edition). San Diego, Cal.: Academic Press.

Spiegel, D., and Kato, P.M. 1996. "Psychosocial Influences on Cancer Incidence and Progression." *Harvard Review of Psychiatry* 4(2): 10–26.

Sundberg, J. 1988. *Hope in Times of Grief*, p. 34. Colorado Springs, Colo.: Waterbrook Press.

Weil, A., Personal Communication, August 2012.

Chapter 7

Caras, R. Quote from Wise, R. 2011. *Wise Quotes of Wisdom*, p. 46. Bloomington, Ind.: Author House.

Fine, A.H. 2008. "The Gift of Love: Dogs Make Us Feel Needed and Give Us Devotion." *Dog Fancy* 39(7): 44.

Fine, A.H. 2010. *Give a Dog Your Heart and Love Will Come Your Way*. Claremont, Calif.: Healing Paws Press.

Fine, A., and Eisen, C. 2007. *Afternoons With Puppy: Inspirations from a Therapist and His Animals*, pp. 165–166. West Lafayette, Ind.: Purdue University Press.

Hugo, V. Quote from Thomas, J. 1915. "Brotherhood." *Scottish Rites Bodies of New York* 4(2): 14.

Kübler-Ross, E. 1969. *On Death and Dying*. New York: Macmillan.

Kübler-Ross, E., and Kessler, D. 2005. *On Grief and Grieving: Finding the Meaning of Grief Through the Five Stages of Loss*. New York: Simon & Schuster.

Mears, B., and Bidoulph, D. 2000. *Love Stories of Pets and People*. New York: Rescue Team Publications.

Melson, G.F., and Fine, A.H. 2010. "Animals in the Lives of Children." In Fine, A.H. (ed.), *Handbook on Animal-Assisted Therapy: Theoretical Foundations and Guidelines for Practice*, pp. 223–247. San Diego, Calif.: Elsevier.

Milito, M. 2011. *Clarice and Friends . . . How They Helped Mend the Hole in My Heart*. Self-Published.

Podrazik, D., Shackford, S., Becker, L., and Heckert, T. 2000. "The Death of a Pet: Implications for Loss and Bereavement Across the Lifespan." *Journal of Personal and Interpersonal Loss* 5: 361–395.

Remen, R. Quote from Goodreads. www.goodreads.com/quotes/30853-every-great-loss-demands-that-we-choose-life-again-we. Accessed August 28, 2012.

Richardson, I.P. Quote from Mears, B., and Bidoulph, D. 2000. *Love Stories of Pets and People*, p. 114. New York: Rescue Team Publications.

Sharkin, B.S., and Knox, D. 2003. "Pet Loss: Issues and Implications for the Psychologist." *Professional Psychology: Research and Practice* 34(4): 414–421.

Townsend, I. 1986. *Separate Lifetimes*. Exeter, N.H.: J.N. Townsend Publishing.

Chapter 8

Angelou, M. Quote from www.brainyquotes.com. Accessed August 2013.

Einstein, A. Quote from www.brainyquotes.com. Accessed August 2013.

Fine, A.H., and Eisen, C. 2007. *Afternoons With Puppy: Inspirations from a Therapist and His Animals*. West Lafayette, Ind.: Purdue University Press.

Gaither, G. Quote from www.brainyquotes.com. Accessed August 2013.

Hoff, B. 1982. *The Tao of Pooh*. New York: Penguin Books.

Marston, R. Quote from www.brainyquotes.com. Accessed August 2013.

Richter, J.P. Quote from www.searchquotes.com/quotation/There_are_souls_in_this_world_which_have_the_gift_of_finding_joy_everywhere_and_of_leaving_it_behind/230069. Accessed August 28, 2013.

Wilde, O. Quote from www.brainyquotes.com. Accessed August 2013.

APPENDIX

 PAWS FOR THOUGHT:
Cherishing the Moments

This PAWS for Thought section will help you integrate the practical ideas identified in *Our Faithful Companions*. These exercises are enjoyable and will bring you closer to your companion animal. Taking the time to reflect on your relationships and optimally engaging with your pet will lead to richer experiences in the future. So take a moment . . . and PAWS. It will help you cherish and preserve your experiences. Reflect and respond. Remember — a moment taken now may be the key to a future relationship or may enhance a current one. For every action, there is a reaction, and the actions you choose will have a direct impact on your relationship with your pets.

• PAWS FOR THOUGHT:

Consider your earliest memories with animals. How old were you when you forged your first meaningful relationship with a pet or even felt connected to wild animals? It might be your first puppy kiss. How did you feel about that animal? Did you consider the animal to be a friend or confidant? What were your experiences with the animal — did he join you on adventures or brighten your mood? How did your connection to animals change your childhood? Have you maintained relationships with animals since childhood? Why or why not? What parts of your life are or would be enriched by having a kinship with an animal?

• PAWS FOR THOUGHT:

Just as we humans form attachments to our animals, animals are doing the same toward us. Our pets rely on us for safety, food, health, and emotional well-being. Consider your relationship with your pets. If you were your pet, would you feel secure, healthy, and happy? What can you do to ensure the greatest contentment possible for your pet? When you put yourself in your pet's shoes, what to you see about your daily life? Do you walk enough (with your dog)? Do you relax enough? Are you at home as often as you'd like?

- ### PAWS FOR THOUGHT:

Add a physical activity with your dog or cat to your routine this week. (If you have a cat, maybe you can find an interactive toy to play with or play bubbles with him.) Record how often you do it and how you feel when you're done. Did the activity enhance your mood? Did it enhance your pet's mood or offer him needed exercise or quality time with you?

- ### PAWS FOR THOUGHT:

Because healthy people often are more hopeful and engaging in life, think of a project you can do in your community that would express hope and compassion to animals in need. For example, you could make blankets for an area shelter, collect supplies for a wildlife rescue center, begin a regular volunteer commitment, or take part in an annual dog walk to support your local humane society. Do the project, and try to spread hope and compassion to another person. Then you have doubled your impact for the animals and have passed your hope on to someone who will likely do the same.

- ### PAWS FOR THOUGHT:

If you have a dog, try this experiment. Take a walk without your dog on a trail or through a park. Keep track of the percentage of people you meet who have a conversation with you. The next day, take the same walk, and do the same. Notice whether walking with the dog increases or enhances your interactions with other people. Did you feel differently after each walk?

- ### PAWS FOR THOUGHT:

Draw your family tree and include past and present pets. How would you draw them into the connections of your family? What did each pet mean to you? To other family members? What role did they play in your family?

- ### PAWS FOR THOUGHT:

Exercise is an important part of keeping you and your pet healthy and happy. Whether you exercise together, such as taking a nice walk, or you help your pet to exercise separately by playing a fun game of laser chase, doing so regularly can provide many benefits. Use an exercise journal to keep track of the fun things you do together. It will help you figure out what you and your pet enjoy the most. Then do more of these things to grow the bond between you.

• PAWS FOR THOUGHT:

What does your pet love more than food (besides you)? Nothing! Try out this simple and healthy homemade pet treat. You can even try a bite yourself if you want, as all ingredients are human grade. Treating you and your pet to healthy and fun snacks such as these is a great way to cherish the bond. Look for other recipes of special treats online or at the library.

"Frosty Bites" Ice Cream (*Grain Free)
- 32 ounces low-fat vanilla yogurt
- 1 ripe mashed banana
- 2 tablespoons peanut butter
- 2 tablespoons honey

Combine all the ingredients together in a blender. Pour into paper cups or an ice-cube tray and freeze. Share with your pet on a hot summer day or as a fun reward any time.

• PAWS FOR THOUGHT:

Not only is physical exercise important for your pet, mental exercise is as well. Companion animals are intelligent creatures who can get just as bored with the same routine as you can. Try setting up a "scavenger hunt" for your pet. Start by hiding some of his favorite treats in the backyard, a room in the house, or even his enclosure (for smaller pets). Once he learns the game, start hiding some favorite toys as well. Make sure to give lots of praise when your pet finds each item. It can be entertaining for you to watch him hunt down his prizes and rewarding for your pet when he finds the treat! A friend of mine always ends his walk with his pet with a scavenger hunt for treats, thereby giving his dog both physical and mental exercise daily.

• PAWS FOR THOUGHT:

Since everyone is on social media these days, why not make an account for your pet as well? There are many famous pets on Facebook and Twitter, so why not yours? You could add pictures, create a funny bio, and post silly updates on your pet's behalf. Then, you can have fun going through and adding lots of friends and followers for your pet.

- ## PAWS FOR THOUGHT:

Gear up for some good old-fashioned snuggle time. We often are so concerned with getting things done and keeping everyone happy that sometimes we forget to just slow down and enjoy the little moments in life. Set aside a good chunk of time to just snuggle up with your animal. Pick a time when you know he is most likely to cooperate, such as after a meal, and settle in and snuggle. If your animal still does not want to participate, use the time to simply sit and enjoy watching him do whatever he does. It'll be a good change of pace for you both.

- ## PAWS FOR THOUGHT:

The hardest part about our relationship with animals is that they just don't live as long as we do. Even with the great advances in veterinary medicine, we still have to say goodbye long before we are ready. One way to help with grieving is by cherishing the memories. Start by working on a scrapbook now with favorite pictures, mementos, and stories of your animal. Try to add to this collection every month. When you do eventually have to say goodbye to your friend, it will be a great way to remember and reflect on the wonderful relationship you had.

—

A downloadable pdf file of *The Healing Workbook* (which also appears on the following pages) is available FREE online at:

http://www.alpinepub.com/healing_workbook-pdf-file.html

Print out as many copies as you need and bind or put in a notebook Make one for each pet, or each child can make their own memory book.

A Note To Parents

As our pets generally have shorter life spans than we, our children are likely to witness important life cycle events—such as birth, serious illness and death—through experiences with their family pets. For many children, the loss of a pet will be their first experience with death and, for many, the outcome may be the same as experiencing the loss of any other family member: a sense of emptiness and pain.

It is important to allow children to grieve. We can help our children by allowing them to express themselves in different ways, from discussions with close family and friends, to reading books (such as Give a Dog Your Heart), drawing pictures and writing poetry. Art activities and other media such as scrap booking can be very valuable in the grieving process. This is why we have included a memorial book activity that you can help your child create to celebrate and remember his or her beloved companion.

We shouldn't hide information about an animal's illness and/or death from children out of desire to "protect" them from an upsetting loss. Some families begin to prepare for the end of life by saying their good byes but in no way does this guarantee that it will make it easier for a child to accept the inevitable. When the death isn't of natural causes or when a pet is euthanized, some children find it particularly difficult to understand. Phrases such as "putting to sleep" can confuse young children, and even frighten them.

I recommend that parents answer children's questions, using simple, clear and accurate information geared to the development stage of the child. Parents also need to reassure children that the pet's death was not their fault. Having parents who are supportive and help the child work through any sense of guilt can be critical to the child's well being.

PAWS for THOUGHT
THE HEALING WORKBOOK

A few guidelines to consider:
Children ranging from the ages of two to three "do not have a true concept of death," so they should be told that their pet has died and will not return. Parents shouldn't be afraid of expressing their true emotions. This may help children express their own grief.

Children who are a bit older (four to six) usually begin to have a better understanding of death, but may lack an understanding of its permanence. We need to help a child realize that their pet is not coming back, but also help them understand that they didn't do anything to cause their pet to die.

Over the years I have supported my own sons as well as many of my patients, formally and informally, who have experienced the death of a beloved pet. Pain is a real feeling; this unfortunately is unavoidable. What is avoidable are the possible mishaps that we may make trying to protect our child from this life event. Help your children not only mourn the loss of their beloved friend, but also cherish the time they had together. Use the following pages to memorialize their special friendship.

They will not forget or replace their beloved companion; but rather, in time, healing eventually comes. As the day comes so does the night followed again by day. This is life. There is an old proverb, "Don't mourn for me that I am gone, but be happy for the time we had together." Perhaps hard to put into action, our role as parents must be to console our children, but moreover, to help them understand their loss by helping them realize the significance of the pets in their lives.

CAPTURE the MOMENTS

PAWS FOR THOUGHT
THE HEALING WORKBOOK

Remembering my special friend

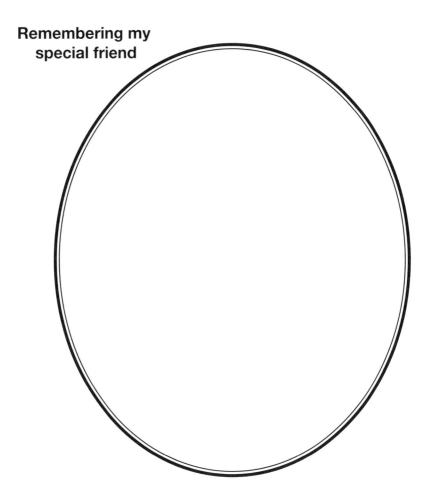

This is a picture of _____. My special friend.

CAPTURE THE MOMENTS

PAWS FOR THOUGHT
THE HEALING WORKBOOK

My favorite memories of my pet are...

Draw or paste a photo of your pet here

CAPTURE THE MOMENTS

# PAWS for THOUGHT

Special tricks my friend could do...

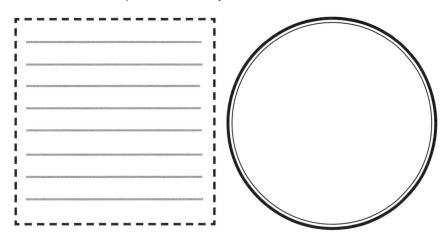

Things we would do together...

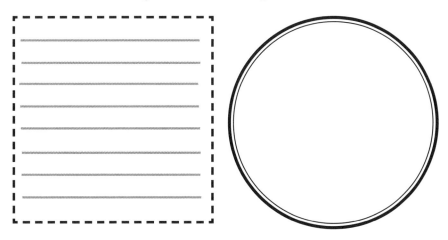

CAPTURE THE MOMENTS

PAWS FOR THOUGHT 🐾

Special times we have shared...

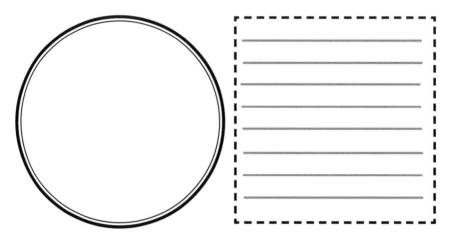

My pet's favorite things to do...

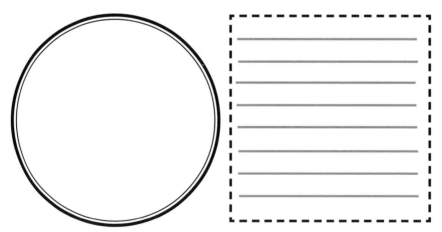

 CAPTURE THE MOMENTS 🦴

ABOUT THE AUTHOR

Psychologist Dr. Aubrey Fine has been in the field of Animal Assisted Therapy (AAT) for over thirty years. His work and insight into AAT and the human/animal bond has placed him at the cutting edge in the field. His greatest asset is his capability to translate his insights in a warm and receptive manner.

Over the past 30 years, Dr. Fine has researched and studied the value of Animal Assisted Therapy with children as well as the elderly. In addition, he has strongly integrated the foundations of AAT into his clinical practice, which primarily focuses on the treatment of children with attention, behavioral, adjustment and developmental disorders. Over this period, he has applied AAT with a variety of children with diverse forms of etiology and has witnessed many moving outcomes as a result of incorporating animals as therapeutic agents.

Dr. Fine has been on the faculty of the California State Polytechnic University since 1981, where he is presently a Professor in the Department of Education. His leadership among faculty and teaching excellence earned him the prestigious Wang Award in 2001, given to a distinguished professor within the California State University system, in this instance for exceptional commitment, dedication, and exemplary contributions within the areas of education and applied sciences. Dr. Fine has received numerous other awards for his professional contributions including the Educator of The Year Award given by the California Learning Disability Association.

He is the editor of *The Handbook on Animal Assisted Therapy*, the most widely accepted book on the subject, now in its third edition (Elsevier/Academic Press, 2010), and has published several other books, numerous articles, and video documentaries on related subjects such as parent/child relationships, learning/attention disorders, and sports psychology.

Dr. Fine serves on numerous boards and advisory committees related to human animal interactions, including the American Veterinarian Medical Association's (AVMA) steering committee on human animal interactions, and the Board of Directors of Pet Partners (previously the Delta Society).

For continuing resources on the human animal bond, and to follow Aubrey's work in this area, you are encouraged to go to *aubreyhfine.com*.

.